LEARNING
AT THE
SPEED
OF LIGHT

Published in the United States by
Hudson Whitman/ Excelsior College Press
7 Columbia Circle, Albany, NY 12203
www.hudsonwhitman.com

Interior and cover design by
John Barnett, 4eyesdesign.com

LCCN: 2017952139
ISBN (PB): 978-0-9898451-2-0

DEDICATION

This compilation of histories and recollections on the evolution of online learning is dedicated to two extraordinary men, Ralph Gomory and Frank Mayadas. With the support of the organization of which they were a part—the Alfred P. Sloan Foundation—Ralph and Frank, in little more than two decades, have done more to increase access to education (at all levels) than anyone in memory. To them, we offer this collection of essays with gratitude, in the hope that their work, as recorded here, will persist.

RESULTS

As can be seen in various accountings, somewhere between a quarter and a third of *all* enrolled higher education students, of which there were more than twenty million in 2015 (NCES, Fast Facts), were enrolled in at least one online course in fall 2014. According to the Babson Survey of Online Learning, the actual number in 2012 was 7.1 million. Additionally, more than 2.6 million were completing their *entire* degree online in 2013 (NCES, Fast Facts).

THE HISTORY

In addition to providing millions of dollars in grant money ($72 million to 346 projects) to institutions that have traditionally been seen as leaders in the adoption of innovation ("If it's okay for Berkeley or Harvard, we might want to follow their lead"), the Foundation created, and for many years supported, a national survey of attitudes and acceptance in regard to online learning, as well as the consortium known as Sloan-C. Together, these initiatives provided objective data about acceptance and growth while mobilizing the "true believers" to share lessons learned, as well as to promote expansion of the revolution and the unprecedented access it offers.

Ralph Gomory

Ralph Gomory's name is less well known to those of us in the online sector than that of Frank Mayadas. Yet, as Frank will quickly attest, there would not have been the kind of rapid growth and acceptance that we have seen if not for Ralph and the Anytime, Anyplace Learning project that he designed and then implemented with Frank.

Having been IBM's senior vice president for science and technology prior to being named as Sloan's President, Ralph brought an extraordinary academic and professional background to the foundation. A graduate of Williams, Cambridge, and Princeton, as well as a veteran of the US Navy, he had served in a series of research posts with IBM. As director of research, he oversaw IBM's Zurich Research Laboratory and work that received two successive Nobel Prizes in Physics.

Coming to Sloan in 1989, Ralph invited Frank, also at IBM, to join him in "retirement." Frank accepted in 1992.

Frank Mayadas

Before joining President Gomory at Sloan, Frank spent twenty-nine years at IBM, heading research operations and serving as an advisor to the company's corporate management team on matters of strategy and management. At Sloan, he joined with Gomory in the establishment of the Anytime, Anyplace Learning initiative (a.k.a. the

"Asynchronous Learning Networks" initiative), the annual survey and report of online growth (the Sloan/Babson Report), the Sloan-C Consortium, of which he was the founding president, and *The Journal of Asynchronous Learning Networks*.

The Team
As the face of Sloan to participating institutions, Frank has become known as the "father of online education in America." Yet, this paternity must be shared with the man whose ideas ALN sprang from, and who ensured that the all-important financial support followed Frank's assessments, Dr. Ralph Gomory.

The Future
Together, Gomory and Mayadas have carried out a revolution in American higher education. While too modest to be comfortable with this fact, their legacy speaks for itself. Nearly all regionally and nationally accredited institutions, along with entire secondary and elementary school systems, now offer online instruction to varying degrees. The "father" and "godfather" of online learning deserve to be recognized, now and in the future, for bringing this phenomenon to reality, and also for doing so in such a short period of time.

Well done, gentlemen.

LEARNING
AT THE
SPEED
OF LIGHT

HOW ONLINE EDUCATION GOT TO NOW

JOHN F. EBERSOLE
AND
WILLIAM PATRICK
EDITORS

CONTENTS

ACKNOWLEDGMENTS

I would like to personally thank the contributors for giving so generously of their time and expertise, and for remaining committed to the project even after John Ebersole's untimely death. What a tribute to the bonds of friendship and professionalism.

I would also like to thank the talented production team for starting and finishing this project with me: John Barnett, Melissa Mykal Batalin, Sue Morreale, Jessica Knight, and Heather Dubnick.

Susan M. Petrie
Publisher and Managing Director
Hudson Whitman/ Excelsior College Press

In addition to those listed above, I would like to thank William Patrick for working tirelessly to help bring this project to completion. We would also be remiss if we did not include all of the technical experts who were also part of this REVOLUTION. Without their creativity, commitment, and collaborative efforts, we would not have gotten HERE. That includes faculty, instructional designers, software and hardware developers, illustrators, technical and business people, and those who helped with regulatory issues. At one point in preparing this, I thought I might have the space to list everyone by name. However, I not only find I don't have enough space, but am fearful my recall would be insufficient. Thus, our amazing contributors will stand as surrogates for the many. We are indeed grateful to our authors and the substantive way they responded to our requests, and believe that together we have created a book of truly long lasting relevance to higher education.

John Ebersole

"Sometimes the fall kills you.
And sometimes, when you fall, you fly."

—*Neil Gaiman*

INTRODUCTION
In the Beginning

John F. Ebersole

The delivery of instruction by computer can be traced from the 1980s. My own experience started in 1985 while serving as dean of the School of Management at John F. Kennedy University, then in Orinda, CA.

JFKU's president, Dr. Donald MacIntyre, had met and developed a relationship with a fellow Marin County resident by the name of Ron Gordon. Ron was CEO of the San Francisco-based start-up, TeleLearning. Founded in 1982, the venture intended to use computer technology to deliver instruction. Toward this end, it created The Electronic University Network (EUN) the same year. This network included major colleges and universities from around the country. Ron sold them on the idea of participating in both an emerging technology and outreach to a national market. The nearby Stanford School of Engineering was one of the first to sign on, and its doing so made the attraction of others more likely.

Ron had previously served as CEO of the electronic game company ATARI (in the 1970s) and had accumulated some wealth with that enterprise's success. A serial entrepreneur and master at marketing, Ron, along with a group of investors, had formed TeleLearning after he left ATARI.

With a roster of big-name schools to point to, Ron proceeded to do what he did best: launching a marketing and sales effort to America's top corporations. His vision that employees could complete or acquire a degree through computers, modems, and telephone lines, was infectious.

By the time that he had enlisted forty Fortune 500 companies, it was clear that there was a market for electronically mediated instruction *and* that the MBA was the credential of choice. While encouraging, this news was frustrating in that all the network had to offer were standalone courses. There was no MBA. This was where MacIntyre, JFKU, and I entered the picture.

Once aware of Ron's need, and the potential that it represented, Don was anxious that JFKU become a part of what had the potential to be a large-scale, national experiment. He offered Ron the MBA he needed, subject to approval by our accreditor, the Western Association of Schools and Colleges (WASC). It then fell to me to make the case for approval to that body.

Appearing before the association's executive director and chairman, I presented the reasons for approving our offering as essentially an experiment, from which all of higher education might learn. While extremely skeptical, the "researcher within" the two men prevailed. John F. Kennedy University was authorized to offer its MBA, so long as all requirements were met (albeit electronically), and the institution provided the association with quarterly reports.

The EUN was now in business. In addition to niche courses from big-name institutions, it had the graduate business degree from a regionally accredited source, as desired. In return, employers such as Pepsi, Frito Lay, and Freuhauf offered to pay the costs associated with employee enrollment.

This all occurred in 1985. By 1986, JFKU was ready to launch its pioneering MBA, or at least it thought it was. Within days of accepting enrollments, it was clear that this "experiment" would not unfold smoothly.

A great number of students had neither personal computers nor modems, and employers were unwilling to go so far as to provide this equipment as part of their support. The cost of most commercially available equipment was prohibitive for the majority of the growing number of degree seekers. As a solution, Ron placed the university in contact with a South Korean supplier, which offered the university's students both pieces of equipment (CPU and modem) at a reasonable price. The only problem was the firm's requirements that orders be placed in bulk and that all shipments to the US go to a single, West Coast address (to reduce shipping costs). JFKU's School of Management and its Access to Learning project soon became the site of a shipping and receiving operation for the needed electronics. With this problem resolved (sort of), others emerged.

The creation of lesson templates, such as those shown in Stephen Andriole's article, the identification and training of faculty, and the process for communication between students and faculty were all problems that followed. The TeleLearning programmers, working with JFKU's faculty, were unable to stay sufficiently ahead of the pace of instruction. Thus, students found themselves waiting weeks for the next lesson or next course.

While enrolled students were growing increasingly dissatisfied, the recruiting of new students slowed as word of the problems spread, and the TeleLearning/JFKU team ran out of marketing money. This was the beginning of the end. Ron's fellow investors soon elected to sell TeleLearning, for pennies on the dollar, to Dr. Steve Eskow, the former president of Rockland Community College in New York, and his partner, a former publishing executive. Unfortunately for the Eskow team, their purchase carried no obligation for JFKU, which announced its termination of the program once current students were taught-out. There was still no other online source for either an accredited MBA, or any other degree.

Although the electronics had worked more or less as intended, software programming and many of the basics of new enterprise creation (such as sustained marketing and supply chain management) were the effort's undoing. In the end, MacIntyre moved from JFKU to become the first chancellor of the University of Phoenix's evolving international expansion. In making his departure from JFKU, he was offered the intellectual property that had been created with TeleLearning (under a joint ownership agreement), which he took with him to the University of Phoenix and its parent, the Apollo Group.

All of this took place within a span of just three years. By the 1990s, a new day was dawning. It is here that this collection of remembrances and recollection picks up, reviewing and assessing two decades of more successful experimentation and academic program launches (such as those at Drexel, Penn State, UMUC and UC Online, (which connected the UC system's Center for Media and Independent Learning into a trove of AOL-delivered online courses, but not degrees). Most of these early attempts (especially those that became successful, and that still exist) were funded by the Alfred P. Sloan Foundation, at the direction of its visionary leaders, Ralph Gomory and Frank Mayadas.

The early '90s also saw much failure, as is often the case in moving new ideas to reality. The most notable of these were Columbia's Fathom, NYU Online, and the California Virtual University (which really never got off the ground). Babson, Cornell, Duke, and the University of Illinois found ways to learn from their missteps and remain in the market, albeit largely with non-credit offerings that met faculty criteria and limitations.

In looking back over the past thirty years, it isn't hard to see that the move toward online education has followed significant distance education patterns of the late nineteenth and early twentieth centuries. As Michael G. Moore , pointed out in his seminal work *Distance Education: A Systems View*, with Gregg Kearsley, the correspondence course was the earliest form of distance education. The University of London is credited with having awarded an entire degree based on study from correspondence courses, as early as 1850. Huge correspondence course operations could be found at the open universities of Turkey, India, and the Commonwealth countries of Great Britain, as well as in the University of California system (which did not convert to online technologies until the mid-1990s), until the beginning of the twenty-first century.

Acceptance of the correspondence course as a legitimate form of learning grew in the US when William Rainey Harper moved from heading the Chautauqua Institute, where correspondence courses were used for religious education, to the University of Chicago. His advocacy of correspondence study would later guide such institutions as the University of Wisconsin, the University California, BYU, and the Department of Defense. Credit accumulation through paper and pencil "correspondence" study from the US Armed Forces Institute (USAFI) was especially necessary to the highly mobile members of the armed services. I know this from personal experience, having survived a year on an island in Alaska. However, it was not possible to complete a degree with such credits until the creation of Regents College, now Excelsior, in 1971.

"Correspondence study," which continues to be a US Department of Education classification for technology-delivered instruction, was followed in the late 1960s and '70s by other forms of distance education. Instead of exclusively mail-dependent communication, both Canada and Australia found ways to use telephone lines, radio broadcasts, and video tapes, in that order, for providing access. In the US, Colorado State and the University of Colorado, Colorado Springs, teamed with Jones Cable to offer something known as Mind Extension University, which was accessed in multiple communities nationwide via cable TV. CSU, Fort Collins was a pioneer in getting its televised MBA accepted under its accreditation from the American Assembly of Collegiate Schools of Business (AACSB).

The engineering disciplines within higher education developed the next generation of distance education, using video technology under the direction of Lionel Baldwin, CSU's then just-retired dean of the School of Engineering. Supported by such institutions as Stanford, the Illinois Institute of Technology, Georgia Tech, and Colorado State, to name but a few, they created the National Technological University (NTU), which went so far as to gain Higher Learning Commission (HLC) accreditation and the authority to award its own graduate degrees. In this case, the instruction originated with such faculties as those of Berkeley, Stanford, MIT, and IIT, and was delivered through videotaped lessons that were then rebroadcast via satellite from the NTU campus, adjacent to Colorado State. These would downlink to VCRs and classrooms in major corporations across the nation, as well as to institutions overseas.

Glenn Jones, the power behind Jones Cable and Jones International University, along with Lionel Baldwin, the former CSU dean and NTU's founding president, were followed in the pioneering ranks by John Sperling, founder of the University of Phoenix (UoP). These three were not only early higher education entrepreneurs, but also important foundation builders for the online revolution. Glenn recognized the value of moving to the Internet first, seeking regional accreditation from the HLC for his Jones International University, which has since closed, before John Sperling's move online but *after* the University of Phoenix had become the first national, for-profit, online institution to gain regional approval.

John Sperling and UoP contributed little to the online movement initially. The university had far too many real estate leases to embrace the full potential of online learning in the early years. However, as those leases expired, and UoP started to realize the savings presented by the Internet, enrollments took off.

Sperling, while always controversial, deserves greater positive recognition than he has received for his success in drawing the attention of traditional institutions such as Berkeley, Colorado State, and Boston University, to name only those where I served, to the adult student. Starting from a base in the San Francisco Bay area, Sperling, a San Jose State economics professor, saw the need and the potential in serving adult learners. Beginning with the University of San Francisco, where Don MacIntyre was then provost, he added Saint Mary's of California and Regent University of Colorado, all Catholic institutions (two Jesuit and one Christian Brothers), before the Western Association of Schools and Colleges

(WASC) shut down his operation (then known as the Institute for Professional Development, or IPD). He was offering degree programs with little or no faculty oversight and was the hiring authority for instructional faculty. He argued, with some basis, that faculty oversight would essentially kill the effort. Few professors were interested in the night and weekend instruction required by those adults working full time. Unlike non-profit John F. Kennedy University, which encountered little difficulty in obtaining WASC recognition, Sperling and IPD weren't able to shake the stench of making money off of education.

Sperling, Jones, and Baldwin all focused on the working adult. While not totally ignored by traditional institutions, older students found many more choices for non credit courses than for either graduate or undergraduate degree programs—such as those offered by these pioneers. Today, the adult students (age twenty-five to sixty-five), whom Sperling and MacIntyre sought to serve in the 1970s, represent nearly 80 percent of all degree-seeking students, once part-timers and commuters are included. And as the eighteen-to-twenty-four-year-old population continues to shrink, more of those who criticized Sperling and Jones now see the wisdom of their early focus.

Unfortunately, Colorado State and NTU both fell victim to their inability to adapt to online, Internet-based learning. Prior to the web movement, faculty had been able to offer their instruction even at a distance without any special preparation or extra effort. A lecture before video cameras was only slightly different than one in a traditional classroom—and there was often no difference, with cameras mounted in the back of a regular room. Sure, the homework came via US mail, but that was about it.

With online, there was much work that had to be completed in advance of a class, especially if the students were to be retained. During the late 1990s at CSU, I found few instructors interested in the work, or in the risk of embarrassment that came with building a web-deliverable course, for which I was empowered to offer a $1,000 incentive. My successors found it necessary to create an entirely new institution—CSU Global—as a way to break up the Fort Collins faculty love affair with really bad video, available in either VHS or broadcast form.

Instructional design materialized as a real and highly valued profession in the early 2000s. Under the influence of this group, web-based instruction evolved from electronic correspondence courses to enhanced PowerPoint presentations, and then into the multimedia, Internet-specific classes of this last decade.

The electronic correspondence courses, which the UC system perfected when it converted delivery of nearly 1000 courses from US mail to AOL, proved to be no more effective instruments of instruction than their paper-and-pencil predecessors. Pre-conversion, the Center for Media and Independent Learning had a completion rate of 47 percent. After spending millions in Sloan Foundation money, the completion rate was essentially the same. Clearly, faster feedback was not adding to this learning process, as anticipated.

Recognizing the need for a more sophisticated instructional experience, faculty sought to incorporate PowerPoint to make more visual impact, and without requiring much additional work from them. These courses produced slight improvements in both learning and retention. However, their lack of interaction was still a problem. Not until instructional designers were given a greater voice in the development of interactivity and improved options for color, motion, and graphics did we see real progress in enrollments and completion rates. This "third phase" of design is now giving way to a model that incorporates simulations and serious games into the design, while also offering a host of assessments and feedback features.

Today's online courses (not to be confused with MOOCS, Massive Open Online Courses), have become so sophisticated that they put most traditional courses to comparative shame. For instance, a new online student may well go through an assessment process that measures academic strengths and weaknesses, as well as offering an individual fit with the online format. Contrary to the views of critics, those in this business are among the first to say that online study isn't for everyone. Aspiring enrollees who need remediation, typically in math or composition, are now made aware of online writing laboratories and Khan Academy resources, as well as given access to 24/7 tutorial support. Today's students may also receive coaching as well as academic advising. These coaches provide scheduled, proactive contact with students (weekly, for those having trouble), check on student progress, ask about areas of difficulty (both academic and with life), and offer both insights and encouragement. Faculty, academic advisors, coaches, tutors, and librarians all stand ready to assist with online student success today.

The regulation of twenty-first-century online learning has presented as many hurdles to model adoption as faculty acceptance. Three factors have combined to confront state and federal regulators simultaneously: the rapid expansion of online delivery; the ability, thanks to technology, to serve students anywhere, thereby creating truly transnational institutions; and the growth of proprietary education, as profit-focused entrepreneurs have recognized the reach and efficiency of online education.

The combination of for-profit providers, serving working adult students nationally with online technology, has raised multiple concerns. This perfect storm of forces has left many state regulators feeling completely overwhelmed, with some still questioning the need for change. As for the US Department of Education, it has declared war on for-profit schools and, in an attempt to reduce their role in serving older students, has produced a plethora of regulations intended to control the proprietary schools, but applicable to everyone. Compliance with these often-questionable regulations has driven up the cost of education and reduced access, as institutions retreat within their own state's borders rather than meet costly new requirements. Look at Paul Shiffman's and James Hall's article to see how the sector is striving to bring about informed and responsible compliance with one of the least-needed and most-costly of the new rules: state authorization.

Over thirty years, many talented, dedicated, and creative individuals, both from within the academy and without, have learned from each other's failures and successes and have built on the work of those who have gone before. In the pages that follow, we learn directly from some of these talented contributors what it was like to be an early participant in what has become a revolution in the delivery of instruction, providing new forms of access to millions of students, and allowing for the management of time as well as the spanning of distance.

One of the first institutions to see the potential in online learning was Penn State University. Gary Miller, the recently retired director of the World Campus, explains what it was like, organizationally as well as technically and academically, to embrace this new methodology, starting in the summer of 1996. He explains that the impetus for PSU's early explorations emerged from its land-grant mission and its history of involvement in various forms of distance education.

Like Penn State, the University of Maryland University College (UMUC) was also an early adopter. Patricia Wallace's tenure as the college's chief information officer from 1991 to 1999 overlaid the institution's period of construction for an initiative to extend access to its older, post-traditional students, both domestically and globally. Echoing Gary's experiences in State College, which were unfolding in parallel with those of UMUC, Patricia lists some of the many challenges which had to be overcome and outlines the phenomenal success which this trail- blazing effort was to realize.

We break with the historical accounting format in our interview with Charles "Chuck" Hill, one of the first online instructors and, to my knowledge, *the first* to teach in an online degree program (MBA) from a regionally accredited institution. Chuck is a friend and colleague who taught human resource management in the School of Management for little-known John F. Kennedy University (see above). The university had no day classes nor full-time faculty. As described in the introduction, this is where Chuck and I both received our baptism in the use of electronic technology to provide access and learning.

His interview, from the perspective of an adjunct instructor, describes the instructional process and offers insight into the motivation for becoming an adjunct, that category of instructor that has become an indispensable part of the online movement. Without adjuncts—and their interest and desire to be a part of the early efforts described here—we would not have anywhere near the progress we have realized. Certainly, the slow acceptance by traditional, full-time faculty continues to be a concern. Chuck and I would both go on to share our experience in this arena at UC Berkeley Extension and, in his case, UC Irvine, where he worked with Gary Matkin, another of our authors.

Veterans of the UMUC move online, Julie Porosky Hamlin and Gerald Heeger, provide insights into and details about the rise of Quality Matters (QM), in the case of Julie's chapter, and a broad exploration of online learning's larger place in higher education, in Jerry's interview. Julie provides a clear picture of the need to address the perception often raised by those critical of online learning: that it offers an inferior learning experience of lower quality than that found in a classroom. Recognizing the importance of quality standards and procedures for assuring that those standards are met, QM reflects the concern of many that there be no compromise in the quality of the learning experience due to the means of access (i.e., computer vs. classroom). Julie traces the evolution of the Quality Matters organization from its start with twelve schools in Maryland (MarylandOnline), to a national entity with hundreds of members.

Jerry Heeger's interview provides another change of pace to our series of essays, both in form and content. He provides a thoughtful and introspective account of his career and his involvement in continuing higher education. Against this background, he provides a macro-picture of his journey along the electronic highway, from NYU Online to UMUC, and from UMUC to the entrepreneurial work of Randy Best and Academic Partnerships. Jerry's comments refer to colleagues at various institutions across the nation, and illustrate the web of connections and relationships that have facilitated sector evolution. He also notes, as do others throughout, the critical role played by Frank Mayadas, Ralph Gomory, and the Sloan Foundation, in bringing online education to a sustainable point.

An early participant in the pre-computer world is my long-time friend and colleague, Susan Kryczka, who describes her early involvement with televised instruction, the National Technological University, and its approach to graduate engineering instruction at the Illinois Institute of Technology. She also describes her moves to Northeastern University and later to Boston University, along with her role in introducing the online model at both institutions.

Chris Dede is a tenured faculty member of the Graduate School of Education at Harvard. He has held the Timothy Wirth Professorship in Learning Technologies since 2000. He is considered one of the leading voices on the intersection of learning and technology in America today. His work in helping the faculty at other institutions overcome their skepticism of online learning has made a powerful contribution toward the goal of attaining greater faculty buy-in. Chris's research has focused on three aspects of what are emerging as new areas of academic specialization: emerging technologies, leadership in educational technology implementation, and effective policy for educational technology implementation. As a scholar in this sector, Chris not only chronicles the successes that have resulted, but also reminds us of the significant work yet to be done. His central thesis is that we are adopting technology more quickly than we are learning how to use it.

Jim Hall and Richard Bonnabeau provide a comprehensive overview of the State University of New York's (SUNY) efforts to embrace online learning. Well before today's attempt to create Open SUNY Online, the SUNY system developed Empire State College, of which Jim was the founding president, as a laboratory for experimentation with distance education. It also served as a precursor to the SUNY Learning Network, described so well by Eric Fredericksen in the chapter that follows.

Jim and Richard provide both a detailed history of the Empire State founding and a description of the rich environment for innovation that existed in New York State in the early 1970s. They also deal with issues of pedagogy and student performance within the models that emerged.

Between the period of development at Empire State College and the Open SUNY initiative, championed by former SUNY Chancellor Zimpher today, we find the SUNY Learning Network of the 1990s, which Eric Fredericksen, its founding director, details in his chapter. Facing many of the same issues as Gary Miller at Penn State and Jerry Heeger at UMUC, Eric takes us down familiar paths as he, too, deals with a skeptical and fearful faculty, a lack of resources, and the challenge of creating the right organizational structure. Not included here is the closing of the SUNY Learning Network, which followed Eric's time as director, and its transformation into Open SUNY. The political factors of this repositioning, like the closing of the Texas TeleCampus (see Darcy Hardy's chapter), provide insights and lessons learned in the sustainability of these undertakings in the face of politics and shifting priorities.

Throughout this book are frequent mentions of the many contributions made to online learning by the Alfred P. Sloan Foundation. Initially titling its initiative, the Asynchronous Learning Networks (ALN), the Sloan Foundation also created the professional network known as Sloan-C ("C" for consortium), of which John Bourne was the founding director. Meg Benke, Kathleen Ives, and Jill Buban, in a later chapter, describe the evolution of this consortium into the OLC, or Online Learning Consortium, as it has grown beyond the early ALN.

The annual survey on the state of online learning in America, also known as the Sloan Report, is described in Jeff Seaman's chapter. In both instances, the move away from the Sloan name is in keeping with the foundation's wishes and in recognition that the ALN, the consortium, and the annual survey have all evolved to require broader, ongoing support.

In "The Creation of Sloan-C," John Bourne provides a detailed look at the history, mission, and evolution of the initiative, including the thinking behind its creation and the work that is has furthered. John offers an impressive accounting of the numerous Sloan grants made to create and maintain the consortium over its life (from 1995 until 2013). Emphasizing the depth of the foundation's commitment, it also underscores the Gomory/Maya-das belief that the recipients of the foundation's largesse had a role to play in expanding awareness, acceptance, and advocacy for this new form of learning facilitation.

Darcy Hardy's interview chronicles the rise and fall of Texas's UT TeleCampus, which was strategically positioned within the UT system to assure access to resources, minimize the "selling" that would be needed to create multiple campus-based programs, and to send a signal to system members that this was important. The success of this approach, according to Darcy's account, would appear to be the reason for its eventual demise. Having stimulated online programming at its various campuses, the system's role was thought complete by its chancellor, and it was closed in 2010. In describing her career since UT, Darcy illustrates the many ways that the knowledge developed in the creation and operation of one of these initiatives (such as the TeleCampus) migrates both into government (various agencies in Darcy's case) as well as business (Blackboard).

In his discussion of online and open education, Gary Matkin, a long time friend and a former boss to both me and Chuck Hill, discusses the arrival of online education and the lessons that might be relevant to the emergence of Massive Open Online Courses, or MOOCs, and open (read "free") learning generally.

Gary makes a case for "universal learning" and the role that the open educational resources (OER) and MOOCs may play in achieving this objective. His advocacy for MOOCs and OER participation may not be well received by all. MOOCs must also pass through the phases of skeptical analysis and pilot efforts that we have seen with mainstream online advances. As others have noted, the advent of MOOCs has brought with it much conflation as to what online learning is and is not. This is thought to have added fuel to faculty opposition as the pedagogical weaknesses of MOOCs are often attributed to the older, instructor-led courses that now serve millions of higher education enrollees.

Those of us who were, or still are, skeptical of online learning must bring the same openness to new thinking, which we have asked for "traditional" online methods, to that of MOOCs. While not yet clearly understood, their role in achieving universal education is promising. Building upon the experience of establishing a "node" in the ALN, Gary sees many parallels with what MOOCs and OER face today.

Little mentioned in the evolution of online learning is the business vendor, that is, the company that creates or modifies software, examinations, or proctoring services to facilitate broad, credible learning outcomes. These are the providers of services and products that have also been just as essential to the revolution as those of the academy. Where would we be today without the contributions of e-learning (once known as Real Education), Embanet, WebCT, Pearson/Vue, ProctorU, and yes, even Blackboard, the learning management system (LMS) provider we love to hate, and Canvas, which is now taking the LMS market by storm.

The next interview in this cavalcade is a representative of the vendor community that has contributed so much to the revolution. Carol Vallone was the founding CEO of WebCT. She is a serial entrepreneur with a host of start-ups to her credit. She describes her career in innovative software development and what it was like to build and see one of the most popular learning management systems (second only to its eventual acquirer, Blackboard), take root in higher education. Along the way, she discusses the changes occurring today within the academy from a business point of view, and the growing popularity of competency-based education (CBE), an arena in which she is attempting to recreate the success of WebCT. Heading the start-up, Meteor Learning, she and her team have founded an online program management (OPM) firm that supports both the student and instructor in navigating the CBE process. As with MOOCs and OER, CBE represents yet another variation in the use of online technology to further higher education goals.

Stephen Andriole's chapter, "Learning from Screens," is an account of Drexel University's dive into the online pool. Also starting in the early 1990s, Andriole provides well-illustrated examples of what it is like to be on the receiving end of online learning. He ends his piece with the disquieting observation that the last two decades are but "the beginning of major educational disruption."

Another contribution to the field has been an annual survey that provides insight into its changing status. Over its decade-long life, the annual survey on online learning has had different names and sponsors. Initially created to support the work of the Sloan Foundation, the highly-regarded report that came from this survey, was known, at least informally, as the Sloan Report. This later gave way to the Babson Report, in recognition of that institution's role in hosting the survey and its administering staff. Jeff Seaman describes how he and his wife, Elaine Allen, have evolved this must-read source of information about the sector's progress, as well as some remaining challenges, such as faculty acceptance. In addition to describing the difficulty of just defining distance and online instruction in the early years, Jeff goes on to explore trends the survey has helped to identify, as well as detailing the economic factors that must be considered. What may strike some as unsettling in Jeff's interview is the news that the survey is being taken over by the federal government and the Department of Education and its Integrated Postsecondary Education Data System (IPEDS).

Meg Benke, Kathleen Ives, and Jill Buban have joined forces in the next-to-last chapter to describe the evolution of the Sloan-C Consortium now, as developed by John Bourne and Frank Mayadas, into the Online Learning Consortium, headed by Kathleen. They discuss areas of similarity and difference, along with future areas of emphasis, such as advocacy for post-traditional students broadly, not just those online. The three authors describe areas of expected research and publication, as well as incentives for participation. A profile of member institution demographics reflects how large and diverse the consortium has become in just over two decades.

In the final chapter, Paul Shiffman, CEO of the Presidents' Forum, describes the ten-year effort to create and build support for an oversight framework that would allow online serving institutions to meet the regulatory requirements of the various states in which they have students. Interestingly, this effort started voluntarily in 2006 as an attempt to simplify what at the time required separate scrutiny and approval from each of fifty-four different jurisdictions (states, plus territories and the District of Columbia). Passage of the Department of Education's program integrity regulations gave this effort added impetus as failure to comply with the state authorization rules could now result in loss of Title IV entitlement. Previously, there had been no such penalty for a failure to obtain a state's approval. As of this writing, more than forty states have adopted the State Authorization Reciprocity Agreement, or SARA framework.

I hope you will enjoy reading this important history of one of higher education's most successful revolutions, which is providing access and instruction to millions of Americans. This work is too important to be forgotten.

THE PENN STATE WORLD CAMPUS
A Profile in Institutional Innovation

Gary E. Miller

Executive Director Emeritus
Penn State World Campus

When The Pennsylvania State University first began to explore the idea of an online campus in the summer of 1996, the university was already a leader in distance education. Nevertheless, online learning—embodied in what was to become the Penn State World Campus—was a change that proved to be, if not disruptive, transformational within Penn State's historic mission as a land-grant university.

A BRIEF HISTORY
Penn State's commitment to serving students at a distance dates back to 1892, when it was one of three universities (the other two being the University of Wisconsin and the University of Chicago) that pioneered independent study by correspondence, using an

innovative new delivery system—Rural Free Delivery (RFD). Penn State's Home Reading Program in Agriculture was, like RFD itself, a response to the rapid urbanization and immigration that marked the Industrial Revolution. There was a concern that the country's agricultural production could not keep pace with urbanization. RFD was designed to improve the quality of rural life—to "keep them down on the farm", as the old song says, and improve home life and agricultural production.

Over the decades, Penn State's correspondence study program grew well beyond its agricultural roots. By the 1990s, the program served more than 18,000 learners from all fifty states and twenty countries around the world.

During and after World War II, Penn State innovated with new technologies. During the war, Dr. Ray Carpenter had experimented in the use of film for military training. After the war, as the university struggled to accommodate large numbers of new students on campus through the GI Bill of Rights, Carpenter was instrumental in creating the University Division of Instructional Services, which provided film, graphics, photography services, and video production support for on-campus courses. During the 1950s, the university addressed student demand for high-enrolling courses by interconnecting twenty-four classrooms with a one-way video, two-way audio network that allowed faculty to teach larger numbers of students in traditional-sized classrooms.

In 1965, the university launched its own public television station, which served the largely small town and rural central Pennsylvania area. The station delivered video instruction to the area's public schools and also offered a service called University of the Air that combined broadcast video lessons and periodic meetings at local campuses to deliver credit and noncredit courses to adult students.

The 1980s saw more innovation driven by new video technologies of satellite and cable television. The university created a new Division of Media and Learning Resources that combined the production and delivery resources of public broadcasting, the Division of Instructional Services, Independent Study by Correspondence, and the university's audio-visual library. It also partnered with cable television companies to create PENNARAMA, a statewide instructional cable television service, and began to offer both credit courses and noncredit teleconferences nationally over satellite. Video lessons were now integrated with correspondence study materials, so that no classroom meetings were required. The new unit reported to the vice president for continuing education (later renamed outreach).

In 1992, the university-wide Task Force on Distance Education, noting that distance education should be considered as a central strategy for growth, recommended that current distance education initiatives and resources be integrated into a Department of Distance Education within the domain of Outreach and Cooperative Extension. The university-wide Distance Education Advisory Committee was created to help move distance education into the institutional mainstream.

By 1994, considerable energy surrounding distance education was focused on interactive video systems—including dial-up video teleconferencing—that allowed institutions to distribute live classroom sessions to sites around the world. Penn State equipped all of its twenty-four campuses for interactive video and shifted its satellite-based distributed classroom programs to industry sites to dial-up services. At the same time, the university was experimenting with the use of computer-based learning on campus. It established a computer-based learning laboratory to help faculty members experiment with online applications.

ONLINE LEARNING AS A DISRUPTIVE INNOVATION

In June 1996, Penn State president Graham Spanier returned from a conference at which the Western Interstate Commission on Higher Education (WICHE) announced its plan to create an online institution: Western Governors University. President Spanier called together a small group that included the provost, the executive director of computer and information systems, the budget officer, vice president for outreach, James Ryan, and me in my role as associate vice president for distance education. He laid out what he saw as the university's options given the emergence of online learning as a potential change agent:

- The university already had a diverse distance education program rooted in correspondence study and in video distribution. We could experiment with a few courses via online learning and see how the field developed.
- We could stick to our current media and program design for distance education and stay out of the online movement.
- We could invest heavily in online and transform our distance education program to one that was totally online.
- We could decide to get out of distance education altogether.

At the end of the conversation, we agreed that the first two options were not realistic. If we stayed the course and just experimented on the fringe with online, or if we simply avoided e-learning, the group agreed that we would likely be left behind by the technology revolution. Our realistic options were to make a significant investment in online learning or to abandon our distance education mission. We agreed on the former. Outreach vice president Jim Ryan and I were asked to develop a talking paper, and, in his "State of the University" address at the beginning of fall semester, President Spanier noted plans to explore the creation of an online "World Campus"—a name suggested by Fred Gaige, who was then chancellor at Penn State's Berks Campus.

THE STUDY TEAM

Spanier appointed a study team to develop plans for the World Campus. The study team consisted of twenty-one members, including leaders of all the major university units that might be affected by the innovation and whose support would be critical to success. Included were the university budget officer, director of educational technology services, dean of international programs, dean of libraries, vice provost for undergraduate programs, dean of the graduate school, representatives of key academic colleges and the faculty senate and graduate council, and key outreach staff in marketing, development, and distance education support services.

The study team met once every two weeks over dinner, from November 1996 through March 1997. The result was a sixty-six-page report that envisioned how the World Campus would help Penn State "become a national leader in the integration of distance education into the fabric of the 21st-century land-grant university." The vision was supported by six objectives:

- Matching the assessed needs of employers and individuals with academic resources in which Penn State has an acknowledged leadership position.
- Using a variety of technologies to create a distance learning environment that encourages active and collaborative learning through a variety of appropriate technologies.
- Focusing on the needs of employers and individuals and using a wide range of program formats and institutional partnerships to meet those needs.
- Employing a curriculum team approach that supports faculty initiative and encourages innovation.
- Generating revenue for participating academic units to stimulate ongoing academic innovation and program development and support.
- Measuring the impact of technology-based program designs on the efficiency, effectiveness, and productivity of learning.

The report also established guiding principles for faculty participation, student access, funding, and governance. It described how programs would be identified, the curriculum team approach for developing courses, organization and staffing, funding, and criteria for success. The report was presented to the faculty senate, the graduate council, and, ultimately, to the university board of trustees, which approved us to move ahead.

AT&T INNOVATIONS IN DISTANCE EDUCATION PROJECTS

One factor that informed the study team's discussions, and thus helped to prepare the way for the World Campus, was a national three-year Innovations in Distance Education (IDE), led by Penn State and funded by the AT&T Foundation. This had begun in 1995, when the focus was on interactive video networks as an emerging innovation that would allow the university to link individuals and groups in live distance education classes. IDE brought together a national group of leaders from eleven land-grant universities and eight historically black universities to make recommendations on institutional policy and planning innovations that colleges and universities would need in order to develop or expand media-based distance education programs. The project centered on three invitational symposia that, as it turned out, overlapped with the planning for the World Campus.

The first symposium, held in 1995, focused on administrative and financial policy issues affecting the growth of distance education in their institutions; the second, in 1996, examined the role of faculty and policies needed to support faculty in development and delivery of distance education programs; the third, held in 1998, looked at distance education from the learner's perspective, focusing on the learner's participation in courses, curriculum development, and learner support policies.

The IDE recommendations, coming as they did from a community of peer institutions, helped create a context for the study team's work. For instance, at the first symposium the institutional representatives agreed on an over-arching principle to guide the development of distance education at an institution: "Distance education will be an integral part of the mission of higher education; a key component of the institution's overall goal of improving the teaching and learning process; and a significant component of the teaching, learning, and administrative environment of the twenty-first century university" (Distance Education and the University Culture, p. 6). The second symposium focused on faculty support and arrived at three model policy statements that related to faculty support services, faculty rewards, and the need for an institutional commitment to ensure support across all relevant disciplines. The third symposium focused on learner support and resulted in eight model policy statements designed to ensure quality in terms of defining and reaching learners, providing access to learning resources, and maintaining and assessing quality.

THE SLOAN FOUNDATION

While these early steps were being taken, we also benefitted from a growing relationship with the Alfred P. Sloan Foundation's Asynchronous Learning Networks (ALN) initiative, led by Dr. Frank Mayadas. Penn State had an early Sloan ALN grant in 1993-94 for a media-based distance education program designed to prepare engineering graduates to take the professional licensing examination for engineers. The program was delivered largely by video; the real innovation was the use of online technology for students to take sample tests.

In 1996, the university received a second Sloan Foundation grant to develop an online version of one of our most popular video-based distance education programs—the Postbaccalaureate Certificate in Acoustics (Noise Control Engineering), offered by Penn State's College of Engineering. This, the university's first fully online program, was designed as part of a contract program for employees at companies involved in submarine technology development. It began development while the World Campus was still in planning, and rolled out as part of the World Campus' first semester.

While the study team was at work, we met individually with the deans of each of Penn State's twelve academic colleges to identify undergraduate and graduate degrees and certificate programs that might be appropriate to offer online. This generated about ninety ideas. The university received a Director's Grant from the Sloan Foundation to conduct secondary market research on these programs. Our goal was to ensure that programs launched in the first few years of operation would have a high chance of both initial and sustained enrollments and sustained support within the academic unit. For each program, Outreach marketing staff explored the national reputation of the program; faculty support; competing distance education programs at other institutions; the availability of a defined, reachable target audience; and possible partners, such as employers or professional associations. The results of this research helped narrow the list to twenty-five programs that became the focus of the first few years of program development.

By the time the study team report was approved, we were ready to submit a proposal to the Sloan Foundation to fund the first round of program development and operations. The grant was approved in June 1997, and the World Campus launched in January 1998 with forty-four student enrollments in four programs.

SUCCESS FACTORS
Program Positioning

One of the first four programs—the Undergraduate Certificate in Turfgrass Management—illustrates the initial program development strategy. Penn State has a longstanding, internationally reputed program in turfgrass management. Many golf course superintendents around the country and beyond are graduates of the program. The lead faculty member for the World Campus programs, Dr. Al Turgeon, is internationally known in the field and was an advocate for innovating with online technology. There was little competition among US institutions. Finally, the Golf Course Superintendents Association of America agreed to endorse the program for its members. All the ingredients of success were present: a highly regarded academic program, led by a well-known and innovative faculty member, targeted to an identifiable, reachable audience with support from well-placed alums and a national professional association.

Supporting Students

From the outset, World Campus programs benefitted from Penn State's long history in serving students at a distance. A strong student services infrastructure, evolved over the past century to support correspondence study, was already in place and was easily adapted to the needs of the World Campus. The staff was already expert at enrolling students at a distance, providing texts and other materials to distant students, proctoring examinations at a distance, and, perhaps most important in the long run, advising both prospective and continuing students, recognizing that, for many adults, taking college courses on top of other job, family, and professional responsibilities was a high-risk venture.

The Course Team Approach

Few faculty had experience in developing or teaching courses online. Penn State adopted a course team approach in which the World Campus staff provided a program manager who worked closely with the lead faculty member in the academic unit. In addition, the World Campus provided, for each course, an instructional designer, media developer, editor, and other support staff to work with the faculty member. The course team stayed in place as the program rolled out; it was assumed that a new course might need significant revision after the first offering and then updating every few years. Over time, some academic units decided to invest in their own instructional designers, who were embedded in the academic unit. However, the World Campus continues to maintain a central instructional design and development staff to ensure that all faculty members have support for course development and delivery.

Mainstreaming Technology

From the beginning, the university was committed to ensuring that the technology that would be used for distance education would be fully integrated into the university's infrastructure. The learning management system was mainstreamed in the university's central information technology unit, which had already been working with faculty to encourage the use of computer-based learning, especially in large classroom lecture courses. This encouraged faculty to develop online innovations for their on-campus courses that they could easily transfer to a World Campus course. Alternatively, it also made it easy to incorporate elements of World Campus courses into their on-campus counterparts. This also protected student data and discouraged departments and individual faculty from putting data on non-university servers. The result was an ongoing partnership between the World Campus and Information Technology Services. In 1999, the president charged a Web Strategies Task Force with exploring how to further enhance access, quality, and service for the Penn State community through the use of web technologies.

GOVERNANCE AND POLICY

Once the World Campus was approved, many members of the study team became the core of the university-wide World Campus Steering Committee that served to identify policy and governance issues. A key principle was that the World Campus would work within the governance culture and policy structure of the university in general. This extended to the World Campus the longstanding principle of shared governance, in which academic units were responsible for academic quality, while the World Campus, as an administrative unit, was responsible for non-academic issues such as infrastructure, marketing, student services, registration and records, finance, etc. It was also important to establish working partnerships between the World Campus and other administrative units, including Information Technology Services, the registrar and bursars offices, the library, and other campuses in the university's twenty-four-campus structure.

Academic Program Approval
All programs offered by the World Campus had to be housed in

an academic unit (or units, in the case of some interdisciplinary programs). They also had to be approved by the faculty senate (for undergraduate programs) or the graduate council (for graduate degrees and postbaccalaureate programs). To facilitate this, World Campus leaders were appointed by the provost to serve on the faculty senate and the graduate council. Being at the policy table allowed the World Campus to be present to discuss issues as they arose.

One issue arose early on at the graduate level: how to deal with the residency requirement embedded in all graduate degree programs. After discussions at several graduate council meetings, it was agreed that the purpose of a residency was to introduce the graduate student to the academic culture in which the graduate would be operating upon completing a degree. However, this was not necessarily a factor for professional degrees. Since the World Campus made it possible for students to study without leaving their workplace, the graduate council ruled that the World Campus could offer professional master's degrees (master of engineering, master of education, master of business administration, etc.), but not academic degrees (master of arts, master of science).

Finances

One fundamental assumption of the World Campus Steering Committee was that the World Campus should not be built at the risk of other academic commitments. The World Campus should be prepared to assume all financial risk. At the same time, the academic unit should benefit financially when it offered successful programs. Historically, academic units had not benefitted from distance education programs. Instructors were given extra compensation to develop and teach distance education courses, and the delivery unit—Outreach—bore the total financial risk and kept the proceeds. As the World Campus was being conceptualized, that all changed. The university approved a revenue sharing policy that outreach had developed with its Coordinating Council for Outreach and Cooperative Extension—the internal governing board that included associate deans from each academic college.

Initially, the Coordinating Council approved a *net* revenue sharing plan. Outreach would cover all costs and then share the net revenue with academic units. It didn't work. Academic units, fearful that the World Campus would always find costs to eat up all revenue, became overly cautious about spending, especially in areas like marketing and support. So the council reconsidered and agreed on a new *gross* revenue sharing policy, under which the World Campus would have primary responsibility for cost but the sponsoring academic unit would receive a specific percentage of each tuition dollar, depending on the degree to which it had a financial investment in the program. For instance, if the World Campus paid all costs—including faculty salaries for development and instruction—the academic unit would receive 10 percent of the tuition revenue. If the academic unit shared the financial risk—by funding faculty salaries, for instance, or by funding its own instructional designers or taking on other responsibilities—it would receive a higher percentage of the gross. This approach created a true partnership in which both the academic unit and the World Campus shared an interest in growth and long-term success.

Campus Relationships

Penn State operates as a single institution geographically dispersed, with a main campus at University Park, and twenty-three smaller campuses scattered across Pennsylvania, offering undergraduate and, in some cases, graduate degrees. The World Campus was planned as the twenty-fifth campus. The question arose: would the World Campus create internal competition with these campuses? To avoid that problem, the university created the Campus Course Exchange—a system by which a physical Penn State campus could include a specific World Campus course in its own schedule and offer it as a local course, collecting the tuition and paying a standard fee back to the World Campus to cover the cost of instruction. The mechanism was not widely used, but it did help to ensure that the World Campus would not unfairly compete with our traditional campuses.

Copyright Policy

The university also recognized the need to update its copyright policy to include technology-based courseware. It determined that, when the university initiated the development of courseware—essentially assigning a faculty member to develop a course—the resulting material would be considered a commissioned work, with the university owning the copyright. When a faculty member initiated the courseware, using university technical resources, the university did not claim copyright, but did claim the right to use the materials in university courses.

LAUNCHING THE WORLD CAMPUS

The World Campus launched in January 1998 with forty-eight student enrollments in the first four certificate programs: Chemical Dependency Counseling (College of Education), Fundamentals of Engineering (College of Engineering), Noise Control Engineering (College of Engineering), and Turfgrass Management (College of Agricultural Sciences). Additional programs—certificates in Geographic Information Systems (College of Earth and Mineral Sciences) and Electrical Engineering (College of Engineering)—launched in the fall.

By the end of summer, the World Campus had generated 108 student enrollments. By November, it had generated 3,335 inquiries from all fifty US states and sixty countries around the globe. It also generated forty-six inquiries from US service members posted outside the US. Of course, the most important success factor for the World Campus was the degree to which we helped students succeed in meeting their educational goals. For our students, the World Campus was not simply an innovation; it was chance for them to achieve their educational dreams. One early student, a school teacher, bought her first computer in order to gain access to the World Campus. Another, one of our early Turfgrass Management students, was in the military and continued with the program when he was posted to Iraq.

THE WORLD CAMPUS TODAY

Today, the World Campus offers more than forty undergraduate degrees, minors, and certificates and more than sixty master's degrees and certificates, plus its first doctoral degree in nursing. In the academic year 2014-15, it served 15,491 unique students (not including students from other Penn State campuses who took occasional World Campus courses) in all fifty states and eighty-one countries around the world, making it the second largest of Penn State's twenty-five campuses. *US News and World Report* ranked it the best provider of online bachelor's degrees in the United States. It also ranks in the top ten military-friendly campuses.

The success of the World Campus can be traced to many factors, including the quality of Penn State's faculty and academic programs, strong faculty support for course development and delivery, and the longstanding commitment to student support. To those, I would add the early commitment of Penn State's leadership to (1) start with a vision, (2) engage a broad leadership community in defining how to achieve that vision, and (3) ensure that World Campus policies were well-integrated with the university's policy and governance culture. This early mainstreaming set the stage for the effective institutionalization that has allowed for ongoing innovation.

UMUC'S VIRTUAL UNIVERSITY
Expanding Access for Nontraditional Students

Patricia Wallace

Former Associate Vice President and Chief Information Officer
University of Maryland University College

The mission of University of Maryland University College (UMUC) has been, since its founding in 1947, to bring higher education opportunities to nontraditional students who don't neatly fit the picture of typical, full-time college students enrolling in a university right out of high school. "Nontraditional," of course, covers considerable ground. It might describe a mid-career manager seeking to switch careers, or perhaps a young Marine corporal stationed in Okinawa who wants to earn a bachelor's degree. The term also applies to working parents with young children, farmers who live far from any city, nuclear power plant employees who staff the night shift in remote locations, entrepreneurs seeking to start their own businesses, or retirees who want to study humanities now that they have more time to indulge their passions. These are the kinds of students who flock to UMUC and who early recognized the enormous value of distance education and online learning when UMUC became an enthusiastic pioneer.

This chapter explores the early history of UMUC's groundbreaking, student-centered efforts to make higher education more accessible to its nontraditional students, examining the major successes as well as those initiatives that did not work out well. After first emphasizing a distributed learning model, in which faculty traveled to hundreds of remote sites around the world to teach small classes, UMUC embraced a fully online, virtual university that now brings together faculty and students from literally every continent. UMUC's experiences with technology platforms, curriculum development, faculty training and logistics, assessment strategies, student services, and other areas shed light on the many challenges that surfaced during this tumultuous beginning of online learning and the successes that followed. I served as UMUC's chief information officer from 1991 to 1999, and before that, was a faculty member and head of IT in UMUC's Asian Division, so I had a front row seat during this period.

UMUC'S ORIGINS

How did a university come into existence with a mission to serve nontraditional students across Maryland and then around the world? In 1947, UMUC began as the College of Special and Continuation Studies, initially as part of the University of Maryland College Park. This new division's mission was to reach out to mature, working adults around the state who could not enroll as full-time students on the main campus, but who could take one or two courses—provided they were offered at convenient times and locations. In the first years, students enrolled in courses offered in the evenings and weekends on military facilities such as Fort Meade and the Pentagon, business premises such as the Calvert Distilling Company, and also in communities far from the College Park campus, such as Salisbury on the state's eastern shore, and Cumberland in Maryland's western panhandle.

The response from students was overwhelming, particularly among military students, many of whom were just returning from World War II, eager to get their careers back on track. But many military members were still overseas at bases in occupied Germany, Japan, and other locations. They, too, sought opportunities to pursue their degrees, and, in 1949 at the request of the Pentagon, the college began sending professors first to Europe, and then to Asia, scheduling courses at large military bases, former Nazi barracks, remote outposts in South Korea, Department of Defense high schools in Japan, and, by the 1960s, even tents with makeshift blackboards in Vietnam's war zones. UMUC officially took on its current name and became a separately accredited, degree-granting institution of the University of Maryland System in 1970, building on rapidly rising enrollments and a steady mission to continue serving nontraditional students. (Hudgins, 2008; Parker, 2006; University of Maryland University College Self-Study, 1986, 1996, 2006).

DISTRIBUTED EDUCATION

An early hallmark of how UMUC approached its mission can be called distributed education. Rather than establishing a large, centralized campus with multiple buildings for classrooms, labs, and offices, the university made agreements to schedule small classes at many different sites that would be more convenient for students to access. This approach called for faculty who were willing to travel, and who were flexible enough to adapt to a myriad of classroom conditions. For the overseas programs, UMUC recruited some faculty who could move to a new military base every eight weeks, which was the length of the academic terms.

Many of these facilities were very well-equipped, such as the UMUC headquarters in Adelphi, Maryland, and the many military education centers constructed for the larger bases. But others brought surprises that required faculty to improvise in innovative ways. Blackboards and chalk, for instance, might be in short supply. One faculty member I met carried his own portable mimeograph machine to reproduce handouts and tests, modeled after an early, manually operated Chinese version.

Classes were typically small and personal, and the adult students left their rank or status markings outside the door. For example, faculty addressed military members as Mr. or Ms., regardless of rank, and CEOs and office clerks sat side by side. These status-free environments encouraged a classroom norm in which students could freely express themselves.

While the classes were enthusiastically welcomed by students in many remote areas, the distributed education model had limitations, particularly because of the difficulty of offering a range of courses at small sites. At most locations, lower-level courses in subjects such as math and English attracted enough students, as did the foreign language courses at the overseas military bases. But options narrowed for upper-level courses, especially at smaller sites and for students interested in majoring in less popular fields.

In the early 1990s, UMUC began experimenting in Maryland with technology-enabled distributed education models to fill some of these gaps. One approach deployed audiographics, in which students convened at a few sites to listen to a live audio lecture delivered by a professor at a central location, and broadcast, along with slides, to students at other sites. While that technology made it possible to expand access to more course options, it was not very well received by students or faculty. Students at remote sites felt disconnected, with little opportunity to interact with other classmates or the professor. One administrator who evaluated the system for its potential for use at isolated nuclear power facilities said the system was, at best, marginally acceptable for people in desperate need of a particular course.

By the mid-1990s, UMUC took advantage of an interactive video network (IVN) to enhance the distributed education model, a technology launched by the University System of Maryland (Teaching Meets Technology, 1995). This network added video interaction using cameras and TV monitors at a handful of locations in Maryland, so students and professors could see one another during the class. While IVN offered richer communication channels, the system was expensive to implement and cumbersome to use. It also limited access to the few sites with installations. While quite useful for special-purpose niche applications, this kind of proprietary video network could not scale to meet the growing needs for working adults around the world.

BUILDING THE VIRTUAL UNIVERSITY

Recognizing that its student body needed flexibility and easy access, UMUC began experimenting with a variety of distance education options before most academics were even using that term. The overriding goal was to provide working adults the opportunity to engage in higher education independent of the constraints associated with time and place. For example, UMUC tried "newspaper" courses, first in the European Division in the 1970s, and a few years later in Asia. The military daily *Stars and Stripes* was enlisted to provide reading assignments and faculty commentary while exams were administered in regular classroom settings. With few takers, this approach soon faded.

More successful were early efforts modeled after Britain's Open University, in which students could earn credits through structured independent study guided by tutors and relying on television lectures, videotapes, texts, and radio broadcasts, without actually attending classes. In 1991, UMUC became the first university to offer a degree-completion program through the National University Degree Consortium, with students taking advantage of some course materials offered through cable and satellite television, supplemented by telephone conferencing and voice mail.

A key breakthrough for UMUC's vision for the virtual university emerged as students and faculty gained access to the Internet, and rapidly adopted e-mail. Faculty in both the Asian and European Divisions began offering courses that relied on e-mail interactions, and they also used mailing lists called listservs to engage students at a distance and distribute materials. The technology at the time was variable, to say the least, and military students also had to comply with varied regulations about its use. One faculty member teaching business courses in Europe recalled the frustration of trying to e-mail course materials, and frequently running into blocks due to limits on file sizes (James Stewart, January 11, 2016, personal communication).

UMUC's vision for the virtual university, from early on, was far more than simply experimenting with a few online courses that might supplement the curriculum for students who enrolled mainly in face-to-face classes. Many other universities were approaching online learning in that way, or as a backup for regular classes that might be interrupted by inclement weather, pandemics, or other emergencies. Understanding the needs of nontraditional students, UMUC's leadership envisioned a much broader concept, one that embraced full degree programs as well as a rich complement of easily accessible student services, to include registrations and financial aid, academic advising, remedial programs, library resources, and even extracurricular activities. A fundamental component of this vision was the technology infrastructure, and UMUC took on this challenge.

THE TYCHO SERIES
Creating the Infrastructure for the Virtual University
E-mail certainly paved the way for faculty and students to communicate on an "anytime, anywhere" basis, but its limitations as a means to manage a classroom, let alone whole academic programs and student services, were noticeable. Rather than relying on the myriad e-mail and mailing list systems that were popping up, UMUC launched an initiative to create the technology infrastructure that, once students logged in, would simulate actual classrooms and even a whole campus. We named the software series "Tycho," after the colorful sixteenth-century Danish astronomer Tycho Brahe, who made remarkably accurate and comprehensive observations on the planets and other astronomical bodies, without the assistance of telescopes. Brahe was the last of the "naked eye" astronomers. In the IT department, we created a new unit called Learning Applications, Development, and Support (LEADS), and John VanAntwerp led

the team. He was an enthusiastic evangelist for the potential for the virtual university; before coming to UMUC, he worked on the original Plato project at the University of Illinois, another pioneer of innovative computer-based education.

The first iteration of UMUC's software was built for DOS computers, programmed in the C language as a client/server application. Students installed the software on their PCs, and then dialed into one of UMUC's hundreds of modems at the (then) breathtaking speed of 1200 baud. Once logged in, the student could enter his or her classroom, view the syllabus and other course materials, engage in discussion forums, join study groups, contact the professor and classmates, and participate in other activities. An important design principle was that the software must be able to run on the kinds of computers that students actually had, and it should not require them to purchase high-end machines to take classes.

Early on, in 1994, we were invited to do a live presentation for the University System of Maryland Board of Regents, to show them what the future might hold for UMUC's vision for using the Internet for higher education. Our team carefully set up the laptop, projection screen, modem, and telephone line, and we crossed our fingers that all would work as planned. It did, and the next day's headline in the *Diamondback*, the University of Maryland College Park's campus newspaper, read "Regents Get Glimpse of Future Cyber-Campus" (Crecente, 1994).

As technology changed, Tycho evolved with it, with releases for the Windows operating sytem (WinTycho), MacIntosh (MacTycho), and eventually WebTycho, which was first built using the Lotus Domino application development platform, and later converted to IBM's Websphere, with Oracle as the underlying database. (UMUC finally retired WebTycho in 2014 after a remarkable lifespan, and the university migrated its online programs to a commercial learning management system.)

While the software was continually improved and new features added, the main components continued to stress ease of use. Students had access to all the major elements of the course, including materials available to all students such as faculty announcements, syllabus, and course content, and also privately submitted material, such as messages from the faculty, teaching assistant, or other students, as well as grades and feedback on assignments. Students could enter the chat room to engage in pre-arranged synchronous sessions with classmates or faculty, and faculty could use that functionality to hold online office hours, supplemented by telephone calls (SchWeber, n.d.).

Faculty tools were also critical to the success of this early virtual campus, and faculty input was vital as the software progressed. Faculty could post announcements, add content items, assign readings from the library, lead interactive conferences, post grades, and return assignments with feedback. They could also copy key aspects of their classes from one semester to the next, avoiding unnecessary reworking. The early versions of Tycho were primarily text-based, but the system began to support more multimedia once it was converted to a graphical and then web-based platform. Faculty could add images, audio, and video to course content, and students could embed such elements into their postings and online profiles. All these features continue as core elements of modern learning management systems.

THE CHALLENGES OF THE EARLY VIRTUAL UNIVERSITY

Skepticism among educators about the effectiveness of online learning ran high in the 1990s, even among some UMUC faculty and administrators, and it presented an important challenge. Some faculty scoffed at teaching classes while relying mainly on a text-based medium, which lacked the rich communication channels as when faculty and students shared the same physical classroom. Stripped of all the nonverbal communication associated with facial expressions, gestures, and eye contact, how could faculty create the positive learning environment of a live class? Other faculty, however, became champions, embracing the medium's potential for a new kind of learning environment—one in which students took on more responsibility for their own learning, and faculty could serve more as the "guide on the side" rather than the "sage on the stage." The text-based online environment was also liberating to many mature working students who felt a bit awkward attending classes filled with eighteen- to- twenty-two-year olds. Faculty frequently remarked that shy students were more willing to participate in a virtual class where what they said (or typed) was more important than how they looked.

Early empirical research on the effectiveness of distance education compared to face-to-face classes began appearing, but results were highly variable, and the methodologies used to make comparisons and draw conclusions were often flawed. For example, researchers were rarely able to randomly assign students to treatment groups, so self-selection confounded the findings. Also, "distance education" describes an enormous variety of activities. Nevertheless, meta-analyses that attempted to identify effect sizes based on dozens or hundreds of studies most often found either no significant differences for learning outcomes, or a slight improvement for online students. (e.g., Bernard et al., 2004; Means, Toyama, Murphy, & Baki, 2013; Williams, 2006).

From a psychological standpoint, many argued that online environments would hinder learning, but the research did not support that conclusion. In fact, several aspects point toward certain advantages for students. For example, most of the communication inside a virtual class is asynchronous, so students have ample time to think through their posts and improve them through edits. They can also craft a persona for their profiles that shows them in the best light and boosts their confidence. For UMUC in particular, another advantage is a high level of diversity in the classes, with students enrolling in the same class who come from many different racial, ethnic, and cultural backgrounds, who follow different career paths, and who live in geographically distributed locations. That diversity enriches the class discussions, and often motivates students to be more creative, work harder, and perform at higher levels than they might otherwise (Lount & Phillips, 2007; Wallace, 2013).

Another challenge involved faculty training and development, which not only required faculty to learn new technology skills, but to acquire new techniques for effective teaching and class management in the new medium. For the virtual university, UMUC did not follow the broadcasting model, in which much of the delivery involves one-way transmission of information, an emphasis on multimedia presentations, and also large class sizes. Instead, UMUC leveraged its traditional learning model, with small classes and much interaction between students and faculty, and also among students themselves (Allen, 2001). As a result, faculty needed to learn how to use Tycho for intensive interactions, group conferencing, online chat sessions, messaging, and breakout study groups.

Development efforts for the Tycho series relied heavily on input from faculty, so the software was continually improved to support their needs and the kinds of interactions that defined UMUC's approach. One key ingredient, for example, was that the user interface for communication must be very simple to use, posing a short learning curve for both students and faculty. People quickly tuned out if the software was overly complicated or if the technology became a burden and an obstacle to learning.

As for pedagogical strategies, faculty began learning how to adapt their styles to the new environment and even to leverage some features of it to improve on traditional classes. One element, for instance, was simply an emphasis on timeliness. In face-to-face classes, students generally ask questions during the class session or wait for the professor's weekly office hours. Online, however, students quickly learned that they could send questions to faculty at any time of day or night, and often receive responses within a few hours. A graduate student stationed on the remote island of Kwajalein in the mid-Pacific, for example, recalls how valuable her professor's timeliness was to her: "As a long-distance learner, nothing is worse than being stuck on something and unable to proceed without clarification from a professor" (Eve Cran, January 31, 2016, personal communication).

Instructional design and development for the emerging online environment presented a third challenge, but UMUC's experience with innovative, technology-based approaches helped prepare the institution to make this leap. UMUC's Center for Instructional Design and Evaluation, for example, had already developed interactive videodiscs that were used as course materials for some undergraduate programs, so it readily supported the demands of virtual university courses at the undergraduate level. Online graduate courses were mostly developed by the faculty themselves.

The challenges of designing, building and supporting the technology infrastructure went well beyond what traditional campuses faced at the time. For example, UMUC at first assumed much of the responsibility for helping students connect to the Internet and to our servers in the Adelphi data center. That involved implementing a massive telecommunications infrastructure with racks of modems installed at many locations around the state, so that students could dial local phone numbers and avoid long distance charges. It also involved a relentless need to increase the number of lines and upgrade the modems as speeds improved. The breathtaking growth in the number of students enrolled in online courses, however, along with the widening reach to students far removed from our Maryland sites, soon overtook our determined efforts to support the demand. Fortunately, the private sector was stepping into this market space and building out their own dial-in modem infrastructure, so that students had many options to connect to the Internet with local phone numbers.

Capacity planning was at the forefront because of such rapid growth. In 1994, UMUC had 110 online enrollments. That number grew to more than 60,000 by FY 2001, which represents an astonishing 54,000 percent increase in just seven years (Allen, 2001). Each semester, the capability of UMUC's network and server to support the ever-growing traffic was stretched thin, requiring very frequent upgrades. Eventually, UMUC moved to clusters of synchronized servers, and students took advantage of faster Internet connections. The sheer pace of change, not just in the technologies themselves, but in students' access to it, was an important element in UMUC's infrastructure planning and decision-making. For instance, many wanted to add voice capabilities using VoIP to Tycho's functionality, but that feature was delayed because most students were still relying on dial-up connections and so would not be able to use the feature ("Going the distance to set up Tycho in Japan," 1997; Shank, Precht, Singh, Everidge, & Bozarth, 2008).

The ease with which students can now obtain a wifi connection, not just in their homes, but in coffee shops, airports, or simply by launching their own hot spot with a smartphone, makes people forget how frustrating connectivity was in the 1990s. UMUC's technical support team worked tirelessly to help students and faculty connect to the virtual university, and patience was a precious commodity. Challenges for UMUC were particularly acute because of the university's worldwide reach, especially to military facilities with secure networks. One student, for instance, who was trying to submit a final project so he could graduate, was on the aircraft carrier Kitty Hawk when it was deployed in the Persian Gulf, and the UMUC technical team worked closely with the military engineers so he wouldn't miss his graduation date.

As substantial as the challenges were, the benefits to UMUC's students were even greater. Students in all 50 states and on every continent, who might never have been able to pursue a degree in the past because of their situations, could do just that.

CONCLUSIONS

UMUC has a long and colorful history of serving nontraditional students in innovative ways, always working to make higher education accessible to this distinct population. The university has won numerous awards for its efforts. For example, in 2015, the World Affairs Council named UMUC "Educator of the Year" for its role as a leader in innovative education models.

Overcoming the many uphill battles of those early years, the virtual university quickly became the most significant component in UMUC's programs. Online learning and the virtual campus may not be the environment of choice for many traditional students, but for certain populations it is remarkably effective and welcome, especially for those who don't quite fit into traditional settings. For example, highly gifted students who become bored in grade-level classes often blossom in online learning environments in which the pace and content can match their abilities (Wallace, 2009). UMUC's mature working students, juggling work and family responsibilities, are another population that benefits from the flexibility of online learning.

By 2014, UMUC's online enrollment exceeded 243,000, with students taking 981 distinct courses. The institution offers seventy-four undergraduate and graduate degree and certificate programs, and all but one can be completed online. (The exception is the Doctor of Management program, which has some residency requirements.) I continue to teach online courses in the UMUC graduate program, and I very much enjoy how the virtual university environment enables new ways of communicating, learning, and teaching. In addition to frequent asynchronous communications, I hold live webinars each week with webcams and audio, so students can experience interactive sessions and discuss more spontaneously. Most students now have high-speed Internet access, but glitches happen, just as they did in the early days. One student, for instance, put his phone on hold while he left his computer for a brief break, so the class audio was flooded with hold music until he returned. These sessions are also recorded so students who can't attend—often because they live in distant time zones—can view the video at a convenient time.

UMUC continues to innovate, and the latest strategic plan calls for striking initiatives, some of which harness the power of big data and data analytics to provide individualized education tailored to each student. With personalized analyses, UMUC is striving to match each student with the classes, course sequences, and targeted assistance that will enhance student success. The educational journeys of UMUC's nontraditional students will continue to follow many different paths, but almost all of them—from Russian Siberia to the state of Maryland, and from military bases in Japan to outposts in Afghanistan—travel through the virtual university.

ACKNOWLEDGEMENTS

Personal communications with many faculty, students, and administrators who were involved in the emergence of UMUC's virtual university in the 1990s were an important source of information for this chapter. Particular thanks go to Nicholas H. Allen, Eve Cran, John Gustafson, Christine Hannah, Paula Harbecke, Julie Porosky Hamlin, Paul Hamlin, Julian S. Jones, Gary E. Miller, James Stewart, Wayne Precht, and John VanAntwerp. I also want to thank several people at UMUC who provided important historical documents, including Stephen Miller, Renee Brown, and Alexander Pirella.

REFERENCES

Allen, N. H. (2001). Lessons learned on the road to the virtual university. *Continuing Higher Education Review, 65*, 60-73.

Bernard, R. M., Abrami, P. C., Lou, Y., Borokhovski, E., Wade, A., Wozney, L., Wallet, P. A., Fiset, M., & Binru, H. (2004). How does distance education compare with classroom instruction? A meta-analysis of the empirical literature. *Review of Educational Research, 74*(3), 379–439.

Crecente, B.D. (1994, October 10). Regents get glimpse of future cyber-campus. *The Diamondback*, University of Maryland College Park.

Hudgins, S. (2008). *Beyond the ivory tower: The first sixty years 1947-2007*. Adelphi, MD: University of Maryland University College.

Lount, R. B. J., & Phillips, K. W. (2007). Working harder with the out-group: The impact of social category diversity on motivation gains. *Organizational Behavior and Human Decision Processes, 103*(2), 214–224. doi: 10.1016/j.obhdp.2007.03.002

Means, B., Toyama, Y., Murphy, R., Bakia, M., & Jones, K. (2010). *Evaluation of evidence-based practices in online learning: A meta-analysis and review of online learning studies*. Washington, DC: US Department of Education.

Parker, M. L. (2006). University of Maryland University College (UMUC), USA. In S. D'Antoni (Ed.), *The Virtual University: Models & Messages*. UNESCO. Retrieved from http://www.unesco.org/iiep/virtualuniversity/media/document/Ch11_UMUC_Parker.pdf

Phillips, K. W. (2014). How diversity works. *Scientific American, 311*(4), 43–47.

SchWeber, C. (n.d.). The WebTycho model. Retrieved from http://www.c3l.uni-olden-burg.de/cde/wtmodel.htm

Shank, P., Precht, L. W., Singh, H., Everidge, J., & Bozarth, J. (2008). Infrastructure for learning: Options for today or screw-ups for tomorrow. In S. Carliner & P. Shank (Eds.), *The e-learning handbook: Past promises, present challenges.* San Francisco, CA: Pfeiffer.

UMUC Strategic Plan 2015-2018. (2015). University of Maryland University College. Retrieved from http://www.umuc.edu/umucfuture/upload/umuc-strategic-plan.pdf

University of Maryland University College Self-Study. (1986, 1996, 2006, 2016). Report to the Middle States Association of Colleges and Schools, Commission on Higher Education.

Wallace, P. (2013). Nurturing innovation through online learning. In L. Shavinina (Ed.), *The Routledge enternational handbook of innovation education,* (pp. 430-441). New York, NY: Routledge.

Wallace, P. (2009). Distance learning for gifted students: Outcomes for elementary, middle, and high school aged students. *Journal for the Education of the Gifted, 32*(3), 295–320.

Williams, S. L. (2006). The effectiveness of distance education in allied health science programs: A meta-analysis of outcomes. *American Journal of Distance Education, 20*(3), 127–141. doi: 10.1207/s15389286ajde2003_2

AN INTERVIEW WITH CHUCK HILL

Former Director
International Alliances and Business Development
Distance Learning Center, UC Irvine

Chuck Hill was interviewed by John Ebersole and William Patrick.

JOHN EBERSOLE: My recollection is that you came to the San Francisco Bay area from Seattle, and took a position initially as a vice president in a hospital, running the HR department. What brought you to teaching?

CHUCK HILL: Actually, you did, because I had left that hospital and I had taken a better-paying job as the assistant general manager at AC Transit, the local bus company, which was the most miserable job I had ever had in my life. As assistant general manager, I had human resources and I had training, safety, security—I had several departments working under me. You called me up one day after you had made the transition from Kennedy to Berkeley and you asked if I would be interested in helping to sell customized training programs. I remember distinctly saying, "John, I'd love to work with you and I'd love to work with Berkeley because I understand they've got a great retirement system, and I'm in misery over here where I am."

JE: But before that earlier job as a full-time VP of HR, what brought you to teaching in any format?

CH: I had always taught, ever since I had gotten out of college. I used to teach for Sullivan's Opportunities and Industrialization Center. That was when Dr. Leon Sullivan had these industrialization centers going around inner cities and teaching job skills to inner-city minority residents. Anyway, I have always taught on a part-time basis ever since I graduated from college. But I remember telling you, "I don't know anything about selling," and your response, in the usual Ebersole manner, was, "Well, you buy training programs as vice president over there, don't you? If you can buy them, you can sell them." And that's kind of what sealed the deal.

JE: Tell me a little more about why you wanted to teach. What is it about teaching that has kept you at it for so long?

CH: The sense that you're making a difference—the "Aha!" moment when you see a student's face light up and they say, "Oh, I think I understand what you're saying now." Or they recount some experience at work that makes the point that you had made two or three lectures before about some issue or other, and you see that recognition appear on their faces: "Oh, this all makes sense now." When you see people get it, to use common language, I just get a lot of joy out of that. It's very rewarding.

JE: And you don't get to see that happen online in the same way. What attracted you to try online teaching?

CH: Well, the notion that we could use the resources of an institution like Berkeley and we could extend those resources to people who otherwise would never have an opportunity to have that experience.

Now at Kennedy, near the beginning, it was the notion that here we are able to, through computers, give people the chance to experience what I've seen in the classroom. We were not at all satisfied with a primarily text approach. We didn't want students sitting there and reading off of a computer. We wanted interactivity. We wanted chat groups. We wanted simulations. Graphical design. Lots of pictures. We wanted to offer a compelling experience rather than an "Oh, God, I've got to read all of this" kind of experience.

Actually, I didn't know how I was going to feel about not being able to see their reactions specifically and so forth, until I started getting some of their written work, and I found their written work to be much more in-depth and much more thoughtful than the work I had been receiving in the traditional classroom—particularly with some of the Asian students, whom we were having difficulty drawing out. They tended to not to want to stand out, so I had to really draw them out if I wanted them to participate in the classroom. But online I was getting a considerable volume of material from the students who otherwise in a classroom were very quiet. That was a pleasant surprise for me and I thought, *Even though I can't see them, I can feel them. I can see where this online business has opened up something that has allowed them to express themselves far more than what I have experienced in face-to-face classroom.*

JE: What were some of the other differences, aside from this inability to see the student, that you experienced as an instructor?

CH: What I anticipated to be a barrier—the slowness of the computers, the need to have a modem and other, various pieces of equipment so they could be online; to make everything work together—was not. I thought all of that would be enormously frustrating for students, and I assumed that they would try it for two or three weeks and, once they had experienced forgetting their passwords or the modem not working or the line being broken, that they would just say, "The hell with it. I don't really need this." But that was not my experience. In fact, my experience was the further away the students were, the more tolerant they were of the technical difficulties we were having.

JE: That's a great insight. What did you find the same about online and classroom teaching, anything?

CH: What did I find to be the same? I think the sense that in a class of, say, twenty people, there are four or five who are really, really engaged, and who take a leadership role and can be counted on to start discussions and to offer feedback and to have insights and to be very active participants. Then there will be a group of seven or eight who, with the normal prodding, react as typical students. But then there are four or five who, no matter what you do, are maybe here or not here and sometimes they're just out there like lurkers.

JE: Chuck, I don't know if it was you who told me this or not, so here's a case where I need you to refresh my memory: I had somebody tell me once that they felt they were better organized in the classroom because of having taught online. Was that you?

CH: No, I don't think that was me who made that comment, but I have certainly had that same experience. The rigor that we had to develop, to make sure that we were offering a good experience online, far exceeded the rigor or any kind of approach that we used in a classroom. We were pretty much left to do our own thing when we went in the classroom, but there were rubrics and other things that we had to follow to do an online class that far exceeded any requirements or outlines or stipulations that we had in the traditional class. After having taught online, I got used to adopting those online approaches for the face-to-face teaching as well.

JE: I remember one basic story from your time at John F. Kennedy University, but I've forgotten some of the details about the Russian student you had who, if I remember correctly, was at Moscow State University. Do I have that right?

CH: Yes. There was a student whom I got in touch with and said, "Hey, I don't have your midterm exam," and he wrote back, "I'm still waiting for it to print out." He had this dot-matrix printer and it tied up their system for an entire weekend. We're talking 300 baud modems and 256k RAM. When I apologized for not anticipating the inconvenience of tying up their system for over seventy-two hours, the student quickly informed me that it was not an inconvenience: after all, he now had access to US-based higher education and that was certainly worth waiting for an exam to print, even if it took the entire weekend. One of the lessons I learned from that was this: the greater the distance between learner and content, the greater the learner's tolerance for bugs in the technology. That realization served me well over the years.

JE: What kinds of students did you have in the 1980s and '90s? Were they a different kind of student than we have now?

CH: Let me answer it a little differently. I do know that some of the correspondence students and the students who were doing any form of distance learning back prior to 1995 or so were largely military, and displaced people who were in places where they wanted to continue their education. They had veterans' or some other type of benefits that could help them out financially, and their motivation was a little different, I think. There were classifications that they could achieve if they crossed certain thresholds of learning. They weren't stand-alone students in the community deciding to beat the traffic and take a correspondence course. They were physically removed from the campus—true distance students.

JE: Yeah, because today, I think it's as much about moving time around as it is spanning distance. But I think that's a really good observation— the early students were truly distance students. What's validating about that, Chuck, is when I left Berkeley and went to Colorado State, they had made this huge commitment to video. Try as I might, I didn't have the resources or the influence to get them to stop video and move to online. And the video instruction that we were offering was god-awful: we had a couple of cameras mounted in the back of the classroom, and we just videotaped the instructor giving the standard lecture. But there were absolutely no production standards at all on those videos. I used to say that we'd lose a third of the class within the first two courses. After that, you could almost guarantee that the rest would stay with you because they had sat there through thirty to forty-five hours of really bad video and they were still doing the work. Either they were really motivated or they had no other alternative.

CH: That's right. And the thing that makes it even more emphatic is that this was the same time that MTV was coming out with high-production, high-quality video stuff, so those students were experiencing the exact opposite on TV. One has entertainment with all sorts of graphics and flash, and here's this class that's putting me to sleep.

JE: Before we move on, is there anything else about the Kennedy experience that stands out for you?

CH: Only that we had these god-awful templates from the EUN— the Electronic University Network—where they were attempting to bring something other than a straight screen full of text to the students. So we had diagrams and templates and other things that were designed to make the presentation of the information more visually interesting. I don't know if that made them more learning-friendly, but they tried to break up that whole screen full of text. I don't think they were very successful. I still have those templates. I thought they were so awkward that I just kept them.

And one other thing: having taught Human Resource Management both in the classroom and online, I was able to compare and contrast student reactions and their performance with the same set of materials. I was impressed that the quality of written work from my online students seemed to be superior to that of my classroom students. Perhaps that was due to the ability to think about, review, edit, and polish their work before submitting it, whereas the classroom students tended to more or less whip things out and submit them in a much more casual manner.

JE: The thing that I thought those EUN templates did best was test the student's patience. You found yourself, as an instructor, waiting weeks for them to do some of those damned templates, didn't you?

CH: I did. The whole thing was so new to everybody.

JE: As you think back over what has now been twenty-five years since we were first wrestling with online learning, has there been anything that surprised you?

CH: We were fighting tooth and nail with the faculty and with the administrators within the university system to gain credibility for what we were doing. They kept saying, "We're not sure you can deliver quality teaching without seeing the whites of their eyes." I can remember going to the UC Berkeley Faculty Senate Committee on Courses. I remember distinctly that I somehow had missed it the day before on my calendar, and I got to work in casual clothes. I looked at my calendar and saw that the meeting was for that day, so I went back home and changed into a sports coat and tie—more formal attire. Then I went to the meeting, only to find a bunch of guys sitting around in sweatshirts and Birkenstock sandals. Then they said, before I could even get started, "Young man, if you're here to explain to us how students interact with computers, save your time. We're not interested. We are only interested in how students interact with instructors and with each other. And I said, "Okay, well I'm pleased to tell you that we're not here to talk about computer-based instruction. All the courses that we're talking about will be absolutely instructor-led courses." And that was the criterion: they wouldn't even entertain discussion of what was then called computer-based learning.

So several of us were fighting with them, and they finally came around. But it seems to me that the corporate world, and the people who were reimbursing students for taking training, came along a lot quicker than we thought they might. I thought we'd have that same battle with the corporate reimbursement world for training and education. Either I missed it or I went to sleep during that period, but it didn't seem to be as difficult a battle as it was internally, with the universities themselves.

But you know what? UC Berkeley Extension was a self-funded portion of the university. We got no money from the university, and we got no money from the State of California. We had to generate our own revenue to pay salaries, light, heat, the whole bit—and we did all of that from student tuition. And so I think, because of that necessity to be self-supported, the faculty members who were opposed to the idea were inclined to say, "Well, you know, if you guys want to try that new age stuff, go ahead."

WILLIAM PATRICK: Chuck, I'm also interested in the early challenges, when you were first teaching online. Would you elaborate on your battles with other faculty members?

CH: They just didn't want to recognize that you could teach this new way and actually have a quality learning experience for the students. They thought it was a fad. They thought it was maybe good for some kind of remedial education. They thought the notion of doing this for some kind of safety training program, where you could expose all the workers of one company to the same exact content at the same time, because they're all online, was probably a good idea. But to distribute actual academic learning material with some rigor—umm, I doubt it. That was the issue. The doubt that you could actually transmit in-depth learning activities through this method, without seeing people, was the stumbling block for them. And of course, underlying this was the idea that maybe the student wasn't really doing the work: maybe it's his wife answering these questions while he's laying up on a couch somewhere, eating popcorn and drinking beer.

It was simply an uphill battle with the entrenched, established older faculty. It was of interest to younger faculty, but their interest did not necessarily convert to them jumping on board, either. Most of the interest converted to, "I want to watch this thing. It sounds promising but I don't know. We'll wait and see."

WP: You've also told me that you were surprised that many faculty members who you knew were really good at face-to-face teaching weren't really any good at online. They just weren't good at communicating that new way.

CH: That was absolutely my experience. I think they were unable to make that switch over because they didn't realize the importance of making a welcoming and friendly environment for students. They were so used to pontificating and lecturing that it didn't come naturally to them to start off a textual conversation by saying, "As we discussed last time, the reason IBM's Watson was so determined only a few computers would serve the world was . . ." They wanted to be more stand-offish. Their language wasn't welcoming or friendly.

Some people just couldn't see the tone that we were after, or what would be compelling for students. Students were too entrenched in the lecture method, where you spit out everything and they sit there passively and then respond on a test.

WP: I think you're making a key point there. Couched in the notion of tone is the idea of whether someone was on board with the way that education was changing at that time. That's a pretty major sea change—we were going from industrial to post-industrial in terms of education, and that meant that lecturing and pontificating were starting to seem obsolete when you compared them with the newer pedagogical methods that online was ushering in. People wanted a different kind of instruction, and teachers either could provide that or they couldn't. So do you think that their identity as professors was threatened by this new mode of teaching?

CH: Yes, I do, but I don't know if I think that in terms of an answer to this particular question. But I definitely think that was one of the reasons they were so slow in coming aboard. There was the notion of, "Well, are you going to replace me with this electronic box sitting on my desk here? What's going to become of me?" In addition to, "What's going to become of my intellectual property when I take my hard-earned and hard-worked-on lecture notes and make them available to just anybody who's on the other end of this communication?" That was a threat as well.

There were some things about it that I couldn't make sense of. I used to ask Gary Matkin and John, as well, "Why do you think it's taking so long to get undergraduate degree programs online?" And their response was, "We'll probably see it happen quicker with the graduate programs than with the undergraduate programs." And I could never quite understand that. Why should the programs that are the most rigorous be the ones that take the risk? I couldn't figure that out.

JE: What I think today, and I'm not sure I thought this at that time, is that it has more to do with age than it has to do with the degree level. I think our older students today are more highly motivated, and they're finding that taking online courses allows them to move time around, and that's critical for them. Whereas the youngsters—even with really good instructional design, I think it's hard to hold their attention. Many of them aren't motivated by the subject matter, and we have not had particularly good luck with the traditional-aged students, the eighteen-to-twenty-four-year-olds. Even with their presumed sophistication with technology, they haven't quite taken to it.

The folks at Teachers College in New York have a center that does research particularly on community colleges, and they did a research project last year that showed that community college students in the classroom did better than community college students online, and I wasn't at all surprised by that finding. The thing that I would like to have seen, which was not there, was what was the age of the student? Assuming that they were probably quite a bit younger.

Chuck, I don't know if you have been disappointed by the fact that our tenured faculty brothers and sisters have taken so long to accept online learning. The latest survey from Babson shows that it still hovers around 30 percent who think that you can learn that way. Have you been disappointed in the way that online learning has rolled out over the years?

CH: I have a little bit of resentment in that what I know to be true in terms of the rigor and the difficulty of taking and completing an online course has not come through to a lot of students. They still believe this is somehow going to be easier, quicker, more efficient, a breeze. I have often had the sad duty of explaining to them, "No, I'm sorry, but you're taking a condensed course from a highly-regarded institution, and it's going to be tough."

JE: You know, I think we can thank the University of Phoenix for that problem, and I absolutely agree with you on it. Phoenix pushed convenience, but in the minds of many people, they interpreted convenience as meaning easy. It's only as easy and as hard as the faculty member makes it. But let me ask you the sixty-four-thousand-dollar question—do you think that real learning takes place online to the same degree that it does in the classroom?

CH: I think that's a function of the quality of the instructors, and if they can create effective groups. A lot of that learning occurs not between the students and the material, but between the students and the students, and the students and the experiences that you push in their way of trying to get through the course. "I want you to go out and do this kind of research project. I want you to go out and investigate this and that and apply so-and-so's theory to that and write me a report." Yes, if the instructors are capable, and if they care about their students, then they can create learning experiences that are equal to, if not better than, the ones that students can get in a classroom.

JE: Let's shift gears to talking about your years of working at Berkeley. You oversaw its online format expansion of the 4-month certificate courses in business and marketing from their classroom version to their Internet-based iteration. It seemed like a good idea at the time, but was it really?

CH: Oh yeah, I think it was. As you know, paper-based correspondence has gone the way of the dodo bird, of course. But we also had another motive in that, and that was the success of our international certificate programs. The number of students for those was just record breaking. And you had done a study, John, of how much it cost them to come to the United States and do those programs, and we kind of deduced from that that we could enroll many more students if we could cut out the travel piece and the residential-living piece. They were paying much more for travel and lodging and food than they were paying Berkeley for tuition. Making those courses available through technology opened up a huge opportunity for revenue production and for an increase in the volume of students.

I was running three and four sections of a marketing class, two and three sections of business, and other certificate programs. We had discovered that many of our students were actually out of compliance with their student visa standing because they were not full-time students. Because of Berkeley extension evening class structure they couldn't cobble together enough of those evening classes to make themselves full-time students.

And so one of our key guys—a guy named Bill Knickerbocker, who worked for you as well—decided that he would try a daytime program. He put together courses so that they could take three and four courses at the same time, through a daytime schedule, and compressed it into a four-month program. He called it the four-month certificate program. It was intense—many courses at the same time, Berkeley Equality—but offered during the daytime so students could maintain their full-time student status. They had enough units that they were full-time students and so they were then in compliance.

That program took off. It was really attractive to international students. Typically, they already had an undergraduate degree from their home university in Brazil or France or wherever. We had a lot of students from Germany, Korea, Argentina, and Brazil. They already had their undergraduate degrees in business, for example, and they came and took our four-month certificate in marketing. That then built a resume that said, "Hey, I've got a bachelor's degree from a local university, but I've got this specialty in marketing from the University of California at Berkeley. That made them hot, hot job prospects back home.

JE: One of the things that I'm hearing from my own faculty here at Excelsior today, twenty-five years later, is that we have stressed standardization of instruction to the point where we have taken all the creativity out of it for the faculty, and I'm afraid there's probably some truth to that. In the classroom, we often decided what we were going to talk about as we came through the door. Here, not only do we have it laid out months in advance, but you can't deviate from it. The experience that one student gets in a class is going to be exactly the same as another student is going to get in that class, and I'm not sure if we haven't taken that to an extreme.

WP: Let me go a different direction. If you remember the ways that you would prepare for face-to-face teaching, how did you have to alter that routine to prepare for online teaching? Can you lay out the differences for me?

CH: Okay, yeah, one of the ways I could do it in a classroom is that I could use an overhead question. I remember once I had a fire chief in the class and we were talking about management skills or supervision or some thing, and I said, "You know how that goes," and the guy said, "No, we don't know, tell us." Then I was stuck. So the notion of using overhead questions and then having to maybe call on someone if the overhead didn't solicit an answer, was one way. But when I switched to online, I had to write question prompts. I had to formulate the question, give it a context, and then throw it out there. I couldn't just do it the way I had done it in the face-to-face classroom. I couldn't just wing it.

One example comes to mind. I was starting to develop these little scenarios where I would take maybe two or three paragraphs—maybe half a page—to set the scene, and then ask the question. For instance, "The manager of a warehouse had this problem and he came to work and he had these three guys working for him and he had one lady working for him and he had this and that . . ." And then at the end there's the question. Well, I was starting to do that to the point where these were getting pretty involved, until I saw this article one day. In it, the president of Starbucks made a comment that they spent more money for employee health benefits than they did for coffee beans last year. And I said, "Wow, let me try something. Let me try to just put that out there to the students online and say, 'What's up with this? Howard Schultz said that Starbucks spent more on employee health benefits than on coffee beans.'" And this was in a class on employee benefits. It elicited the best response of any question I had ever asked, and it didn't need a whole paragraph full of stage setting. So I started changing that whole thing. But my point is that you have to put in a lot more time and energy thinking about the discussion prompt for online than I ever did in the classroom.

JE: You could use that same question in either place, could you not, in either the classroom or online?

CH: Oh, you could, yes. It just happened to be that I wanted to see if I could shortcut all the stage setting and scenario writing and see what would happen. I had about twenty-five students for that course and, to my surprise, one student said something like, "What about auto insurance?" So he missed the whole point. But I didn't have to frame it, and say that benefits are starting to cost us so much now as part of the employee compensation package. They picked up on all that right away and just took off on it. I was really pleasantly surprised.

WP: In that same vein, how was online teaching different than face-to-face teaching for you? How did it change your experience of it?

CH: I wasn't quite as self-conscious online. My experience with the fire chief had really unsettled me because I wasn't properly prepared that night. I went in there, winging it, and got busted, okay?

WP: That's happened to all of us, I'm sure.

CH: Yeah, but online, I could say, "Well, check this out," and refer the students to five or eight or ten things that I had found on the Internet that were on point and on target and much deeper than my spur-of-the-moment conversation might provide. There's a chance to recoup yourself with online teaching, if you will, so I didn't have the same self-consciousness around my preparedness.

And the other thing that I have done is that I have created folders of resource materials, so if a student asks a question about, you know—"How come machine bolts are threaded differently than wood screws?"—hey, I can shoot him, within ten minutes, nine articles on that topic. You can have these wells of resources ready to go. As a matter of fact, one of the things I especially liked about my online teaching was that I tended to use case studies. Whenever I got a textbook, I would always ask for the instructor's manual that accompanied it. Oftentimes, the author of the case study would write an evaluation or an analysis of it and so forth, and I could cut and paste from that author's analysis and add to my response to the student, saying something like, "You did a good job analyzing why the manager did such and such and such, but I thought you could have gone into more depth about it, and see below." And below, I have actually sent him a copy of what the author of the case study wrote in that particular vein, so he has a rich response to his issue.

WP: Plus, you're not being observed all the time. That's the thing about face-to-face teaching that gets on some professor's nerves. Students are always watching, and judging with every question that gets asked—how quickly, or well, or thoroughly will the professor answer this one? Will he stumble if he doesn't have an answer right there? Online, there is a kind of comforting anonymity.

CH: And your answer lives in perpetuity. So you have to be careful because, when you do answer it, it's there forever.

JE: I have done most of my teaching in the classroom, and it occurs to me that it's very ego-satisfying to do a good job there, and I'm not so sure that the ego gets the same satisfaction from doing an online course. Does that resonate with you?

CH: Yes, it does. I'm still waiting for the experience that I've had with the classroom course to happen online, and it's only happened once: I walked into a grocery store and the lady next to me in line said, "Oh, Mr. Hill, I was in your class. Do you remember me?" And I said, "No." And she said, "But I was in your class." So I said, "Oh, yeah, now I remember," but of course I had no idea whether I remembered her or not. She made a big thing about it, anyway, and then she said, "You remember that story you told about XYZ? Well, something happened at work last week and your story made that come alive for me." And that was such a good feeling. It gave me a high all the way through the parking lot and right down onto the freeway. I've only had that happen once in an online course, and that was where a student whom I happened to know was in an online course and I saw him on campus. I said, "What are you doing here?" And he said, "I'm taking a break. In the classroom, I get called on maybe once or twice during the semester. Online, I've got to answer every damned time I log on, so I'm taking a break."

JE: It seems to me that in the classroom, instructors have the whole show on their shoulders. It's how well they can transmit the information and keep the class with them. Online, you're just part of the team, and the real hero is probably the instructional designer who insisted upon interactivity and some exercises and a better visual experience. So it's a case where, online, you've got to share some of that good feeling with the team that helped you build it.

CH: Yes, I think that's absolutely true, and I also think that your skills as an online instructor aren't on display when you're delivering the content because the machine is doing most of that. Your skills are on display when you're attempting to be the editor of the discussion board, and when you show your ability to solicit interesting responses and in-depth questions. Your ability to serve as an editor of that board or that blog or whatever you want to call the location where your interactivity takes place is key. If you can't be the master of ceremonies in a written form, your class won't be that good. I think that speaks to John's earlier question about why traditional classroom teachers didn't do as well online. They didn't understand they needed to master the written communications element—that ability to inspire and entice people to not just say, "Well, I agree with what Susan said." I mean, what value is that? It's a real skill to get that message board going, and going effectively.

WP: Can you give a working example of that?

CH: We're doing a lesson on benefits, and how important employee benefits are. They used to be called perks, or indirect compensation, but they've become 30 to 40 percent of what the company outlays for an employee. They've become just a much larger part of the total compensation package—medical insurance being one example. So there's an illustration at the end of the chapter in the textbook we're using that talks about that Starbucks fact I mentioned before, where the company is paying more for health insurance than they do for coffee beans. How can that be? That's what they sell is coffee. My god. So you get the discussion going around how this has increased over time. Is it out of control? Can we continue this? What's going to happen if medical insurance continues to grow at the rate that it's been growing? I mean, you get all sorts of interesting dialogue about the future of employee benefits just by stating that fact and raising those questions on the message board. Does that help?

WP: But how are you leading the discussion online?

CH: Okay, like this: "Bill, you commented that you agree with Susan. I need you to describe how that works in your experience. You said you've been working in telecommunications—how is that different from health care? Or how is that different from the hardware store that Ralph wrote about in his earlier post from yesterday?" You need to draw the students out.

JE: Final question: how about your own teaching preference? If you had the choice, teaching the same subject matter, for the same compensation, would you prefer to do it in the classroom or prefer to do it online?

CH: Wow, that's a tough one. For the purposes of convenience, I would prefer to do it online. For personal satisfaction and that "Aha!" moment, when you see their eyes light up, I would prefer face-to-face. But five o'clock traffic will change my mind most days, to be honest with you. If I have to fight traffic going across town to get to some damned classroom, I'd just rather go home and sit down at my computer.

QUALITY MATTERS™

Its Role in the Quest for a "Good Housekeeping Seal of Approval" for Online Education

Julie Porosky Hamlin

Executive Director, MarylandOnline

It is sometimes said of a thing that if it did not already exist, it would have to be invented. In retrospect, Quality Matters™ (QM) had to be invented. Simple in concept, though not so simple in implementation, QM began as a set of design standards for online courses and a process for evaluating courses against the standards. The successful creation of an instrument for in-depth measurement of course design quality was perhaps inevitable, but it is an historical curiosity that it did not happen until online education came along. That curious turn of events can be thought about in the context of three successive stages of anxiety about quality in education, stages that do not necessarily occur in the right order.

THREE STAGES OF QUALITY ANXIETY

Stage 1. In Stage 1, a QM-like thing needed to be invented, and was invented, because people in the education establishment were nervous about replacing education in the physical classroom with education delivered online. Significant use of the online medium later spread to other sectors of education, but it started in higher education because that sector, uniquely, is susceptible to pressure from customer-student demand. There came a moment in the early 2000s when student demand for online courses got ahead of the ability of colleges and universities to have all the pieces in place to deliver online courses. Stakeholders, faculty in particular, were skeptical that teaching and learning in an asynchronous, digital medium could be as good as what took place in the classroom and had for a more than a century. Distance education in other forms had been around for decades but had not caught on at the scale of online education. "Online," as it was sometimes abbreviated, was a movement that could not be ignored.

Stage 1 of quality anxiety could be described as a preoccupation with online education being "as good as" face-to-face education. This anxiety gave rise to Russell's formulation of the "No Significant Difference Phenomenon" and the compilation of more than 350 research reports and papers documenting no significant difference in student learning outcomes that could be attributed to the format of educational delivery (Russell, 2001). The misgivings of academicians appear not to have impeded a steady advance in the acceptance of online education by higher education consumers. In halting steps, the regional accrediting commissions also came to accept it. Throughout most of higher education in the US and other countries, parity was achieved between courses taken online and those taken in classrooms on the ground. Today, at most institutions in the US, academic transcripts do not indicate whether course credits were earned online or in the physical classroom.

Stage 2. With general acceptance that online courses were or could be "as good as" face-to-face courses, the comparison framework shifted in Stage 2 of quality anxiety to whether online courses were as good as one another. The awareness of differing levels of quality in online courses and programs was raised when organizations including the Sloan Consortium, Southern Regional Education Board, Council of Regional Accrediting Commissions, and others began publicizing principles of good practice for online education. The principles could be used in building a case against diploma mills. Online delivery was growing up, getting better. Expectations for quality were higher. The focus for organizations engaged in online quality assurance (QA) progressed from "Calm down, everything's fine!" (Stage 1) to "Hmm, let's have a closer look" (Stage 2).

Stage 3. In Stage 1 of higher education's quality anxiety, it had not escaped online education's pioneers and advocates that the "is it as good as?" question combined with the documentation and assurances demanded by accreditors, state higher education coordinating commissions, and academic officers amounted to a requirement that online education meet higher expectations than does traditional education. The irony of that proposition is that the vast majority of colleges and universities in the US and other countries set no explicit standards or only minimal standards for course effectiveness in content and delivery, nor are course effectiveness evaluations conducted by independent evaluators against a set of standards. Before being allowed to teach in the face-to-face classroom, historically, faculty have not been asked to demonstrate a knowledge of effective construction of course content and an ability to teach effectively. This odd fact has long been higher education's dirty little secret.

The creation of Quality Matters, a faculty peer review process guided by an instrument for measuring online course effectiveness, forced the irony to the surface. In Stage 3 of quality anxiety, people in the higher education community who were paying attention to the online movement had begun to notice that if standards like QM's were to be applied to online courses, they could be applied to traditional courses, most of which had not previously been subjected to a quality review.

It would be unrealistic to hope that a QM-like process would substantially impact the practices of a higher education establishment whose members had been complicit for centuries in the dirty little secret of low quality expectations in teaching and learning, but growth in QM subscribership indicated new awareness of the fact that tools exist for measuring quality. Had the advent of online education not given rise to the need for a QM-like instruments and had QM's standards and processes not been created and nurtured with steady refinement and increasing depth, Stage 3 of quality anxiety—a healthy anxiety—might not have been reached. The notion that something as difficult to pin down as course quality could in some way be measured, in traditional as well as online courses, began to be credible.

Defining and measuring quality is by no means easy. Why it had to be done has been suggested, and how a group of educators in Maryland went about it, leading to the birth of Quality Matters, will be explored next. In the US, no uniform process or set of standards exists for certifying, across disciplines the quality of online courses, or of any courses; even the standards and processes of the institutional accrediting commissions vary from region to region. Quality Matters certification is worth examining because it comes as close to universality as any "seal of approval" yet devised in the online education community. The number of institutions in the US and abroad subscribing to QM standards and processes has grown steadily over the past 10 years, reaching 1,038 as of 2016.

THE QM STORY

QM's Parentage

In 1999, at the dawn of online education nationally, representatives of 12 colleges and universities in Maryland came together in the tradition of grassroots movements to consider how they might benefit from one another's efforts and find areas of cooperation in online delivery. A consortium comprising all 16 community colleges in the state, the Maryland Community College Teleconsortium

(MCCT), had been formed two years earlier, and representatives of its schools sought to work with the distance education leaders at UMUC, an institution that already had a well-developed infrastructure for online delivery and a number of online courses. Representatives of three other universities in the state joined UMUC and the MCCT group, and the consortium MarylandOnline (MOL) was established and incorporated as a non-profit. Later MCCT and MOL merged under the name MarylandOnline. MOL's purpose was to provide its member institutions support and advocacy for online learning.

At the time, online-focused consortia were forming in other states, but, unlike MOL, most were created through an act of the executive or legislative branch of state government or by multi-institution system offices. MarylandOnline was unusual in that the impetus for cooperation had come from online education practitioners and advocates at the member institutions. The grassroots nature of MOL's launch is important to bookmark, because grassrootedness is a thread that has continued in the Quality Matters program.

Though MarylandOnline as an organization had not been anointed by the Maryland Higher Education Commission, the Commission supported MOL's early work through two generous grants between 1999 and 2002. The first project commissioned MOL, through a train-the-trainer model, to prepare hundreds of faculty at Maryland institutions for online teaching, and the second deployed faculty teams from MOL colleges to identify shareable online learning objects in specific disciplines (Shattuck, 2007).

Following these successful projects, one of MarylandOnline's next undertakings to leverage consortial advantage was the establishment of a process, building on work done by MCCT, for sharing online courses among the sixteen community colleges. Later named the Seat Bank, the process enabled colleges to "buy" and "sell" student seats in one another's online courses, with the course transcripted as if taken at the student's home college. The Seat Bank allowed the colleges to offer their students access to online courses beyond those available at the student's home college, thereby saving on the costs of online course development in the early days of online education. The hosting of inter-institutional online seat/course sharing by MOL was the triggering event for what would become the Quality Matters program.

Getting to "As Good As"

In the academic world, the use of the word "share" in conjunction with the word "course" is cause for pause. To be comfortable with inter-institutional course sharing, a faculty member would need to be reassured an *online* version of ECON 101 at a sister institution, to be taken by a student enrolled at her own college, would be equivalent in content and quality to the ECON 101 she herself teaches at her college. Equally, there would need to be a way to confirm the standards for quality of an online course at college A were the same as those for an online course at college B. And there it was: that word "quality." How to assure it?

Jurgen Hilke, a distance learning administrator at Frederick Community College, proposed a way to address the QA challenge. Representatives of MOL colleges would put their heads together and develop a course review and improvement system for the shared MOL online courses, with course reviews to be carried out by faculty experienced in teaching online. An important founding premise, according to Hilke, now considered to be "the father of QM," was that the participants must own what they were creating (J. Hilke, personal communication, February 18, 2016). The review process would encourage feedback that would lead to course improvement strategies. From the outset, what Shattuck (2007) has termed the seed idea for Quality Matters had two components: not only would the process aim to assure the quality of what already existed, it would also focus on course improvement. The concept of continuous quality improvement (CQI) remains at the center of Quality Matters.

Another central part of what would become the QM process was faculty peer review. In the fall of 2002, peer reviews were piloted at three Maryland community colleges, using a checklist of what to look for, a worksheet for the instructor whose course was being reviewed, and a step-by-step guide to the process (Shattuck, 2007). Each review team included three members from the MOL community, one of whom was a content expert in the subject matter of the course under review, and all of whom had current experience in teaching online. The course instructor, though not a reviewer, was considered part of the team; the instructor would receive feedback from the reviewers (Shattuck, 2007). Transparency became another central tenet of the process that would eventually be known as QM.

A Community of Practice for Online QA Wins a Grant

Through these early reviews, a community of practice for quality assurance was formed and a structure for peer review built. The MOL work group was well positioned for the next milestone on the way to the creation of Quality Matters. In 2003, MarylandOnline leaders applied for and won a three-year, $509,177 grant from the US Department of Education's Fund for the Improvement of Postsecondary Education (FIPSE) for a project to extend MOL's work in quality assurance. The goals of the project, "Quality Matters: Inter-Institutional Quality Assurance in Online Learning," would be to develop a rubric of standards, create a process for peer review using the standards, and disseminate results (Shattuck, 2007). The quality assurance process developed by the Maryland project team could potentially benefit institutions throughout the country.

Mary Wells of Prince George's Community College and Christina Sax of UMUC were co-principal investigators, leading a project management team that in turn formed three committees to carry out the work: (1) The Tool Set Committee would develop a set of standards and processes for peer course review. The committee was tasked to review all nationally accepted standards of good practice in online distance education that existed at the time, create a rubric of standards to be used by peer reviewers, and develop supporting documents. (2) The Process Committee would create the procedures necessary to carry out the various course review activities, with a focus on course and peer reviewer selection and certification processes. (3) The Training Committee would develop and implement the training curriculum for peer course reviewers and the faculty whose courses were being reviewed (known as "course developers") (Shattuck, 2007).

Chocolate chip cookies would provide a useful analogy for how to think about and measure quality. During the project, future reviewers sat in small groups around a table with the assignment of sampling an array of chocolate chip cookies from various sources and then rating the cookies on the five criteria shown in Figure 1. Eating the cookies and matching the taste experience with the criteria in the Cookie Rubric approximated the process reviewers would engage in when they opened an online course and applied the criteria that made up QM course standards. It would not be sufficient to make an individual decision about texture or taste. Again approximating

CHOCOLATE CHIP COOKIE RUBRIC

http://www.teachervision.fen.com/lesson-plans/lesson-4522.html

	Delicious	Good	Needs Improvement	Poor
Number of Chips	Chocolate chip in every bite	Chips in about 75% of bites	Chocolate in 50% of bites	Too few or too many chips
Texture	Chewy	Chewy in the middle, crisp on edges	Texture either crispy/crunchy or 50% uncooked	Texture resembles a dog biscuit
Color	Golden brown	Either light from undercooking or light from being 25% raw	Either dark brown from overcooking or light from undercooking	Burned
Taste	Home-baked taste	Quality store-bought taste	Tasteless	Store-bought preservative aftertaste— stale, hard, chalky
Richness	Rich, creamy, high-fat flavor	Medium fat contents	Low-fat contents	Nonfat contents

Figure 1: Chocolate chip cookie rubric.

a review team, members of the group around the table were asked to discuss and justify their ratings. The requirement for discussions among review team members continues to be a component of QM peer review.

Grant Project Results

Though the QM project was centered in Maryland, its reach went beyond the state's borders. At the end of the three-year period of the grant, 694 peer reviewers from 154 institutions in 28 states had been trained, and 111 reviews had been conducted of courses from 29 different institutions, 18 in Maryland and 11 in five additional states (MarylandOnline, 2006). In the final report to FIPSE, five main outcomes were listed for the QM project:

THE PROJECT

1) fostered inter-institutional, inter-segmental collaboration; 2) promoted faculty acceptance and adoption of standards, a rubric and a process for assessing online courses; 3) created a discriminating rubric based on national standards and research literature; 4) developed a replicable process for using experienced peer reviewers to review courses and provide guidance for improving them; and 5) impacted online teaching positively as evidenced by the data collected over the project term. (US Department of Education, 2016, para. 4)

The project team's liaisons at FIPSE were impressed by the conduct of the QM project, and team leaders were invited to present at a FIPSE conference on the components of a successful funded project. The project also received awards from three different distance education organizations. Word of the Quality Matters project continued to spread.

Kay Shattuck, a member of the grant project team and now QM's director of research, has chronicled QM and identified four phases in QM's development between 2002 and 2006: emergence of a peer review system from a seed idea; development of the program, with federal funding; implementation and dissemination; and transformation to a nationally recognized program (2007). In the transformation phase, MarylandOnline faced the question of what to do with the intellectual property called Quality Matters that had been created in the grant project.

Post Transformation: The Next Phase
One option was to do nothing, and simply allow the QM rubric to live on in the public domain, as required in the terms of the grant, as an instrument for use by the online community at large. Another option was to sell the rights for use and further development of QM; MarylandOnline had been approached by owners of an online education start-up. During the grant period and before, excitement and momentum had built, and the project team members together with the nearly 700 trained peer reviewers across the country constituted a small army of QM adherents. Stop the momentum now? Ron Legon, president of the MarylandOnline Board and a respected academician and online education pioneer in the state, led the initiative to move QM to self-sustainment. As the grant was ending, the MOL Board voted to allot $20,000 to help QM continue as a non-profit entity under a scenario in which institutions could subscribe to QM's course evaluation services for a modest fee. The post-grant QM was born.

Quality Matters did not need to use the allotted MOL money. With a staff of three, only two of whom initially were paid, in 2006 QM successfully began selling QM subscriptions that included peer course reviews to institutions, mainly through word of mouth. It was quickly apparent that among US institutions conducting online education, a pent-up demand existed for a turnkey approach to evaluating quality in online education, for the Stage 1 reasons discussed earlier in this chapter. Administrators at institutions offering online education not only had to quell the concerns of their own faculty and administrators, but also had to satisfy their regional accreditors that the online courses were "as good as."

To the present, Quality Matters evaluation is considered akin to accreditation review, and the regional accrediting commissions came to recognize QM's role in working with institutions on continuous quality improvement. Perhaps the most significant indicator of QM's influence on quality assurance practices is the fact that at a number of subscriber institutions, as reported by their QM coordinators, QM standards are used not only to evaluate existing courses but also to design new online or face-to-face courses. Figure 2 depicts CQI as carried out in a Quality Matters peer course review.

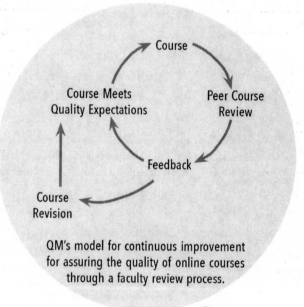

Figure 2: CQI in a peer course review.

The QM Rubric Then and Now: More than a Checklist

The Quality Matters model rests upon the all-important rubric of standards. The Quality Matters Rubric for Higher Education (https://www.qualitymatters.org/rubric), the first QM rubric to be developed, has changed little in its basic structure since the grant period. The standards also have not changed fundamentally, though they have been updated and fine-tuned in successive reviews and revisions since

2003. The fifth and most recent edition is organized around eight General Standards incorporating forty-three Specific Review Standards, ranging from as few as four to as many as nine per General Standard. Critical to the relationship among the General Standards is the concept of alignment among five of the standards to ensure that course elements directly support course learning objectives.

A weight of 3 (highest), 2, or 1 point(s) is assigned to each Specific Review Standard, and a course is considered to meet QM standards if 85 percent of total available points (the total has varied from edition to edition) are assigned by the review team and if all 3-point standards are met. A course review management system (CRMS), software developed by QM, compiles the ratings assigned by reviewers. An online course that has met the standards is eligible to display the QM certification mark.

An element of the rubric that has changed with successive editions is the Annotations that accompany each Specific Review Standard. Originally rather informal notes on what is meant by a standard and what to look for in evaluating a course, the Annotations have expanded and become more formal, essentially codifying what must be taken into consideration in applying a standard, in several cases with examples. The inclusion of the Annotations sets the QM rubric apart from many other lists of standards and best practices. A number of QM users have commented that they consider the Annotations to be the most powerful part of the rubric.

To date, the higher education rubric has been revised no less often than every three years. In keeping with QM's emphasis on its community roots, the year-long review and revision process is undertaken by a committee of 15 to 20 made up primarily of experienced reviewers representing different types of QM subscribing institutions. As part of the process, the entire QM subscribership also is surveyed, with detailed questions asked about the effectiveness of the rubric and how it is being used. Importantly, a rubric review and revision is more than tinkering at the margins. The committee is invited to put nearly every aspect of the rubric on the table, from the content of standards to assigned weights.

DESIGN, NOT DELIVERY

Because instructor effectiveness is a component in overall course effectiveness, QM has had to make a distinction between "design" and "delivery" as the focus of the formative evaluations it conducts. The QM process evaluates the design aspect of a course, which includes the instructor's role in planning and the layout of instructions and course components. It does not review implementation of the design or course delivery elements, such as amount and quality of the instructor's interaction with students.

The fact that QM review is not intended to evaluate or certify instructors themselves may be a key to its usability and acceptance. The focus on design allows QM review to be collegial and separate from the performance evaluation processes of the institution. As review team members and rubric review committees have realized, the line between design and delivery is sometimes difficult to draw.

Another line sometimes difficult to draw is that between course design and course content. For the most part, the higher education rubric standards and review do not evaluate course content, as it is considered separate from course design; but the clienteles of other QM rubrics have requested that the standards and review address content. The matter of whether content should be evaluated in the higher education review remains somewhat controversial and has been addressed by rubric review committees.

The foundational aspects of the QM approach have been distilled in the "Underlying Principles of Quality Matters," shown in the Appendix at the end of the chapter.

QUALITY MATTERS 2.0, 3.0, AND ONWARD

In the first few years, the number of QM subscribing institutions grew rapidly; in later years the rate of increase leveled off, but growth has been steady throughout the ten post-grant years. Currently, from its various spheres of operation, QM has 78,000 account holders. Beyond this group, the number of QM users in institutions and organizations is too large to be quantifiable.

Statewide subscriptions. An interesting chapter in the QM story had to do with the creation of statewide QM subscriptions. Following Hurricane Katrina, Louisiana appropriated funds for online learning so the state's colleges and universities would be able to continue operating online if physical access were disrupted by a future hurricane. Mike Abbiatti of the Louisiana Board of Regents used some of the appropriation to provide QM services to all the public higher education institutions in the state, and in so doing negotiated with QM for a statewide contract that would cost considerably less than forty-plus individual subscriptions. The agreement, which included designation of a lead institution to relieve some of the administrative burden on the QM staff, became the model for statewide agreements, which now exist in about twenty-five states (R. Legon, personal communication, February 17, 2016).

Leadership and governance. From the outset, QM's leaders encountered unanticipated challenges to the business model. Among them was the early discovery that some subscribing institutions would find it more cost-effective to train members of staff to conduct QM reviews than to pay the QM front office to manage the reviews. Thus QM adjusted, offering both QM-managed services and self-service models. In a number of institutions, QM has scaled; to meet individual institutional needs, it is being used in ways not originally envisioned. Five variations on the use of QM have been identified. Among them are developing course templates based on the QM rubric and annotations, and conducting a limited number of official QM reviews to establish benchmarks against which to informally evaluate a larger number of courses (Shattuck, 2015).

QM's success, starting in the early post-grant years, owed to the resilience and creativity of its two leaders. Ron Legon, the first executive director, was joined by Deb Adair, administrative director; Adair brought experience in leading a non-profit organization and in teaching online. The two had complementary sets of expertise; a chemistry for making wise decisions, balancing risk-taking with being careful; and an utter belief in the efficacy and potential of the QM program.

As QM higher education subscriptions grew and new QM ventures were launched, the need for appropriate governance for an organization like QM became apparent. In 2014, the MarylandOnline Board restructured the relationship between itself and QM. Legally, QM would be a supporting organization of MOL, but it would be separately incorporated, with its own governing board.

QUALITY MATTERS TODAY

During the decade from 2006 and 2016, QM developed new products and services that tracked with the evolution of online education and subscribers' use of it.

New QM clienteles. Beyond higher education, QM recognized other clienteles seeking quality assurance in online education and sought partners in developing QM tools that would be relevant and responsive. In collaboration with the Florida Virtual School and the International Association for K-12 Online Learning (iNACOL), a QM rubric of standards and review process were developed for K-12 education. The rubric is now in its third edition. QM partnered with John Wiley & Sons to create a rubric and review process for educational publisher-produced online courses. The University Professional and Continuing Education Association (UPCEA) was QM's partner in producing a rubric and process tailored for online continuing and professional education (CPE). The CPE rubric encompasses MOOCs (Massive Open Online Courses), a delivery format generating considerable buzz and experimentation.

The rubric of standards and review processes for each of these constituencies are reviewed and updated every few years. The latest edition of the flagship higher education rubric incorporates the newly embraced delivery format of competency-based education (CBE) in its standards. The CBE standards were developed in cooperation with a study group representing QM subscribing institutions that offer competency-based education.

QM program certification. In 2015, QM launched program-level certification, its most significant new product since the unveiling of the higher education rubric more than ten years earlier. (https://www.qualitymatters.org/program-reviews). Four individual certifications are offered: Online Program Design, Online Teaching Support, Online Learner Support, and Online Learner Success. A task force of representatives from QM institutions developed and extensively tested the program certification standards and process.

Professional development. Supporting the QM review activities is a substantial lineup of professional development offerings designed for QM peer reviewers, institutional coordinators, and others. In response to subscriber demand, QM in 2016 launched its Teaching Online Certificate, a set of seven workshops aligned to QM's Online Instructor Skill Set. The certificate serves instructors in both higher education and K-12. A digital credential (badge) is awarded for completion of each workshop and for the complete set. Though this initiative may seem to contradict the QM mantra of "design, not delivery," it does not do so because instructor performance in a course is not being evaluated.

New QM communities. In 2013, QM established the QM Instructional Designers Association, providing a professional umbrella for a cohort that has been integral to QM's work throughout its history. Individual subscribers are another newly recognized community. QM subscriptions are now offered to accommodate individuals who want to be part of the QM network but are not affiliated with a subscribing institution.

International initiatives. A few institutions outside the US subscribe to QM, with some subscriptions leading to international partnerships. A promising collaboration executed in 2015 has QM partnering with Fudan University in Shanghai to create a cultural adaptation of the QM rubric and process for delivery in China. A lesson learned in the initial explorations with Fudan was that there are aspects of the QM model that cannot simply be translated; instead, they must be "recultured." Examples are the extent to which the teacher is to be treated as an authority figure and conventions related to learner interaction (Gao & Legon, 2015). QM expects future international partnerships in other countries may likewise entail reculturing.

Annual and regional QM conferences. Quality Matters holds an annual conference, with the eighth held in 2016. Conference attendance has grown each year, reaching over 600 in 2016. Smaller regional conferences also have been held the past few years. The tracks in the 2017 annual conference illustrate the topics explored at a QM conference: (https://www.qualitymatters.org/events/attend/qm-connect-conference)

A broadened QA focus. In the past few years QM has broadened its focus beyond its own proprietary resources and services to address quality assurance more broadly, in a national and international context. Its representatives are invited to participate in initiatives related to quality assurance in online education, such as the Bill & Melinda Gates Foundation-supported Landscape Project to assess the status of competency-based education, and they are turned to by the media as spokespersons on the subject of online quality assurance. Last year QM was invited by the US Department of Education to participate in ongoing conversations on outcomes-focused quality assurance and innovation in quality assurance related to the Department's Educational Quality through Innovative Partnerships (EQUIP) program. QM also was invited to join a confederation of higher education associations holding meetings to explore quality assurance frameworks for new, non-traditional forms of educational delivery.

THREATS TO THE QM SEAL

Can QM Standards Be Tied Directly to Student Learning Outcomes?
Documenting the impact of QM on student learning has been a preoccupation. During the grant period, the project team invited proposals for action research, and eight projects were funded (Shattuck, 2007). All revealed positive impacts, but a direct link remains difficult to confirm. A common question posed by institutions considering the adoption of QM is whether it can be shown that applying the QM rubric to an online course improves outcomes such as learner retention, grades, and satisfaction (Legon, 2015).

It is generally agreed that the components of QM implementation should be considered inputs in a process designed to achieve quality outputs (Adair & Shattuck, 2015). One area in which these inputs have been shown to have a direct influence is faculty satisfaction and behavior. Recent studies have documented the influence of both service as a QM peer reviewer and participation in QM professional development on actions undertaken by faculty members to improve their courses and their teaching, face-to-face as well as online (D. Adair, personal communication, February 19, 2016).

At the top of QM's current research agenda are studies to determine the effectiveness of the inputs in producing desired outcomes for students, teachers, and institutions (Legon, 2015). A major study has been commissioned to measure the impact of the QM rubric, and initiatives are also underway in QM to add the student voice to discussions about quality and how to evaluate it. Documented results of a decade of QM-focused impact studies can be obtained at qualitymatters.org.

Is QM Built to Last?

Another threat has to do with possible obsolescence. In a sense, QM is a legacy model. The monolith that has been instructor-led education in a physical or online classroom, the model on which QM is based, could splinter into a multiplicity of new student-driven, individualized forms of online education. The rather sudden popularity of competency-based education, a format that has been in existence for decades without such popularity, can be taken as a sign of restlessness with the legacy model. For some time, commentators inside and outside education have asserted that simply transplanting the basic format of a classroom course into an online course shell fails to use the full potential of the online medium for achieving superior learning results. Such criticism points toward a fundamental remaking of the educational process. Should such a revolution—or speeded-up evolution—occur, would a QM-like instrument and process remain relevant? The fact that QM has already incorporated instructional formats such as MOOCs and CBE in its rubrics suggests Quality

Matters will continue to stay abreast, or even ahead. So far in its short history, QM has demonstrated an organizational mindset of openness and a willingness to experiment.

QM AS A BELIEF STATEMENT AND A SEAL OF APPROVAL

This chapter has summarized how Quality Matters came into being, caught on, and grew, as well as what its future challenges may be. To an extent, answering the question "What is Quality Matters?" always has been difficult. A program, a system, a model, a process?

Quality Matters has been framed by Adair and Shattuck (2015) as "a belief statement put into practice and made tangible":

- a belief that online courses should reflect in their design what research has revealed as important for student learning,
- a belief that instructors best serve their students and each other through peer review and feedback focused on continuous improvement, and
- a belief that a shared understanding of quality can support diverse pathways to meeting standards of excellence. (p. 159)

From the beginning, a "Good Housekeeping Seal of Approval for online education" was also a handy way to describe QM. Legon identifies two factors responsible for a growing familiarity with the QM seal as a symbol of course quality. One is the absence, to date, of any competing form of recognition. Another is the rapidly expanding number of faculty and instructional design advocates (more than 45,000 now QM-trained) making conference presentations and publishing on their individual or institutions' accomplishments using QM (R. Legon, personal communication, February 17, 2016).

Quality Matters can be credited with helping to start the conversation about quality assurance in online education and with advancing the state of the art in educational quality assurance in a broader sense. The conversation will grow more urgent, and responsive quality frameworks more essential, as forms of educational delivery become more various and exciting.

APPENDIX
Underlying Principles of Quality Matters

The Quality Matters Rubric and processes are:

CONTINUOUS
- The Quality Matters process is designed to ensure all reviewed courses will eventually meet expectations.
- The process is integral to a continuous quality improvement process.

CENTERED
- On research - the development of the rubric is based in national standards of best practices, the research literature, and instructional design principles.
- On student learning - the rubric and process are designed to promote student learning.
- On quality - the review sets a quality goal at the 85 percent level or better (courses do not have to be perfect but better than good enough).

COLLEGIAL
- A Quality Matters review is part of a faculty-driven, peer review process.
- The review process is intended to be diagnostic and collegial, not evaluative and judgmental.

COLLABORATIVE

- The review is based on collaboratively identified evidence found in the course rather than the personal preference of an individual reviewer.
- The review is flexible and not prescriptive (there are many ways to meet each standard).
- The review team consists of experienced online instructors as reviewers in communication with the course developer. (Quality Matters, n.d.)

REFERENCES

Adair, D., & Shattuck, K. (2015). Quality Matters™: An educational input in an ongoing design-based research project. *The American Journal of Distance Education, 29,* 159-165. doi: 10.1080/08923647.2015.1061809

Gao, Y., & Legon, R. (2015). Internationalizing Quality Matters™: The China case. *The American Journal of Distance Education, 29,* 210-219. doi: 10.1080/08923647.2015.1061809

Legon, R. (2015). Measuring the impact of the Quality Matters Rubric™: A discussion of possibilities. *The American Journal of Distance Education, 29,* 166-173. doi: 10.1080/08923647.2015.1061809

MarylandOnline. (2006). *Quality Matters: Inter-institutional quality assurance in online education: A project of MarylandOnline: Summary—final project report: November 2006.* Largo, MD: Author.

Quality Matters. (n.d.) Underlying principles of Quality Matters. Retrieved from https://www.qualitymatters.org/research-grants/fipse/principles

Russell, T. (2001). *The no significant difference phenomenon: A comparative research annotated bibliography on technology for distance education* (5th ed.). Chicago, IL: IDECC.

Shattuck, K. (2007). Quality Matters: Collaborative program planning at a state level. *Online Journal of Distance Learning Administration, 10*(3). Retrieved from http://www.westga.edu/~distance/ojdla/

Shattuck, K. (2015). Focusing research on Quality Matters. *The American Journal of Distance Education, 29,* 155-158. doi: 10.1080/08923647.2015.1061809

The advantages of rubrics. (n.d.) retrieved from https://www.teachervision.com/teaching-strategies/advantages-rubrics-part-one-five-part-series#what_is_a_rubric

U.S. Department of Education, Fund for the Improvement of Postsecondary Education. (2016). *Quality Matters: Inter-institutional quality assurance in online education* (FIPSE Database). Retrieved from http://fipsedatabase.ed.gov/fipse/grantshow. cfm?grantNumber=P116B030646

INTERVIEW WITH GERALD HEEGER

Former President
University of Maryland University College

WILLIAM PATRICK: When you talk about the early days of online learning at New York University, I think that's an interesting story.

GERALD HEEGER: Well, it is, but to fill in a larger background, I really believe that one of the key elements of success for literally all of the contributions in this book, *Learning at the Speed of Light*, is the fact that most of the places where online learning began, or at least took some early steps, were in places that were essentially marginal. I don't mean that as a derogatory category. We can go back to my example and see that the School of Continuing Education was certainly not the dead center of learning at New York University in the mid-'90s. And the continuing education units at the University of California, whether they were at Berkeley or UCLA or Irvine, were the same way—somewhat marginal, each one functioning with very different rules. But the common situation was that not being central to the institution, in a kind of

100

back-handed way, allowed the leaders there to have more freedom for innovation.

WP: Do you think there was also an element of "What-do-we-have-to-lose?" on the part of these marginal educational communities?

GH: Yes, of course. There was certainly a piece of it that we would have to describe as "What-do-we-have-to-lose?" The other piece of it—and I include myself in this category, though I don't know how many others gravitated toward leadership in continuing education the same way as I did—is that they're really an interesting group of people. But they're not traditional academics. I was trained as a political scientist in South Asian Studies at the University of Chicago. In the end, I decided not to do that, although I have worked as a professor of political science on the faculty at the University of Virginia. I believe that the commonality I'm talking about is that many of the people in continuing higher education were nontraditional, and so had a greater sense of risk-taking. They were in positions that were institutionally less central, and that combination made for fertile ground for trying new things.

And let's remember the money part of it. The characteristic of not being a school or a program that was seen as part of the core institution or system meant that essentially that school or program had to be largely self-supporting. In such a situation, some people can become very risk averse; others, the opposite. For me, there was a sense of, "Let's try new things. Let's get that new program, because we can't survive just doing imitation traditional academics."

WP: Innovation can be exciting for many people, of course.

GH: Yes, it can. However, when you look back at innovation, there is a tendency to create a storyline that makes the outcomes of innovation more or less inevitable. That's how it works retrospectively in your head, but in some ways I think that narrative misses much of the drama and it misses most of the contributions that people have made.

WP: And perhaps it misses the random nature of history as well.

GH: I don't think innovation comes in big choices. Innovation comes out of a slowly dawning big idea that appears in a series of small steps. I was very struck, for example, by Gary Matkin's letter to you about his planned contribution to this book. In the middle of that e-mail, he enumerates seven or eight things that he wanted to capture as part of UC Irvine's growth online. Gary is very gifted, but, for me, issues such as the impact of technology on the university or the impact on access—or more broadly, "What does all of this mean for the faculty and for students?" or, ultimately, "How should online learning be organized within the university?"—all of these revealed themselves in a series of small steps. The trick is making the right choices as you hit each of these small steps and coming to grips with whatever each of the small steps gives you . . . you know, you make a small step, and the next question becomes, do you understand what that step gets you into?

I'll use an example. When I arrived at UMUC as its new president, I discovered that there was a sizeable online program that had been started under Ben Massey, who was my predecessor, and it was largely coming out of faculty in the Overseas Divisions of UMUC. By that time, I had already begun to sense that, "Okay, now it's 2000, and this online learning thing is going to get pretty interesting, and UMUC needs to have a bigger presence in it." I had already started some online things at NYU and had gotten involved with the NYU Online initiative. When I got to UMUC, I was trying to carry some of those ideas over.

UMUC is one of twelve degree-granting institutions in the University System of Maryland. Now the second-largest higher education institution in the state (stateside enrollment only) and, during my tenure, one of the fastest-growing universities in the country, UMUC was founded in 1947 as part of the University of Maryland College Park to bring higher education opportunities to adults at times and places convenient to them. It is also very much a global university. Since after World War II, the university has been providing educational services to the military overseas. To serve an adult working population, the university has had to be both innovative and flexible. UMUC has offered courses in a variety of modalities: through correspondence, interactive video network (IVN), interactive televideo (ITV), voice mail, and today, extensively, on the web. This is in addition to traditional classroom courses, executive programs, short residency programs, and accelerated and mixed-format programs.

With the advent of the Internet and online education in the early 1990s, UMUC was especially prepared to launch its virtual university. For years it had been building the necessary infrastructure and the appropriate global orientation to make this possible. It had in place a worldwide faculty and curriculum; a system of distributed learning and support services; and a level of competency in managing both international operations and intellectual capital dispersion that few other institutions could rival, through its fifty-year relationship with the US military. Online learning was the next logical step.

And we found that we were very good at it. Today, the university enrolls 48,000 stateside students and nearly 250,000 worldwide online course enrollments. Because of UMUC's history, online education was not as big of an intellectual leap there as it is at most other universities. No paradigm shift in mindset was required. But, some modest-sized requirements immediately emerged.

Because UMUC offered courses all over the world, it had a widely distributed faculty, and a significant number of those were full-time teaching faculty who taught in places like Germany and England and Japan and Okinawa as part of the tri-branch military contract. It was already clear that the faculty were teaching very different courses under the nomenclature of one particular course or one particular course number. I actually traveled around to all the various areas of UMUC to meet with faculty and to say, "We need to move to a point where the syllabus for a particular course needs to be common." That was something that was both appreciated and resisted, because it challenged people as to how they did their work and what they were comfortable with. Along the way, I began to realize gradually that the issue was really much bigger—online education wasn't about syllabi, and it wasn't even about courses. It's about the faculty role. As you keep growing in the number of courses you offer, you make small steps to support faculty and it begins to dawn on you, "Hey, the faculty role is changing in some fundamental ways. We need to think about how we support faculty and students differently, and better, in the online environment."

My point is that innovation often emerges in modest steps–it doesn't just pop up out of nowhere; it emerges as you make decisions and solve the problems that you see without necessarily devising some big new plan. At least, that was always the way that I tried to work, always trying to be intuitive about where we needed to go. Yes, you go through a strategic plan exercise, but that's very global. The questions for me, at least, are: how does one respond to unique situations, and where are the unique situations that that propel you to take some bigger action? And I believe that this is how this process really unfolded, at least at the institutions where I worked,

WP: Well, in terms of context, let me back you up a little bit so we can make this more chronological. You mentioned the University of Chicago. Were you there for graduate school?

GH: Yes, but before that, I went to the University of California at Berkeley as an undergraduate, and graduated from there in 1965, which was the class of the Free Speech Movement. The university was closed down. That's relevant, I guess, because it's been fifty years. and I have had a lot of time to think about it. That was a time, an era, when systemic questions about the university and how the university treats students were becoming major issues. What do students learn, especially at a big university like the University of California? That was a time when all of those questions came to the fore, just as I was headed off to graduate school.

WP: How did that era affect your ideas about education?

GH: You don't go to a university thinking about the "university." You don't go there with those kinds of big questions. You go there thinking about yourself: *What am I going to major in?* and *Am I any good at anything?* I went to Berkeley in 1961 from Omaha, Nebraska, and just going to California was a revelation in itself. I worried about a lot of things, but I didn't worry too much about what was going to happen after college. I presumed that a college education paid off and that people who got degrees did well. So I figured that all I had to do was finish and then figure it out.

But what the Free Speech Movement did—even in just observing it and sitting around, talking over coffee with other students about what the university should be and could be—was certainly to push the idea of "the university" higher in my consciousness. And the faculty themselves were talking a lot about that, so you just had to listen in. I was not one of those people who viewed the university ideologically. But what did emerge in me was the realization that the university does have a profound social impact, and what a university needs to be should be debated strongly by students and faculty. Don't forget that, in 1965, Berkeley was a university where Clark Kerr was still the chancellor of the UC system and writing about the multiversity: that the university has to be an institution which recognizes that it serves multiple constituents both inside and outside of itself.

So I began to ask those questions, but then I moved to Chicago where I methodically plodded toward my doctorate, and focused on that. But the sense that you were being prepared for the traditional model of the university was very strong at Chicago. It was about training you for the professoriate, and I was studying to be a political scientist, with an emphasis on the politics of South Asia. I did my dissertation work in India. I don't think I really realized it at the time, but I was becoming more and more interested in institutions themselves: what makes institutions work, how do they work, and what are the circumstances that make them change?

I finished that dissertation and came back to America and wound up teaching at the University of Virginia in the Department of Political Science. Eventually, I began to feel like I wanted to do more in administration than in teaching. The idea of shaping programs became more and more interesting to me. Pure opportunity led me to adult students. It wasn't because I suddenly decided that adult students were a unique population toward whom I needed to make a missionary movement. In fact, I distinctly remember that it was while I was at the University of Virginia, in the 1970s, when I discovered quite accidentally that many students actually go to school part time. It just had never dawned on me before. I had always gone to school full time, and it simply didn't occur to me that other people did it differently. *Hey, that's interesting*, I thought.

WP: It's true. In the '70s, that was not the norm by any means.

GH: No. When I moved to Adelphi University, I was first the department head in the Department of Political Science but relatively quickly became the dean of what they called University College, which was their adult division. That's where I began to really think about adult students. I had started teaching at night for these adult classes in University College. Almost all my students were upper middle-class women from Long Island who had stopped out of college when they had married and subsequently used this program to return to school. I began to hear how they integrated education into their lives, and that's when I first began to think about teaching using televised course materials, so I was looking to technology to be some solution for providing content to nontraditional students.

Adelphi was having lots of problems at that time. I had been the youngest dean in the history of the university, and then I became the provost during those difficult years. Eventually I left when a new president came there, and I wound up working at The New School, which was a wonderful experience for me. I had known the people at The New School for a while—David Levy, who was dean of the Parsons School of Design, was there, as was Allen Austill, my predecessor. Both were gifted program developers and continuing-education leaders, and I learned much from them. I spent several years there, focusing on adult students. The New School offered lots of nontraditional courses. Its whole approach, actually, was non-traditional. That's actually where I consistently began to make the acquaintance of people who were in adult learning.

I knew nothing about the University Continuing Education Association until Kay Kohl showed up at my office. We became friends, and I began to get involved in UCEA. Then I was recruited by New York University in 1990 to go there and take over from Harvey Stedman, the dean of the School of Continuing Education, which was very large even then. Again, while filled with gifted academic innovators, the School of Continuing Education was not perceived to be the center of the university, quite obviously. I don't think I'm being harsh when I say that it wasn't perceived to be central to the mission of the university. Nonetheless, NYU made such a big deal out of being in New York City and encouraged the School of Continuing Education to develop important constituencies in the New York business community and, along the way, allowed me to learn a lot about community learning needs.

In the '90s, the recession hit, and we were losing enrollment. That pushed my colleagues and me to begin to think about developing nontraditional programming much more aggressively, and the biggest expansion was in undergraduate degree studies for adults. And then because the Real Estate Institute had already developed a master of science in real estate finance and development, we started to develop very focused, industry-specific master's degrees in a variety of fields. That is actually where I first encountered online learning. Richard Vigilante, who directed the school's information technology program, introduced me to Frank Mayadas at the Sloan Foundation. My school was able to transfer a program in management over from The New School and put it online, and that's when I began to think about what online education could really become.

It is a crass thing to say, but during that time, the only thing that I had to do was to make sure that the School of Continuing Education, (whose name I had changed to the School of Continuing and Professional Studies), could make money. So long as the school generated revenues and didn't outrage anybody, it had considerable freedom to experiment. That's when I first created NYU Online. I thought we could not ask the university to underwrite what seemed to be a costly enterprise and, in the mid-1990s, turned out in fact to be an incredibly costly enterprise. Could we generate enough money? How could we generate the investment? This was not a priority for the university, so we started playing with the idea of going outside and creating a for-profit entity. And at the same moment, I was watching all the things that were going on with the University of Phoenix, which I had never heard of until maybe 1993 or '94, and with other schools as well.

WP: Did you get seed money from the Sloan Foundation during that time?

GH: Yes, we did. If my memory is correct, we got the one of the first Sloan grants in the online learning. If it wasn't the first, it was an early one. We had a very small program to produce certificates of mastery in management. For me, it was a learning exercise. We certainly didn't make money. Frank supported it, and I had the luxury of having access to him. I would meet him periodically. We were in the same city. And Frank was a remarkable leader. Everybody in the field knows who he is, but he's never been completely recognized for all that he did, and for how influential he was in defining the field. Time passes, of course, and new people come into the field, especially in the online learning field, where so many people cycle through. But, in terms of fundamental, intellectual influence, at least in my eyes, he was a critical figure. By just building up programs and encouraging them, and by developing a network of support, I see him as a seminal figure.

It was during this period that I ended up getting involved in a presidential search for UMUC. I wound up there, at UMUC, because the regents were really interested in what I had been doing. There was a feeling among the Regents that UMUC had stagnated a bit (undeserved, I should add), despite its long history with the military and so forth. They were also especially interested in the for-profit, online initiative. So I wound up going there.

WP: Before we move to UMUC, could you give me a short primer on NYU Online? I don't know too much about that.

GH: Curiously enough, I don't either. I started NYU Online with a conversation about funding, talking to the president about going online and taking programs online and creating an online venture. And it wound up with our having conversations with the board of trustees. Ultimately, the university board funded the venture, with the idea that the School of Continuing and Professional Studies would generate courses and that it would funnel the money it made back into the university.

Not too long after I started it, I got recruited away by UMUC, so that's why I don't know as much as I would if I had stayed there. I do know, though, that after I left, NYU Online took a different path, kind of lost its way, and was eventually closed down.

WP: Why did you decide to go the for-profit route with NYU Online?

GH: Well, as you looked around the landscape in 1996 or '97, what did you see? You saw, in adult education, the surge in growth of the University of Phoenix, the surge in growth of these for-profits, which were beginning to do online in a big way. It just seemed that their ability to move faster, their ability to aggregate assets, to grow, was exponentially more favorable to doing the kinds of things we had been talking about in terms of serving the expanding adult population. Again, NYU is a wealthy university, and it's a strong university, but its larger concerns were for the college and in the graduate and professional schools and in making its investments in those areas. So the kinds of things that I wanted to do really didn't seem within reach within ordinary funding from the university.

WP: Well, this was in the early to mid-1990s, and that was the infancy of online, right? Nobody knew what was going to happen with it then.

GH: Right, right. It was overshadowed in some sense by the natural growth of adult education in general, and the sudden sense of that growing demographic.

NYU/SCPS was about developing close contacts with industry and about developing a sense of the kind of programs those industries needed. What kinds of training would people need? And, we had some other advantages. I used to joke a lot that young people would come to New York City from Indiana, and they'd be pretty proud of their degrees from the University of Indiana. They would get into an investment business, and to the right of them an office mate would hang up his Wharton degree and the office mate on the left would put up her Harvard business degree. Of course, the wonderful thing about NYU at that time was that when you got a degree from there, it didn't say what school you came from. Suddenly they had another degree and it was from NYU. I kidded my colleagues in the School of Continuing and Professional Education that we provided "education cosmetology," though I'm not sure you should quote me on that.

WP: Are you sure? That's a pretty good line.

GH: Maybe it's okay. I think it's a very important piece of what continuing education does, and I don't mean that in any derogatory sense. Remember, I came from the University of California, and the University of Chicago, where the continuing education divisions played a critical role in helping people add to their skill sets and played an important role in helping people add to their credentials. It gave them, in the case of Berkeley and NYU certainly, high-end institutions in their credentials.

WP: Absolutely. And let's face it, academia is pretty status conscious.

GH: Oh, incredibly.

WP: Now I'm reading here from an e-mail that you sent to John Ebersole, in which you say, "What unfolded at NYU in the late 1990s was a recasting of risk for the school." It sounds like what you've been talking about is related to that.

GH: That's correct. I think the emergence of the competitive marketplace for the adult student really began to have impact, at least on me, during that time. When you're at NYU, in The New School, you're in the middle of the most competitive adult marketplace in the country, so you've got to be aggressive. But as the for-profit schools and the marketplace grew, we began to think, *Well, how do we maintain ourselves in this larger marketplace?* Now, again, it's a bit opportunistic because we were NYU, for god's sake—in a ten-block area, there were thousands of students—so we didn't need to think of it in terms of distance education. But the idea of moving into new kinds of programs, and the accessibility that technology afforded, made it possible to do this fairly quickly.

My predecessors and I had worked hard to give a lot of autonomy to the students in the School of Continuing and Professional Studies, so we had our own faculty and our own curricula and our own budget. We weren't as dependent as university extension was at Berkeley or UCLA, and we weren't as dependent on having department heads in the traditional divisions sign off on our programs. But the sense of having to be visible and competitive just propelled us to think that we needed to spend more time and effort in growing opportunity. That meant more credit programs, especially more graduate programs in very focused areas. And all of it led to considerations of how we were going to finance the venture. The university wasn't used to huge amounts of investment in our area, and that's what led to the idea, in 1997 or '98, of NYU Online.

But then I left. Maybe I shouldn't have, but I did. The opportunity at UMUC arose, and I was very interested in becoming a university president. I had been down there, and I knew quite a bit about it, and it intrigued me. The chancellor was someone I knew, so I had a sense of the place. The idea of the whole university—UMUC, institutionally autonomous, and separately accredited, set up to deal with nontraditional students—was really engaging. I went there with the idea of taking advantage of that, and I spent the first couple of years there making it very separate, making the curriculum very separate, making sure the faculty knew that they were teaching for UMUC, not the University of Maryland College Park.

And in that context, the university continued to grow. UMUC had its own learning management system. I can't say I was exactly sure what a learning management system was until I got to UMUC. You begin to realize, *Oh, I've got to think this thing through.* I'll give you a good example. You begin to understand the implications of what you're doing, not because you're thinking so globally, at least in my mind, but because you're thinking that you're confronting issues in a unique way. At some point, not too long after I arrived at UMUC, the system began to develop intellectual property rules, as more and more faculty were doing all kinds of interesting things.

But the intellectual property rules being developed by the system were completely antithetical to what we needed at UMUC. We needed to be in control of our content. We couldn't have faculty members control the content, because if they did, we would not have the ability to offer the courses repetitively, in multiple sections. And so we spent a lot of time dealing with the issue of trying to get the Regents and the System to understand the unique needs of a school that was doing much more online work, and why it had to do that, and why it had to have certain kinds of rules, and certain kinds of budgetary rules.

The marginality I mentioned earlier is important here. UMUC received very little money from the state, and it was not the focus of attention in the system. It was essentially self-supporting. So my effort to move online more quickly was not all that controversial. By 2000, we were developing online courses at a rapid pace. We had this large military constituency which gravitated quickly toward it, and so our developing online courses in general allowed us to grow in a fairly quick way. And as we did that, we were forced to think through all of the issues that began to surface then: "Oh, how do we train faculty? How do you manage off-campus students who never come to the campus? How do you provide student services with the technology? How do you do all of these things?" So we did a lot of work on creating the technology infrastructure to support the online learning initiative.

I would say it's opportunistic and judgmental: you see the opportunity, you try to figure out what your choices are, and then you work to implement them. But having the autonomy, that's the thing I keep going back to, because the thing that I have been blessed with is that I have always been in institutions where "adult learner programs" were fairly autonomous to begin with, and the great colleagues I had and I were always able to undertake the kinds of innovations that were necessary to support online learning. To have a whole school, a whole university, devoted to adult students—who had ever heard of that before then? Who would have thought of that? A whole university devoted to adult students where you could invent a whole infrastructure? So you try new things and you learn new things.

WP: How long were you at UMUC?

GH: Six years. Then I was recruited to come down here to Dallas to work for an investment entity that was interested in doing online education overseas. Ultimately, we helped create a system of universities in Latin America, which is now managed out of Miami. That was a great experience, too. It was about acquiring universities overseas and creating alliances and helping to grow online initiatives and developing management structures and things of that sort. And that entity created several other innovative online initiatives as well.

WP: How different was it working for a business like that than working in a university setting like NYU or UMUC?

GH: Well, very different in the sense that when I was working at UMUC, I was the president and I was in control of everything. When you go to work for an investment group, there was a CEO deeply experienced in developing new companies and people with extraordinary business experience. So, I had to adapt to that. And it wasn't always easy. At the same time, it really taught me a lot more about business and about business management and about strategies of growth. As you visit universities, how do you assess them? How do you align with universities? So it was a very different flavor, but many of the same topics continue to be discussed: how do you grow a university online; what is the infrastructure you need; how do you train faculty; how do you recruit students in places that are not as developed or focused, as in Latin America, for instance?

We also created a graduate school of education, called The American College of Education, which had originally been owned by DePaul University. I spent a couple of years being president of that school as we worked our way through re-accreditation where, again, you confront all of the issues that are still relevant today: profit vs. nonprofit; online vs. not online. By the time I got back to some of those core issues, I had really sorted through all the things we're talking about. How do you talk to accrediting bodies about online education? How do you establish credibility and do that?

WP: How do you do that? How do you talk to accrediting bodies?

GH: I think accrediting bodies should have no doubts about online learning by now. Online education is no longer an experiment. It's credible. But there may be a difference in the level of sophistication between the staff of the accrediting body and the faculty who show up for accrediting reviews. The faculty may vary in their sophistication about online education, but the staffs of the accreditors have gotten increasingly sophisticated in understanding what quality means in online higher education. You still need to demonstrate that you meet all the traditional standards of quality and strength, but there's much more openness as to how you present that with accreditors, at least in my experience. But it's still a process of adjustment with new initiatives coming into the conversation: MOOCs and competency-based education, to name but two examples.

WP: What do you see as the future for online learning? Where do you think it's going in the next ten years?

GH: I think it becomes a normal part of higher education. At Arizona State today, it's my understanding that almost all the students are taking at least one online course. It's a huge university that has grown massively under the leadership of Michael Crow, and he's done a lot with bringing ASU online, not only for nontraditional students but for traditional students as well. That integration of online education into traditional universities, I think, will continue and grow despite all of the MOOC effort. I don't mean to dismiss it, but in my mind the MOOC effort was an effort for universities to claim that they were going online without having to pay the price intellectually of thinking through all of the decisions they would need to make if they wanted to really sustain an online program.

WP: Even a pioneer of MOOCs, Sebastian Thrun from Stanford, has discounted them at this point. He's working with Udacity, right?

GH: I think so. That really leads me to the point I was actually going to make. There was some sense that—and I certainly had it for a while—that online education would transform the university as we know it in fundamental ways. I don't think that's happened, and I think, in fact, the intractability of the university, in terms of its resistance to change (although I don't like to characterize it that way), is the problem. The university is a very structured institution that is set in the context of a fairly rigid regulatory scheme which slows innovation.

The university has a faculty which has an inordinate amount of power, and the faculty is very concerned about maintaining its role in the institution. And the university is very worried about how the outside world measures value in higher education, and it tends to use place holders for quality—research productivity, the prestige of the faculty, tuition. Then the university also falls victim to what Ryan Craig of University Ventures, in his book, *College Disrupted: The Great Unbundling of Higher Education*, calls "isomorphism," where a single model, imitative of the elite university, prevails. The tendency has been for universities to absorb change by isolating, rather than to embracing, it.

One challenge for universities to consider is why the faculty needs to be at the same physical location as the university. If an online course is on Latin American economics, why not have a Latin American professor located in Latin America teach it? Expansion of information and communication technologies has not only empowered Western content to permeate world culture—a fact often decried—but also has stimulated new capabilities on the part of developing nations to communicate within themselves, among themselves, and globally. Yet, despite the new level of interconnectedness, of new types of institutions for commerce and for communication, higher education is only a marginal participant. We remain highly localized, closely linked to national and local agendas, consumed by the challenges we face—limited resources, growing demand—but, almost always, inward-facing. Especially for open universities, education capacity building has been a national rather than a global preoccupation.

So far, higher education's most visible contribution to a globalized world is largely a conversation between citizens of the wealthiest and most rapidly developing countries. Countries on the economic periphery, where the demand for higher education is growing most rapidly, remain marginal to this exchange. I would suggest a new collaboration, a "supra-national" university or a network for global, open learning, defined as a set of technologically linked relationships built out of clusters of open universities worldwide. To build such a university, member open universities would agree to pool existing assets and to make them transferable and scalable as a means of building capacity. Faculty from participating open universities, trained in the pedagogy of online teaching, could deliver courses through the web to students not only in their home country, but worldwide.

Students, when admitted to a collaborating institution, could take courses simultaneously or sequentially from both institutions. They would gain exposure to new perspectives and approaches in their international virtual classrooms. They would also be trained in the protocols of learning effectively online and in information literacy, learning how to access and evaluate the extensive resources available on the web. Faculty would benefit from increased opportunities for collaboration with colleagues around the world and would gain expertise in online course delivery to bring back to their home institutions. Courses could be jointly developed and/or delivered by faculty from two or more institutions, adding breadth and cross-cultural perspectives to the classroom. Capacity to put existing courses and degrees online could be built at participating open universities, expanding multifold courses available to students. This network of open universities would bring greatly expanded opportunities to a growing global student body through the large-scale delivery of quality online higher education. It would also create a new level of interconnectedness among participating open universities. In virtual space, a true global dialogue between North and South, East and West could take place and ideas shared and complex issues debated. Students everywhere badly need exposure to ideas and cultures that differ from their own. It is only through technology that this has been possible. Technology has changed the relationship between people and knowledge in ways unimaginable a decade ago. It can reinvent higher education, and it is through the unique innovation that exists in academia that technology can globalize higher education for lifelong learners worldwide.

WP: Going back to an earlier point you made, do you believe nontraditional students still tend to be marginalized somewhat? After all, the vast majority of them are not first-time, full-time, eighteen-to-twenty-two-year-old students at elite institutions.

GH: Despite the fact that they represent the larger numbers, the vision of what a college student is today remains remarkably similar to what it was when you and I went to college. The impact of online on the rethinking of higher education, in the sense of a classic innovation paradigm, is not yet there. I think over time, though, the paradigm of how the university teaches and how students learn is going to change. But the transformation still to occur, at least to me, remains unpredictable.

WP: And that's amazing to me, because online learning has been around for about twenty-three years at this point.

GH: Yes, but again I go back to marginality. The advantage of marginality is that it creates a setting where the people who are participating in the book that you're editing have the opportunity to be innovators. The disadvantage of marginality is that not everybody who needs to know about any innovation necessarily knows, and it all takes longer. I started my career thinking about how developing countries develop. What are the critical leaps that create a transformative environment? The subject of my research work initially was India, and India is a remarkable place because it has been impacted by many civilizations and has gone through many transformative events. The country had the ability to absorb new elements without necessarily being transformed utterly, but over time India has become a transformed environment. Eventually, a critical mass of growth has made the country change in dramatically new ways. We've seen the same thing in China. Transformation is inevitable. Higher education has a similar ability, at first, to resist transformation, but over time, even with such resistance, the university will find itself substantially changed.

WP: But this has been a slower revolution than you initially thought it would be?

GH: Oh, yes, very much so.

WP: Well, sorry to sound cynical, but often it comes down to power and money, and for traditional universities, the power and the money still seem to reside mostly in traditional educational practices.

GH: For now, for now. But at the same time, the structures are changing. The states don't have the money to support the state universities the way that they have always supported them. Private universities are searching for traditional enrollment in more and more desperate ways. Nothing happens quite the way we expect it to happen, but it's a fact. I was reading an article recently about how Illinois is rapidly cutting back on its support of public universities. The Wisconsin idea of the university engaged in economic growth and development is at risk with Scott Walker's governorship. And it's not because people say, "I don't want this to happen." It's because there's a limited amount of money, and people are still wrestling with how that money is going to be spent and what the priorities should be.

WP: Well, this has been instructive and interesting. Thanks so much for speaking with me.

TV TO VIDEO TO THE INTERNET
How Technology Changed Access and Learning

Susan M. Kryczka

Principal Consultant, Elevate Higher Ed
Former Chief Academic Strategist, Educators Serving Educators
Excelsior College

I have been lucky enough to have been part of the evolution of technology-driven distance education from the 1970s to the present. When I think about it, though, my own personal educational experience with learning at a distance began long before that.

I was born and raised in a city that pioneered distance education via live broadcast back in what were still the early days of television. In 1956, Chicago City Junior College (now the City Colleges of Chicago) premiered TV College, a bold experiment offering undergraduate courses and degrees taught live, on television, by faculty. This was offered via the local circuit television facilities available through the Chicago Educational Television Association's station WTTW, Channel 11, which today is the local public broadcasting station affiliate in Chicago (Taylor, 1957). Available to anyone with a television set in the area, these courses were offered to address familiar problems that many community colleges still face today: (1) a lack of physical space on campus to handle degree seeking students due to expected and realized growth, (2) a need to meet skilled manpower needs for local business and industry, and (3) an interest in improving the quality of instruction (Taylor, 1957).

In terms of how the medium might aid in boosting quality, it was thought that the strict time constraints of television would focus instruction, and by utilizing the best faculty available and designing lectures through a team approach, the quality of both teaching and learning would be enhanced. The concept of teaching via television caught on in New York City, also as New York University's Sunrise Semester followed suit broadcasting similar educational programs in 1957.

I remember as a kid sitting on the floor with my brother and sister in our family's one bedroom apartment in Chicago watching a beginning German language course on our small black and white television. Some man was talking to us on TV! The set and presentation were hugely primitive by today's technology standards, but mesmerizing to us. We loved the teacher's enthusiasm, sitting behind a desk and at a blackboard, even if we had no idea what he was saying. We did pick up a few German words. Even during the early days of television, as is the case today, a passionate performer could keep you riveted and engaged, no matter the delivery system.

During the same time in the late 1950s and early 1960s, I also remember watching *College Bowl* with my siblings, the TV quiz show that pitted various college teams from around the country against each other in answering questions about history, literature, math, and science. My parents were immigrants who did not speak English, so the concept of college was totally unknown to me and unrelated to anything in my life. I just remember thinking how old and smart the contestants seemed and how these people were not like anyone I had ever known. I also thought I would never be nearly as brainy as they appeared. We loved that show, too.

I figured out by early high school that college was the great equalizer in America and that it was my best route to achieving more than my parents. (I'm happy to say my brother and sister figured out the same thing.) So I went to college and immediately upon graduation on to graduate school. My path with the Chicago City Colleges coincidentally crossed again in 1976, when I got my first job out of graduate school, managing undergraduate credit courses offered via videotape cassettes through the City Colleges of Chicago's Study Unlimited program. The Chicago City Colleges were focused on making education even more convenient by offering students (in addition to the broadcasts into their homes still going on in the late 1970s, but with more sophisticated productions that were not live), the option of viewing their courses at select local Chicago Public Library locations. Study Unlimited was just that—you were no longer limited by time and place. The neighborhood library offered a free, quiet location to view your courses, study, access a counselor (who was really a coach by today's definition), and take exams when you were ready. The flexibility it offered, to move at your own pace with no set semesters or due dates, might be seen as an early version of competency-based education—no longer seat- or time-based, but more competency-driven.

In 1980, I joined Illinois Institute of Technology's IIT/V system as the manager and later became director of the system. IIT offered programs to a new corporate audience needing advanced coursework. We broadcast graduate courses from campus to business and industrial sites in the Chicago area via microwave signal. Companies such as Motorola, Bell Labs, and Northrup Corporation were hiring engineers straight out of college and needed to ensure that their skills stayed up to date. Most of these companies were located in the suburbs precluding employees from easily driving into campus during the day or even at night. These were live courses televised to select microwave receive sites which allowed one-way video and two-way audio communication. Off-site students could call in questions to the faculty member as they taught a live, small, on-campus class. Complete masters degrees were offered in this manner. Course materials were delivered via courier to off-campus sites or by overnight mail, as this was still before use of the fax machines or computers. Courses were offered during the day and at night, and employers not only paid full tuition for successful completion of the course, but gave students release time during the day, and a bonus or promotion when a graduate degree was completed.

Offering media-based graduate degree programs to industry was not unique to IIT and the Chicago area. Since the early 1970s, a number of major research universities around the country with engineering schools had been offering off-campus graduate programs by live broadcast or videotape. In 1976, a group of ten or twelve schools with these types of programs joined together to form the Association for Media-Based Continuing Education for Engineers (AMCEE). Admittedly a mouthful for a title, it was truly a unique consortium as the group joined together to lease or sell their videotaped engineering and computer science topic-based courses to businesses/corporations and shared marketing expenses by advertising in a combined print catalog.

In 1984, a core of the AMCEE schools joined together to help create the National Technological University (NTU), which was designed to offer master's degrees in engineering and computer science made up of courses from the consortium members. The brainchild of Lionel V. Baldwin, dean of engineering at Colorado State University, NTU was created to serve the continuing education needs of engineers wherever they were, again solving the problem of time and location. NTU was quickly accredited by the North Central Association to grant graduate degrees, and the courses were broadcast via satellite across the country and eventually to other parts of the world. I was lucky enough to have been at IIT when they joined NTU (IIT was a founding member of AMCEE) and in 1984, I became director of the Northeastern University distance learning unit in Boston where we, too, broadcast live graduate courses to local Boston area businesses. Northeastern was also an AMCEE/NTU school.

NTU eventually grew to become a consortium of over thirty engineering schools offering graduate credit and noncredit programs via satellite. The administrators and faculty who were involved in these programs at the member schools were all early pioneers in distance education. The organizational principles behind NTU were fairly radical at the time. While each school was a member of the consortium, each individual institution also ran its own distance education unit, which, we came to realize, could bump heads with NTU. This became particularly evident in places like southern California where the University of Southern California (USC), a regional and national powerhouse in graduate engineering, was also delivering engineering programs via videotape and through live microwave to companies that NTU was also soliciting.The same became true in the Boston, Massachusetts area, where high tech companies were flourishing in the 1980s and the educational needs of engineers were pretty much considered to be the purview of Boston University, MIT, Northeastern University, and the University of Massachusetts Amherst. We loved the idea of being part of NTU as a way of expanding our enrollments, reputation, and reach, but we never dreamed that companies might actually prefer an NTU degree over the regional, known institution. (We learned this lesson again with the growth of for-profit online institutions fifteen years later, never thinking students would choose an upstart over the local entity). Accusations of price cutting (on both sides) immediately surfaced. While we immediately knew we were part of something innovative and exciting with NTU, how to organize and navigate the competitive marketplace in a way that our home institutions (and deans) didn't feel we were working against our own best interests, was a daily feat. Luckily, NTU was governed by a board and president, much like a traditional institution, and the individual universities exercised a degree of governance power with a voice in what programs and courses were offered from what member schools. We had to grow up fast, though in our naiveté we thought all of us were going to reap huge enrollment benefits all of the time. But a surprising thing happened. Besides offering advanced educational programs to engineers, scientists, and researchers, we realized that we were no longer competitive institutions fighting for students but working together to offer collectively the best courses, taught by the best faculty, offered by a separate entity (NTU). We had a place to go to share best practices and even team-taught courses with faculty from two different institutions. When we expanded into new companies with NTU, it had a Wild West feel to it as suddenly we were all over the country offering educational programs and even moving internationally to expand our collective reach. We worked in the trenches, together, especially when it came to helping faculty in a new medium and supporting students at a distance. People talk about "lessons learned"—we were refining those lessons at a rapid speed to keep up with technology. In those days, there were no established best practices and standards. We pretty much ran without a playbook and punted most of the way and learned from each other. NTU provided a real opportunity to collaborate.

We built long lasting professional and personal relationships among the NTU members. The administrators I worked from the University of Massachusetts Amherst, Old Dominion University, the University of Arizona, the University of Michigan, and Purdue University remain good friends to this day. We have all moved on to other schools or retired but the years we spent working together from 1984 to 2000 remain highlights in our careers for the work we did and the alliances we made. I consider myself blessed to have been involved and proud of the work we collectively did in increasing educational access for working professionals.

NTU unfortunately did not survive the advances in new technology. In 2005 it was purchased by Walden University and no longer exists. Of course, all broadcast television, videotape, and satellite programs were eventually inched out by the arrival of the Internet and delivery of programs online. Televised and videotaped instruction was the first step we took to use technology to deliver higher education before the Internet really became widely used as a resource and then as a delivery mechanism for higher education programs.

E-mail was the real forerunner to the Internet. It established a way to quickly communicate via a computer efficiently and suggested links to other resources before we even knew what those resources might look like. I first saw a demonstration of what would later be called e-mail in 1986 at University of Mass Amherst. BIT-NET was an early university computer network founded in 1981 and its first network link was between the City University of New York and Yale University. By 1986, it was being made available to other institutions and NTU was supporting its adoption within the AMCEE/NTU consortium as a communication tool. Again, by today's standards, it was crude and awkward to use, but it was a real advancement for connecting with others. This was before wireless, and all communication was through a hardwire pipeline and phone dial-up. Connections were often unreliable, and getting thrown off was a daily occurrence. By 1990, all the AMCEE/NTU institutions were using e-mail, though I remember I still did not yet have an office desktop computer at Northeastern University of my own, but shared one in a common area with another staff person. We didn't get that many e-mails in those days to really need one. That changed quickly as technology started to move at lightning speed. The use of electronic documents to replace paper correspondence necessitated a desktop for everyone, as did the prevalence of communicating via e-mail. By the early 1990s, everyone had a desk top computer, much like, one day somewhere around 1999 or 2000, everyone seemed to have a cell phone and then a laptop.

We continued to offer live broadcast graduate programs and satellite delivered programs through AMCEE/NTU into the 1990s. In 1998, my unit at Northeastern University offered the first online courses from the university. How that evolved seems now to be a bit of a mystery as this was truly one of those endeavors that occurred entirely from the bottom up. Our distance education unit at Northeastern was keenly aware that to stay competitive, offering courses via the Internet (the term "online" was yet to be coined) was really a necessity. We actually believed we were behind in offering online courses. We talked to a few administrators at Northeastern and without any long-term plan (or funding) we picked some courses and programs and had a graduate student in computer science get content from various faculty members and load it into some templates online that became the course. There was no learning management system

(LMS) as such in place at the time (the term did not exist). The technology was very complicated, requiring the graduate student to also register students into the course that was separate from the registrar's system, but we did launch online courses. None of the systems at Northeastern spoke to each other, there was no such thing as instant access or confirmation of registration, and students were lucky to finally gain access two or three days after registering. Despite this, we were proud to have put Northeastern courses online.

It should also be noted, however, that it was not until a few years later that higher education realized that online instruction would develop a whole pedagogy unto itself and that there were major differences between teaching face-to-face or lecture-based broadcast courses and teaching online. Many of the AMCEE/NTU schools continued to offer courses in basically the same way, by simply streaming lectures via the Internet instead of broadcasting them or shipping videotapes and DVDs. Supporting materials became accessible through websites, but teaching remained the same faculty-centered activity, now simply offered online. Engineering education lost its front runner status as innovator in distance education when it failed to redesign courses to use all the resources the Internet had to offer—multimedia, reduce, talking-head instruction, and a student-centered learning environment within their courses. Other academic areas quickly surpassed engineering in establishing interactive, engaging materials and content that used the best elements of instructional design to connect students with each other and the faculty.

In the summer of 2000, John Ebersole joined Boston University, a neighboring institution to Northeastern University. John had been an associate provost at Colorado State University and an assistant dean and director at UC Berkley. John had two goals in mind, which were supported by BU's administration, build a distance education unit at BU and expand corporate education programs. John arrived in July and by October, I had already met with him about coming to BU to start the online initiative. It was not a difficult decision to leave Northeastern to go to work for John. John is one of those dynamic visionaries who can communicate on a level that everyone can understand. He laid out a vision for me about distance education at BU over breakfast at a local bagel joint. He asked me after about fifteen minutes if this matched my thinking, and I said yes. The deal was done without any discussion of salary or title. I just knew that I wanted to build online programs with John. I accepted a job that didn't exist and gave notice at Northeastern before I had an offer in writing from BU, something I would not recommend to anyone today. I joined BU in November, 2000 as director of distance education.

Boston University had a reputation at the time for being a dynamic institution. Under John Silber, who was president from 1971 to 1996, then chancellor from 1996 to 2002 and again president from 2002 to 2003, BU grew a number of programs and initiatives, bought a lot of real estate up and down the main thoroughfare of its campus, Commonwealth Avenue, and took some calculated risks. Expanding into offering online programs was one of them. I remember meeting with the provost of BU, Dennis Berkey, before I was hired, and he asked me if it wasn't already too late for BU to competitively offer online programs. This was 2000. I assured him that with the BU brand I thought we could be reasonably certain to get enough enrollments to make something of a profit. I laugh when I think about it now. The Internet was expanding everyone's reach, but higher education institutions were still confused about how to market, design, promote, and ensure quality of online programming. The question remained as to how much tuition revenue could be generated through online enrollments.

Luckily, John Ebersole was supported whole-heartedly by the provost in navigating the way forward. BU was also an AMCEE/NTU member, and we continued to broadcast programs via live broadcast to companies with the College of Engineering. At the same time, however, Metropolitan (MET) College, the unit at BU that offered evening, part-time degree programs and continuing education to adults, was looking to move into offering online programs. With no in-place centralized unit to support the necessary design, development, student support, technology, and faculty training and development support to launch a successful online initiative, John Ebersole and the dean of MET College at the time, Jay Halfond (who reported to John), started to think about ways to launch programs without an infrastructure to support it. If we could find a way to outsource everything except content and teaching, short term, while we built up our internal resources to take most of the function back in house, we'd have a sound fiscal foundation. Coincidentally, John was approached by a company he had done some business with while at Colorado State University that presented a business solution for our needs. Embanet offered all the components necessary to launch a successful online initiative. Embanet would grow to become one of the largest online program management (OPM) companies in the US, and was eventually purchased by Pearson in 2012, but in 2001, it was still in a start-up phase with no big name partners, run by its two Canadian founders, Jeffrey Feldberg and Waleuska Lazo. Jeffrey and Waleuska had met as MBA students, where they developed their business model of offering hosted services, an LMS, marketing, recruitment, retention, course design, student support services, and faculty training and support, in exchange for a large percentage of the tuition dollars. For those wanting to get into the business quickly but lacking the start-up cash or the expertise to do so, this offered a possible solution, though it was one dismissed by some institutions as impossible to consider because it was perceived to hand over too much power to a non-academic entity. It was just too radical a concept to consider.

Embanet approached BU, after having spoken to a few other universities, indicating that their research showed that there was a strong market for an online master's degree in criminal justice. MET College had a very small face-to-face, traditional CJ (criminal justice) program and was certainly interested in increasing enrollments. Online delivery offered the promise of new markets outside the Boston area. With a new CJ department chairman in place and just a few faculty, resistance to online delivery of programs was not an issue. I listened to how Embanet was going to work with the university (assuming we went forward with a partnership with them) by essentially paying for every aspect of the development and delivery of the program, with stated enrollment goals for each term, in exchange for a large part of the tuition dollars. I remembered thinking that for traditional institution like BU, there was no way the administration would ever hand over that much control to an outside company. But I was wrong, as both John and Jay immediately saw the benefits (no financial risk to the university while being able to provide a proof of concept in online learning over the Internet). They moved forward with an agreement to develop and launch the CJ master's degree in the summer of 2002. I was amazed, to say the least.

Working with Embanet was an unusual experience. They controlled all aspects of the program except for the content of the course, choice of instructor, and the final admissions decision. In their hands was all marketing, web pages, inquiries, recruitment, and admissions advising. To optimize enrollments and completions, a carousel model of course offerings was employed. No prerequisite courses would be required to take any other courses within the online program. The program was designed with seven week courses, with students encouraged to take two courses each traditional semester, back to back, allowing students to enter in at any term start and continue through. The guarantee was that as long as a student took a courses each consecutive term, they could finish in a year and a half.

Our distance education office in 2000 consisted of one full-time staff member: me. I was also overseeing the technical aspects of broadcasting engineering courses from the College of Engineering at BU as part of our AMCEE/NTU membership. I hired a part-time undergraduate communications student from Northeastern to help me with this. I also started to look to see what departments on campus might be prepared to support us in our eventual transition of services from Embanet to BU. The IT department at BU, while polite and sympathetic to our needs, was honest in their assessment that it would be a few years before they felt confident that they could support online students. At that time, they were using one LMS, WebCT, and had their hands full supporting the few departments that used it extensively. Also, the student information system was not connected to WebCT, so many manual functions still existed. With Embanet, the registrar also had to provide lists of registered students which Embanet manually populated into the LMS they were using at the time, an LMS that had been developed by George Washington University in 1998 called Prometheus. My discussions with the registrar and financial aid offices to resolve the errors caused by manual processes were often painful on both sides. A BU program hosted by an outside entity was viewed internally with some suspicion, as the discussion often revolved around "Embanet students" and how to code them within the system, how drops would be handled with tuition refunds for courses that ran only seven weeks, and how monitoring attendance in regards to financial aid would be handled. BU had a legacy SIS system in place from the 1980s with little flexibility. Our online program did not align with the traditional twelve- or fifteen-week semesters, though summer sessions seem to be accommodated in some fashion. The idea of customer service had not yet penetrated higher education, and there was quite a bit of angst among online students, BU financial services, and Embanet student support services when it came to communicating consistent policies. We came to appreciate that the devil was in the details when it came to the Embanet/BU partnership. It was also apparent to us that online learning was quite different than face-to-face instruction, and numerous support systems needed to be put in place that acknowledged that online students, who would never step a foot on campus, were entitled to a different level of service than those on campus, as was the case at BU, they were paying a premium for the convenience of taking courses online. It was a long learning curve for all of us, one that Embanet helped us navigate.

In the meantime, Embanet course designers, working with the CJ faculty, seemed to have a smoother time of it. Faculty seemed relieved and pleased that the Embanet instructional designers were their partners in creating engaging online materials. It helped that the first course developed and offered was taught by the department chairman who took to the online environment quite well despite having had no previous online experience. We met our modest enrollment targets the first year and continued to grow every year afterward with some terms having ten to fourteen sections of the same course with fifteen to twenty students in each section. Having the department chair offer the first online course turned out to be an excellent idea. He became a champion of online learning not only for his department but for MET College. As of spring 2016, he was still teaching online and overseeing the program.

I continued to plan how to staff the distance learning unit. Overseeing Embanet's many functions became a full-time job and required that we get administrative help. Being mindful of the importance of the role of the faculty, bringing the instructional design function in house became our first priority. One day, a BU alumnus walked into John Ebersole's office looking for an instructional design job, which of course did not exist. He was working as a designer at a local high technology company but always loved the higher education environment. John kept an open door to anyone who wanted to see him, even if he didn't know them, and after meeting with Eldon Strickland, sent him over to meet with me. Eldon became our first instructional design hire. He oversaw the Embanet team's interactions for a few years, increased the number of our unit's designers, and we brought the design function in house a few years later.

Our next hires were student support service staff and a project manager to oversee the staff as well as the other programs that now were coming online at a fast clip. Between 2002 and 2007, we added graduate degrees in computer science, administrative sciences, music education, health communications, and doctoral degrees in physical therapy and music education. We also brought in all outsourced services with the exception of marketing and recruitment; these remained in the hands of Embanet and the other outside partner we used, Compass Knowledge Group (Embanet and Compass would merge in 2010 and, as mentioned, the merged company was bought by Pearson in 2012). BU's IT unit welcomed us with open arms, as we were then able to pay for a full-time staff member who was assigned to support our online initiative, from the tuition revenue we made from our online programs.

John Ebersole and I give Embanet the credit for getting us into the online business and making BU highly successful in those early years. Partnering with Embanet enabled us to learn the business, generate revenue, slowly build our own internal resources, and bring in house many of the services that were required to create a high quality, online learning environment and get our message to the right students. Embanet taught us how to fish. While they didn't plan it this way, we always felt it was important to not remain perpetually dependent on an outside vendor, no matter how good a job they did or how much revenue was generated. By the time I left Boston University in late summer of 2008, the program was generating over $30 million annually in revenue.

Many institutions were and remain committed to finding ways for students to access educational resources. While technology has changed dramatically over the past sixty years, the students enrolled in technology-driven programs remain the same—older, working adults whose family and work commitments make it difficult to attend a campus-based college or university. Employer needs for skilled workers also hasn't changed. What is different is the administration, design, technology, faculty, service support, and skills needed to create even more effective ways to enhance learning at a distance. I feel lucky to have been part of expanding educational opportunities to adult students over my thirty-five-year career in higher education.

REFERENCES
Taylor, J.W. (1957). TV college in Chicago. *The Phi Delta Kappan*, 38, 202-203.

AN INTERVIEW WITH CHRIS DEDE

Wirth Professor in Learning Technologies
Harvard Graduate School of Education

WILLIAM PATRICK: When and how did your interest in online learning emerge?

CHRIS DEDE: I guess I'm going to answer more in terms of distance education, because my interest in online learning was just an extension of my interest in distance education. I began in educational technology around the mid-70s when Apple brought out the Apple I. Before that, I had taken a class in FORTRAN in 1967 that was on punch cards, and I was so appalled by the interface that it drove me completely out of the field. When the Apple computer came along, I saw that you could have a different interface and then I got very interested. The first memory that I have of my involvement in distance education is giving a keynote in 1978 for the Nebraska Educational Television Network. Originally I was more involved with the distance delivery of educational television. Then when online came about, I just sort of moved into that as it happened.

WP: Why have you opted to make this an area of emphasis within your scholarship?

CD: Well, educational technology is my field, and for someone to be in learning technologies and to say, "Well, I have no interest in online learning," would definitely be bizarre. I had started in science education, and I began with learning technologies as a way of enhancing that, but then I got very interested in learning itself and sort of morphed into studying learning and teaching through the lens of technology. In particular, I began to look at emerging technologies, and the 1983 article I sent to you was that sort of emerging-technology emphasis of looking at what was on the horizon and saying, "Okay, what are the strategic opportunities for the field of learning technologies?" Another thing I emphasized in that article was communications technologies.

WP: Let me go on to the third question: how has the field changed during your time in it? Obviously, that's a very broad question.

CD: I think that the most significant change that I would highlight is moving from distance education as a totally separate thing to this continuum with distance only at one end and face-to-face teaching at the other end and a lot of variants in between—blended, hybrid variants. And then the other thing would be not using face-to-face as the gold standard, anymore, where you would say, "Well, face-to-face is the gold standard so is distance education good enough?" But instead seeing online learning as something that has its own strengths and limits, so that in some ways, for some people, online learning is better than face-to-face. In other ways and for other people, online learning is less good than face-to-face. So moving to what works, when, for whom, rather than which is on average better?

WP: I have a question about the second article—"The Evolution of Distance Learning." In the abstract, you say, "However, whether technology-mediated interactive learning (TMIL) creates a global village or an unattractive world of weakened social relationships ultimately depends upon how carefully we think through our design decisions and monitor shifts in interpersonal interaction as they emerge." And then, about five pages in, you have a very interesting discussion about assimilation and pluralism, and I wrote a note in the margin, asking, "What are the social consequences of a widespread reliance on technology?"

CD: I don't claim that I foresaw much about social media. I mean, social media have certainly been much more sweeping than anything that I would have imagined at that time. But I do think that I did see these as high-stakes issues, and part of why I think that keynote address was controversial was because I was saying, "This is about a lot more than just whether people learn face-to-face or they also learn in other ways. This is about a fundamental reshaping of the network of relationships that people have. And I do think that that perspective has been borne out by the evolution of social media, although I certainly wouldn't claim to have forecast what social media would look like.

WP: No, but you're certainly hinting at the boundaries of it. So what do you think, in terms of Facebook and Twitter and other social media? Have they weakened societies? Have they made relationships more or less strong?

CD: I think that they've clearly strengthened social relationships and that they have strengthened the dialogue in societies across the world, so I would say that where I was uncertain in 1996 about the impact of this, that in the way that things played out—and they could have played out in a different way—but in the way that they played out, which was a bottom-up approach to social media, it's been very, very positive.

WP: Even with the last couple of years where ISIS has been using social media to recruit terrorists and all of that?

CD: Well, technology is always a double-edged sword. I mean, you can look at the automobile and you can say, "It's really made a lot of transportation options possible for people." And you can also say, "Look at the dependence on foreign energy; look at the pollution in the atmosphere; look at all the people who die in car crashes." It's never uniformly good or uniformly bad. I think the fact that people wouldn't go back . . . it's not like we see people on a widespread scale saying, "You know, on balance, this social media thing has not been a good idea. Let's stop using it." That's not happening. So I think that we can say, on balance, that it turned out—again, in the way that it came out—to be very positive. If social media had been controlled by just a few groups rather than being a bottom-up, personal expression for people, then I think that my fears about the potential future would have been justified.

WP: Yeah, I understand what you're saying, and not to play ethical or moral devil's advocate, but of course once people are given a powerful tool, there's little chance that they're going to give up that tool. Whether it's a gun or a car or a smartphone, they're not wanting to give those powerful tools up. But I wonder if, on balance, the world is going in a more positive direction given the widespread use of technology. What's your feeling about that?

CD: Well, I think that that's a much more sweeping question than I can handle in this article. That's my answer to that. I think that goes well beyond the issue of online learning. There is a book that came out of Harvard called *The Race between Education and Technology* by Claudia Goldin and Lawrence Katz, but it's not about educational technology. It's about the fact that society is adopting technology at a more rapid rate that it's learning to use technology well, and that book is interesting. It's their attempt to answer the question that you asked. I think there's evidence either way, so I'm not sure that there's a clear-cut answer at this point to the larger question you're asking.

WP: Okay. What's impressed you most about the use of technology in the delivery of education? Which aspect of it are you most impressed by?

CD: I think that learning is incredibly diverse—that people learn in really different ways—and I think that the flexibility of technology, and its capacity to adapt to many different approaches to learning, is very impressive. It has made learning possible for a large number of people who struggled with the one-size-fits-all approach to teaching that was prevalent for so long.

WP: How about the flip side of the coin? What are you disappointed with about technology?

CD: I think the whole history of educational technology, whether online or distance or face-to-face, has been old wine in new bottles, and I continue to be very saddened by the proportion of uses of technology that are simply putting teaching-by-telling and learning-by-listening into new media that are capable of supporting much, much more.

WP: In that context, what have we not been able to achieve? What are you hoping that technology can do that it hasn't done yet?

CD: Well, I think that this idea about personalization—that we really could use technology to personalize learning about people's passions and strengths and styles and preferences—is far from realized. That is the vision that I keep paramount in my mind when I look at my own work.

WP: What about faculty resistance to online learning? So many college teachers are still so resistant to teaching online. Why do you think that's happening?

CD: It's a puzzle. I see it in my own colleagues as well. I think that people believe there's something ineffable about human interaction that just cannot occur online. If you think of education, at least historically, as a personality-directing profession, where people who were particularly good at talking with other people and enjoyed interacting with them and enjoyed helping them to grow intellectually, emotionally, and socially—people who have that profile, people who would naturally be drawn to education as a profession—would be the least likely people to accept the idea that you could actually have richer relationships, at least for some people, online than you could face-to-face.

WP: So they inherently feel there's an alienation involved with the technology?

CD: Yes, they do, because it's so contrary to their own experience. I think that the biggest trap for any teacher to fall into is the belief that every learner is like that person. So these intensely human-centered teachers fall into the trap—that of course their learners must feel the same way they do.

WP: Yeah, they forget that it's heterogeneous.

CD: Absolutely. Or perhaps that people have life circumstances where they would rather have face-to-face but those life circumstances prohibit it, and so online becomes a very valuable alternative for them.

WP: Yup, and in terms of social consequences—you know, what we were talking about before—the more people get familiar with technology, the more they might feel comfortable using it rather than in being in face-to-face classroom situations.

CD: Absolutely. I think a lot of the goal of education is taking you where you're comfortable and helping you to go where you aren't, and unfortunately the faculty who refuse to look at online learning are modeling exactly the wrong thing for their students.

They're modeling an unwillingness to learn rather than an openness to learn.

WP: So how do you think the administrators at various schools could get buy-in from the faculty? How can they get the recalcitrant professors to change their minds about online learning?

CD: Well, unfortunately, I think that what history has borne out is that ultimately economic factors have been the only things that have dramatically influenced the situation. That is, as budgets have shrunk and as institutions have lost their geographic monopolies—so that they face competition where they didn't have competition before—the faculty perforce have had to look at online learning. They don't feel so strongly about it that they'd rather be unemployed. And some of the faculty who have looked at online learning—to their credit—have seen then that they were wrong, and subsequently have become enthusiasts about it. Others are probably still doing it reluctantly, and perhaps not very well, because they are doing it reluctantly. But I think that those are the dynamics that we're seeing.

WP: How successful do you think online learning has been?

CD: I think online learning has been enormously successful, for several reasons. I think that online learning, for some learners, is better than face-to-face learning, even the best face-to-face learning.

WP: Why is that?

CD: Because of their learning strengths and their learning preferences. I think research clearly establishes that. I think that online learning also, as we discussed before, offers options for people who don't have access to high-quality face-to-face learning, and therefore it's very helpful for them as well. And finally, I think online learning has led us to blended and hybrid learning, which I believe are superior to online only or face-to-face only. So online learning has been a necessary vehicle for getting to that middle ground. Someone once said, "I don't know who discovered water, but it wasn't a fish." I think we needed the lens of online learning. Online-only learning provided a kind of lens of getting outside of the fishbowl of face-to-face learning so that we could actually see the water and begin to understand both the strengths and the limits of what was going on with face-to-face learning.

WP: Good point. Do you think hybrid learning is the future?

CD: No, absolutely not. Far from it. I think that the future is much more lifelong learning, in relatively small chunks, of blended where possible and online only where not, that helps people with the knowledge and skills they need for the next couple of years. And then after that, you look again. The 21st century is far too chaotic and dynamic to get a good education once and then expect it to have a long half-life.

WP: So a continuing series of certificates?

CD: Exactly.

EMERGING TECHNOLOGIES AND THE HISTORY OF DISTANCE LEARNING
A Reflection

Chris Dede

Wirth Professor in Learning Technologies
Harvard Graduate School of Education

In 1972, I started my academic career after getting my doctorate in science education. I began in educational technology around the mid-1970s when Apple Computers brought out the Apple I. Before that, I had taken an undergraduate class in FORTRAN in 1967 that was on punch cards, and I was so appalled by the interface that it drove me away from computers until interactive "microcomputers" emerged. I began with learning technologies as a way of enhancing outcomes in science education, but then I became very interested in learning in general and morphed into studying learning and teaching through the lens of digital tools and media. The first memory that I have of my involvement in distance education is giving a keynote in 1978 for the Nebraska Educational Television Network. As the

Internet developed, my focus correspondingly shifted from broadcast media for distance education to interactive learning online.

A theme that has pervaded my professional work across the decades is helping people think strategically, in order to prepare for how rapidly digital technologies were creating future contexts quite different than the present. Some of the things that I forecast about distance learning seem commonplace today, but were seen as bizarre or controversial at the time that they were written.

One example is a paper I wrote in 1983, in which I predicted that,

> Mass telecommunications and computer networking have the capability of greatly expanding the number of students served by vocational, career, and adult educators. Demand for work-related training has always been limited by constraints in the lives of older, working students. Historically, to allow even part of the working population to attend instruction, institutions have had to provide classes at night or on weekends at locations other than the campus; altered admission requirements and formal entry standards; and provided special services such as lower fees, special counselors, financial aid business and job placement, expanded office hours, and child care. While expanding occupationally related education has been seen as an important priority in America's economic productivity, the difficulties of providing increased training using conventional instructional methods have been formidable.
>
> As indicated in the list of modalities earlier, the new communications technologies offer capabilities that may ameliorate some of these problems for adults and workers. Interactive delivery of highly specialized instruction to home and workplace settings will be easy and cheap by the late 1980s. The more basic aspects of training can be communicated by devices (either handheld or home-based) from which students can learn individually at their convenience. Computer networking offers the potential for better "cooperation-at-a-distance" strategies than education/industry partnerships have been

able to achieve with more traditional forms of communication. Students can transact necessary business with different sectors of the institution without having to appear physically on campus. Limitations on time, location, and individualization will be greatly lessened.
(Dede, 1983, pp. 12-13)

At the time, these ideas were controversial in higher education and adult training, and many institutions were slow in realizing these opportunities, to the detriment of the nation's education, adult training, and economic development.

In 1990, the abstract for an article I wrote about the evolution of distance education stated,

This article describes how our present delivery of instruction over distance could become an even more powerful and useful educational medium through incorporating ideas from cooperative learning and computer-supported cooperative work. Advances in information technology that would enhance distance learning include collaborative mimetic interfaces, direct manipulation capabilities, telepointers, automatic electronic archiving, hypertext, and specialized software for different types of interaction. Through incorporating these functionalities, distance learning environments can be designed to have greater opportunities for students to interact than traditional single-classroom settings. By overcoming pupils' segregation into homogeneous enclaves, distance learning can enhance pluralism to prepare Americans for competition in the world marketplace. Eventually, all educational institutions will need to develop students' abilities in distanced interaction, for skills of collaboration with remote team members will be as central to the future American workplace as performing structured tasks quickly was during the early stages of the industrial revolution. However, whether TMIL [technology-mediated interactive learning] creates a global village or an unattractive world of weakened social relationships ultimately depends upon how carefully we think through our design decisions and monitor shifts in interpersonal interaction as they emerge. (Dede, 1990, p. 247)

This was before the World Wide Web and social media, so many of these forecasts were seen as strange and unlikely.

In 1996, I was invited by Michael Moore (long-time editor of the *American Journal of Distance Education*) to give a keynote at a distance education conference that he was holding at Penn State. My talk was so controversial, with some people excited by it and others dismissive, that he dedicated a special issue of the *American Journal of Distance Education* to an article I wrote that was essentially a written version of the keynote address. This article was followed by ten responses—five that were positive and five that were negative – contributed by different people in the field. That journal issue was an attempt at reframing distance education that provoked a lot of debate. Of course, debates are often good for reconceptualization, and the balance between affirming and challenging responses indicated to me that the keynote was about right in terms of the level of forward thinking I offered.

Here are the beginning paragraphs of my 1996 article,

The development of high performance computing and communications is creating new media, such as the WorldWide Web and virtual realities. In turn, these new media enable new types of messages and experiences; for example, interpersonal interactions across network channels lead to the formation of virtual communities. The innovative kinds of pedagogy empowered by these emerging media, messages, and experiences make possible an evolution of synchronous, group, presentation-centered forms of distance education— which replicate traditional "teaching by telling" across barriers of distance and time—into an alternative instructional paradigm: distributed learning. In particular, advances

in computer-supported collaborative learning, multimedia/
hypermedia, and experiential simulation offer the potential to
create shared "learning-through-doing environments" available any place, any time, on demand.
(Dede, 1996, p. 4)

This article speculates about how emerging technologies may
reshape both face-to-face and distance education. Its purpose is to
delineate a three-part conceptual framework (knowledge webs, virtual
communities, and shared synthetic environments) for understanding
the new types of instructional messages that enable distributed learning. Although this study cites leading-edge scholarship to reinforce
its claims, it is a position/discussion piece rather than an inclusive
review of all relevant distance education or educational technology
research. As such, the emphasis is on expanding the reader's con-
ceptualization of "distance education" rather than on proving the
validity of specific pedagogical practices.

While the term "distributed learning" has faded into disuse, the
concept of what is now called blended or hybrid learning was novel
at that time, and established a continuum linking face-to-face and
distance learning, rather than the historical conception that the two
were completely separate (and the latter unequal). My assertion that
online media would reshape face-to-face learning was certainly controversial (as it is to this day among many instructors).

In 2002, some of my doctoral students and I published a book
chapter describing research on our instructional designs that mixed
online media with face-to-face teaching. This was "walking my talk"
in terms of distributed learning and the transformation of face-to-
face instruction. The conclusion of that chapter stated,

Most students feel that something important to their learning is missing in virtual learning spaces, whether synchronous
or asynchronous, if those are the only means of interaction
used. However, less than half of our students ranked face-to-
face interaction as their first choice of learning medium. This

indicates that many students' learning styles are undercut when interaction is limited to classroom settings rather than distributed across multiple media.

Our research also shows that the integration of interactive media into learning experiences profoundly shapes students' educational experiences. Many students reported that the use of asynchronous learning environments positively affected their participation in the course and their individual cognitive processes for engaging with the material. Students also indicated that threaded discussions online often fostered better quality conversations than they had experienced in traditional classrooms.

In addition, students generally felt that the use of synchronous media in the course enhanced their learning experience and complemented other delivery modes used in the course, including face-to-face. They indicated that synchronous virtual media helped them get to know classmates with whom they might not otherwise individually interact within a classroom setting. Synchronous media also provided a clear advantage over asynchronous media in facilitating the work of small groups.

Comparative rankings by students of the eight interactive media we used demonstrate that a threshold of face-to-face interaction seems to empower productive learning via mediated communication, and vice versa. This affirms the fundamental premise of instructional design based on distributed learning: that no single medium or small set of media can facilitate the full range of students' learning styles and needs. Three decades of research in distance education are largely off target because studies have typically compared a single medium (such as face-to-face) to another medium (e.g., videoconferencing) for a group. Some learners are empowered in each situation; others are disenfranchised— the result is generally a finding of "no significant differences." Work in distributed learning suggests that the use of multiple media is significantly better. This has major implications for both conventional distance education and traditional classroom instruction.

(Dede, Whitehouse, & Brown-L'Bahy, 2002, p. 1)

Despite substantial research and experience reinforcing these findings from more than a decade ago, most faculty still are not implementing pervasive blended/hybrid instructional methods in their face-to-face teaching.

REFERENCES

Dede, C. (1983). The reshaping of adult, career, and vocational education by the emerging communications technologies. In N. Singer (Ed.), *Communications technologies: Their effects on adult, continuing, & vocational education.* Columbus, OH: National Center for Research in Vocational Education.

Dede, C. (1990, Spring). The evolution of distance learning. *Journal of Research on Computing in Education, 22*(3), 247-264.

Dede, C. (1996). Emerging technologies and distributed learning. *American Journal of Distance Education, 10*(2), 4-36.

Dede, C., Whitehouse, P., & Brown-L'Bahy, T. (2002) Designing and studying learning experiences that use multiple interactive media to bridge distance and time. In C. Vrasidas & G. Glass (Eds.), *Current perspectives on applied information technologies: Vol. 1. Distance education* (pp. 1-30). Greenwich, CN: Information Age Press.

STATE UNIVERSITY OF NEW YORK, EMPIRE STATE COLLEGE, AND THE TRANSFORMATION OF DISTANCE AND ONLINE LEARNING

James W. Hall
Founding President, SUNY Empire State College

Richard Bonnabeau
Mentor Emeritus
Visiting Professor International Programs
SUNY Empire State College

During the fall and winter of 1970-71, the State University of New York reached out to students with independent study materials and new technologies that led to the creation of an experimental, non-residential Empire State College (ESC). *By combining progressive student-centered principles with traditional distance learning approaches, this SUNY college embodied innovative educational concepts that greatly enhanced system capacities for access and response to new populations of students. Through a student-centered, often highly individualized approach, and employment of a new range of student-driven educational resources,*

Empire helped SUNY test these models and expand its services to the residents of New York. In recent years, as these new approaches have matured, the SUNY System established Open SUNY, involving a much expanded set of its component institutions in external, non-residential study, and potentially global study strategies.

This chapter includes concepts and text portions from a chapter by Dr. Richard Bonnabeau entitled "Conflict, Change, and Continuity: ESC's Goddard College and British Open University Connections," which appears separately in a book entitled *Principles, Practices, and Creative Tensions in Progressive Higher Education: One Institution's Struggle to Sustain a Vision,* edited by Katherine Jelly and Aland Mandell, and published by Sense Publishers. The chapter also incorporates contributions from Dr. Meg Benke, former SUNY ESC acting president and provost as well as director and dean of the Center for Distance Learning during Empire State College's formative transition to online learning. She provided leadership in the development of the SUNY Learning Network and Open SUNY.

NEW YORK STATE AND THE CLIMATE FOR EDUCATIONAL INNOVATION

The State University of New York (SUNY), created in 1948, came late to distance education. Aside from Buffalo, which had a long established noncredit continuing education program, none of the other institutions gave much attention to adult and part-time students. During the 1960s, under its newly appointed chancellor, Samuel B. Gould, SUNY would undergo very rapid growth and significantly increased coherence as an operating university system of sixty-six campuses (four university centers, four medical centers, fourteen university colleges, six technical colleges, thirty community colleges, three specialized colleges, and five statutory colleges administered by Cornell and Alfred University).

Gould's arrival could not have come at a more promising time for innovation in New York. Beginning with Governor Nelson A. Rockefeller's formation of the Heald Commission in 1960 (Henry T. Heald was president of the Ford Foundation), New York State and its new Commissioner of Education, Ewald B. Nyquist, increasingly established an atmosphere for change and experimentation in post-secondary education. One of the Commission's recommendations was that the Board of Regents establish a program of credit by examination. As fully detailed in Donald J. Nolan's (1998) *Regents College: The Early Years*, that single action, and the planful steps taken by the Department of Education to engage all of the colleges and universities of New York in validating the College Proficiency Examination Program (CPEP), established a credibility for external credit evaluation that formed a solid and growing base of acceptance for further experimentation in higher learning. That progressive work culminated in 1971 with the establishment of Regents College, an external degree granting institution.

Entering that fertile environment, Gould aimed to forge a true university *system* that worked collaboratively, sharing resources and programs across the State of New York. At that time an existing independent study program (within the continuing education office) was administered through the system administration. Its course offerings were prepared by individual campuses, but made available in print form to the wider public through a small staff within SUNY system-wide administration.

Gould brought to SUNY his earlier diverse experiences as president of the highly experimental Antioch College, founding president of the University of California Santa Barbara, and president of WNET, New York City's Public Broadcasting System station. Ernest L. Boyer, a highly creative young dean with whom he had worked in California, came with him. Boyer was hired as executive university dean and a few years later appointed vice chancellor for university-wide programs. (Boyer's appointment was the beginning of his ascent to become one of America's most prominent educators in the last quarter of the twentieth century. Boyer succeeded Gould in 1970, followed in 1977 by his appointment as US Commissioner of Education by President Carter. In 1979, Boyer began his tenure as President of The Carnegie Foundation for The Advancement of Teaching. There he had a major impact on the development of educational policy in America.)

Gould, sensing the stirrings of new approaches to instruction and learning in New York State, attempted to enhance the existing continuing education effort by adding the capacity to use televised courses. Modeled to some extent from New York University's Sunrise Semester, these broadcast courses attempted to enhance the availability and accessibility of SUNY to off-campus adult students. Gould committed significant funds to the University of the Air, funding talented staff, costly course development, and distribution over the New York Network. Several years following retirement, Gould chaired a national Commission on Non-Traditional Study, whose report, *Diversity by Design* (1973) summarized the many experimental changes that had or were occurring in American higher education.

Conceptually the linkage of television and education was promising, but by the late 1960s the results were disappointing. Enrollments in continuing education and televised courses were nowhere near initial expectations, and the year-to-year direction was down. Several new national institutions, founded to develop extraordinary filmed courses for television, had expended many millions of dollars provided by foundations, states, and the federal government to design a relatively small number of courses. Though elegant, stimulating, and highly reputable, these courses never attracted a significant student clientele.

Notably, as early as 1968 Boyer had discussed with Chancellor Gould, whom Boyer had known from the time he was the president of Antioch College in the 1950s, the possibility of introducing various progressive alternatives to SUNY campuses, among them experimental units analogous to the University Without Walls. But Boyer became "convinced that what SUNY really needed was a new, free-standing college—a non-campus institution with an integrity and identity of its own" (Boyer, 31 August 1990, p. 2).

FOUNDING A NEW COLLEGE

Thus the SUNY environment was ripe for new initiatives. In the first days of Ernest Boyer's chancellorship, a staff planning retreat explored new directions and options. Among the proposals was one prepared by his assistant vice chancellor for policy and planning, James W. Hall, who prepared a description of a hypothetical new university program. Boyer appointed an eight-member task force from his staff to explore this idea further.

Noting the urgency for action (the considerable behind-the-scenes maneuvering between SUNY and the Department of Education is recounted in Nolan's *Regents College)*, Deputy Vice Chancellor Merton Ertell convened a meeting of the task force on November 3, 1970, and transmitted a proposal to the chancellor by the next day. He offered three alternate models as a basis for a budget proposal to support next steps. The first was to extend the off-campus bachelor of liberal studies program offered by SUNY Brockport; the second was for an extended tutorial program, close in design to that proposed in Hall's earlier memo; and the third was for an open university, modeled on that of The Open University of the United Kingdom, popularly known as the British Open University.. Ertell advised that a final proposal might well include a mix of all three models.

Five contemporaneous developments gave heft to this plan. The first was a public call from the president of the Carnegie Corporation of New York, Alan Pifer: "Is it Time for an External Degree?" (1970, 27 October). The second was the founding of the British Open University, a fresh attempt to redo adult continuing education, then in its initial roll-out. The third was the keen interest of the charismatic state commissioner of education, Ewald Nyquist, in shaking up higher education by recognizing college credit however earned. The fourth was the interest of the innovative governor Nelson A. Rockefeller, who provided strong support for the expansion of the state university. Fifth were the student revolutions of the latter 1960s that had unmoored traditional higher education, challenging many of its existing structures and processes, thereby opening the doors for increased receptivity to change and experimentation.

The Boyer task force, having acquainted itself with the BOU model during the fall of 1970, rejected it as not likely to resonate well with American students. The panel then drafted a uniquely American proposal for a new SUNY non-residential university college. The proposal gained funding from both the Carnegie Corporation and Ford Foundation. These grants funded three experimental models along the lines suggested by Pifer's speech: a degree by examination; a degree by nonclassroom study using various other forms of instruction and learning; and a center for student advisement and referral, including the possibility of a credit bank that could evaluate and assemble the student's credits and competencies.

The first model, realized in Regents College, offered a degree through examination and evaluation. Created by Commissioner Nyquist, it was initially operated by the Regents (the State Education Department), but since 1998 has been an independent entity with a new name: Excelsior College. The second model, SUNY Empire State College, using an instructional/learning model under its own administration and faculty, became the nonresidential campus of SUNY; the third model, an advisement and referral center, functioned for several years under a five-county consortium in central New York coordinated by Syracuse University. Regents and Empire State were designed to work together, with students able to access appropriate services from each as needed. Over the years this collaboration has worked well for students(Nolan, 1998).

Planning for Empire State College continued through the winter of 1970-71, with a prospectus for the new college presented early in February 1971. During this period, the SUNY trustees, the governor, and Boyer's senior staff undertook to establish the legal underpinnings for a new college. The SUNY trustees approved a new nonresidential, degree-granting college on January 27, 1971, and ironically on the same day the board authorized construction of a new campus for SUNY Buffalo, its largest residential campus. Clearly the SUNY system was able to embrace dual goals at the same time. At its February meeting, the trustees approved the name Empire State College, per Boyer's proposal. The New York State Regents (on March 26, 1971) and the governor (on April 30, 1971) made it all official by approving the requisite SUNY master plan amendment. Early in the new year, Hall assumed staff leadership for the experiment, and on April 1, 1971, he officially launched the new enterprise and was appointed president by the SUNY trustees on October 1, 1971.

Hall's background was traditionally academic, holding a PhD in American civilization from the University of Pennsylvania, and untraditionally pedagogic, based upon his degrees in music. The study of music is inevitably student-centered, with teacher and student working together uniquely, building on a student's abilities, goals, and interests through personal guidance and rigorous but supportive criticism. Recognizing that the entire college team was attempting new and untested approaches, he was sympathetic to both the need for progressive educational approaches and for new approaches for access and distance learning. Given the mandate from SUNY, he encouraged experimentation rather than accepting a formulaic set of orders. Hall was a pragmatist, not an ideologue, interested in results by whatever combination of means that would help to achieve the institution's mission.

Significantly, among the first earliest decisions was to discontinue the existing University of the Air and the SUNY Continuing Education office. The SUNY Independent Study Program and many of its staff was transferred to the new college. Initially viewed as a significant resource, the lectures-in-print format of independent study guides was eventually sidelined as the college set out on new and innovative paths of independent study. Thereby, Boyer had radically extended and altered the innovations initiated by Gould.

THE EMPIRE STATE COLLEGE GENOME

Two Hereditary Streams

The original planning group prepared a far-reaching report: *A Prospectus for a New University College: Objectives, Process, Structure, and Establishment* (1971, February 8). From the first, Empire State College's prospectus was inspired and motivated by two inherited educational streams. One stream flowed from the progressive educational values of philosopher John Dewey. It placed the student's learning at the center of the educational dialogue and recognized learning wherever it might have been gained. The second stream flowed from a more traditional pattern of campus outreach, but with radically new processes and tools that held the potential for increasing student access. These characteristics grew from two distinctly different educational philosophies. Although ultimately complementary in function, each represented radically different innovations. While many of these innovations had been attempted before elsewhere, no institution had created a structure within which they could work together to support a student, especially in a projected public institution of considerable size with widely diverse students. These two hereditary streams of educational philosophy and practice, brought together in a single institution, were to dramatically change the character and quality of adult, continuing, and distance education.

The prospectus described these possibilities in dramatically new terms. Among its key points was creation of a new faculty role of *mentor* to work with students in defining an individual study plan as part of a degree program. The emerging definition of the faculty mentor role became central to the spirit of ESC's pedagogy. The term "mentor" is mentioned often in the prospectus and figures prominently in the proposed staffing for a model regional learning center. Such a center was projected to serve some 400 students with a number of full-time mentors and thirty or more part-time instructional tutors, many of them faculty disciplinary specialists. Most tutors would be drawn from other SUNY campuses to work with a single student whose study required that expertise. But unlike many other experimental programs, Empire's mentors were full time. Through the intervening decades, mentor has earned a prominent position in the American lexicon.

A study plan would define the student's educational goals, topics to be studied, and the resources necessary to achieve them. The structure was statewide, offered through regional centers, closer to where the student lived and worked. And a student's prior college-level learning, wherever and however gained, could be evaluated for advanced standing. Only the final one-quarter of the requirements for the degree needed to be earned at Empire State College.

The prospectus was placed before an invited meeting of experienced individuals from three SUNY campuses, a member of the New York regents, and several prominent national educational scholars. Their response indicated strong interest in and support for the enterprise. While it was well to receive such commendations from many directions, including the critical financial awards by the Ford Foundation and Carnegie Corporation, the founders knew that implementation would be challenging. What was needed immediately were individuals who had experience in implementing and managing new approaches defined by the prospectus. Fortunately, several such persons had participated in the meeting that reviewed the prospectus. Fortunately, several such persons had participated in the meeting that previewed the prospectus, and several were considered as possible candidates to join the enterprise.

THE PROGRESSIVE, STUDENT-CENTERED HEREDITARY STREAM

The first hereditary stream placed each student at the epicenter of his or her own education, with the role of the teacher as a mentor and coach. Chancellor Boyer understood and embraced the approach, being familiar with the work of John Dewey and his followers including, especially, Royce "Tim" Pitkin, founding president of Goddard College in Vermont. Significantly, Pitkin became a prime mover in the creation of a national consortium first called the Union for Research and Experimentation in Higher Education and subsequently the Union for Experimenting Colleges and Universities which begat the Union Graduate School and fostered the University Without Walls movement (Benson & Adams, 1987, pp. 208-211). Years later, Boyer noted that "it was the influence of Tim Pitkin that I urged the trustees of the State University of New York to start Empire State College" (Boyer, 1981 8 September, p. 2). Boyer suggested inviting Arthur W. Chickering, a long time Goddard faculty member and colleague of Pitkin, to join the external advisory group in recognition of a prominent reputation gained through his research project Student Development at Small Colleges and the publication of *Education and Identity* (1969).

It would be the progressive stream, fully anticipated by the prospectus, that initially formed the centerpiece of ESC's academic program. And Chickering's vision and leadership were critical to its implementation. He held a principled commitment, rooted in his research, to the centrality of the individual learner and the progressive principles of democratizing education in an era when curricular rigidity was the norm. His background led Boyer and Hall to invite him to accept the position of founding vice president for academic affairs, effective July 1, 1971.

Chickering found much to like in the prospectus's progressive language of learner centeredness and access. His own research, largely conducted in small, often sectarian colleges, as well as unique, often ephemeral, optional programs within larger private and public institutions, needed testing on a larger scale. SUNY had proposed a large-scale public, individual program, unheard of in public higher education. With the prospectus projecting enrollments reaching 10,000 students within three years and possibly 40,000 by 1975-76, the potential was extraordinary, but the challenge would lie in putting into practice progressive principles to a magnitude never imagined by Pitkin. But scale alone was not the only challenge. Innovation to this degree would prove especially difficult in a state renowned for its rigorous regulation in law and practice of its educational institutions.

THE SECOND HEREDITARY STREAM
Access and Innovation in Distance Learning
The second hereditary stream was, at its core, employing distance courses, typically correspondence study at that time, for the purpose of increasing student access to higher learning. Though widely practiced in the early twentieth century, with the growth of traditional campuses, interest in off-campus students declined, especially for adult, part-time, and diverse students. Such forms were increasingly considered inferior to classroom-based education. Despite advances

in audio and televisual technology in the 1950s and 1960s, correspondence study, with the exception of profitable professional education programs, remained of low interest in American higher education. Almost none in the traditional academy considered offering degrees in their entirety for correspondence study. And, given the extremely high student dropout and incompletion rate for correspondence study, such skepticism was generally on target.

In the 1960s, American higher education experienced historic levels of student demand, growing professional and competitive academic departments, and, in the growing mega-campuses, industrial models of learning. Large numbers of new or expanded traditional campuses appeared, built on the assumption of the traditional classroom and providing limited seats in the face of entirely new categories of students. The result was that both of Empire State College's hereditary pedagogic streams, despite occasional lip service, remained marginalized in the mainstream of American higher learning.

Fortunately for Empire State College, all of this was soon to change, and do so dramatically. Several significant forces within the larger social fabric began to erode resistance to experimentation with these two streams of educational philosophy. These forces were first, a rapidly expanding number of increasingly diverse students seeking entrance to the academy (Hall, 1982), second, the new and facile technologies that gained rapid credence as supporting instruments for student access to quality opportunities; third, the rapid breakdown of traditional campus academic authority, initially stimulated by the anti-war protests of the late 1960s; fourth, the demands by older and more diverse students for educational options that provided for flexibility in time, place and method of learning; and fifth, the emergence of a significant number of new, highly experimental institutions and programs (including for-profit versions) in Great Britain and the United States that increasingly demonstrated the capacity to deliver a reputable program of study. In recent times, declining budgets and appropriations has led to increased interest in serving new, often off-campus students, especially adults.

To address the issues of increased academic learning resources and distance outreach, the college assigned two experienced innovative administrators to focus on these college goals. The first administrator was Loren Baritz, who came from SUNY Albany, to head the effort to create highly innovative learning resources, called learning modules, many designed by notable scholars to exemplify the highest quality of innovative educational achievement. The second administrator was William R. Dodge, formerly system dean for continuing education and a member of Boyer's planning task force. He came to ESC with the initial transfer of positions from system administration. Dodge had long experience in creating and managing a traditional continuing education program. But he was interested in developing new strategies for reaching out to distance students and was responsive to progressive ideas to help achieve that goal.

In 1972, Dodge created an experimental statewide center with dispersed small satellites in locations distant from existing regional centers. Each satellite was staffed by one or two faculty mentors who enrolled students in newly developed independent study learning modules, existing SUNY print-based courses, cross-registration courses, and learning contracts with tutors for specialized needs. By 1975, in response to increasing college-wide enrollments, Dodge took charge of an initiative called Extended Programs, a precursor of what became in 1979 the Center for Distance Learning.

FORGING THE ACADEMIC PROGRAM

Based on the prospectus, Empire State College's educational programs were to change almost every practice that was deeply ingrained in traditional American higher education. And each change required design, testing with actual students, and modifications for improvement and wider implementation. Vice President Chickering worked with the faculty to shape the processes for individualized learning. ESC students were expected to write their own study plans and to join mentors in evaluating and writing narrative evaluations, an intensely time-consuming practice. And because the college sought to recognize credit for prior college-level learning, wherever and however earned (sometimes mistakenly perceived as credit for life experience), much work was needed urgently to prepare for the expected onrush of adult students.

For example, within the first month of planning, leading staff asked itself, "If we are not counting credits, and every student has a unique program of study, and each mentor may have a varied sense of normative educational expectations and standards of accomplishment—how will we know when a student has qualified to be awarded a State University of New York degree?" We did not yet have a clear answer to that question. For at least a time the answer was, "We'll know it when we see it!" And, at least for a time, and given the quality of the students we saw, and the professional judgments made by faculty mentors and their committees, that answer was functionally useful. This question was one of the many faced in the first months of intense planning as the academic program was created piece by piece.

Chickering was widely respected for his pedagogical values and vision. The organizational structure of educational delivery was created to support the sense of relatively small pockets of students and faculty working together in regional centers and units that emphasized individual students doing individualized study plans with mentors and tutors. Moreover, the reality of very limited fiscal resources in the earliest days forced a bare-bones structure. As additional faculty resources became available, the model was extended to areas throughout the state, reaching out through approximately forty access points. This lean model yielded very positive results from its earliest days.

What the model did not do, however, was address systematically the matter of the sophisticated resources that would be essential to support what was intended to be a large and growing public, open, access institution of higher learning. President Hall grew increasingly concerned that the model, for all of its strengths, also demonstrated the necessity of establishing a significant body of learning resources, from among which each student and mentor could draw for study. The founding prospectus had envisioned a flexible model that would serve widely diverse students across a broad range of academic specialties, serving many thousands of students by 1975-76 (1978, February 2, p. 12). Hall believed that the mentors, already under considerable pressure to identify the supporting resources, tutors, and learning materials for each student, would find it difficult to sustain such workloads in the years ahead. He also recognized that external regulators would eventually require greater clarity regarding the content, level of study, and qualifications of the faculty.

Indeed, this fledgling institution faced almost immediate public pressure. The State Education Department had awarded provisional authority to offer its programs with a three-year span in which to achieve permanent approval. The New York State education law was unequivocal in requiring *program by program* approval *in advance* of enrolling students. An exception was needed for ESC, but the boundaries needed greater definition and enforceability. The Middle States Commission on Higher Education, the regional accreditor, had also provided a provisional accreditation, requiring a full external evaluation during ESC's third year. Both of these approval and accreditation exercises caused sufficient anxiety among system administrators who had supported creation of the new college.

Moving to strengthen oversight of each student's program of study, the college negotiated an external oversight parameter with the State Education Department. The agreement was to establish broad areas of study, within which certain standards and content expectations would be established by the faculty mentors nominally identified within each broadly defined academic area.

This agreement also prodded Hall to strengthen the educational resources that could be made available to each student, sensing that preservation of the highly individualized approach could falter in the larger world without adequate, professionally designed or identified resources. Chickering offered a principled and rational objection, persuaded that separating prepared resources, apart from the resources identified by each student and mentor, would inevitably undermine the student centeredness of ESC.

Reflecting on the importance of the second hereditary stream, Hall created a complementary office to address that issue. With the chancellor's concurrence, Hall appointed Loren Baritz, a professional historian at SUNY Albany, to the role of provost for learning resources. While Chickering worked with the mentoring faculty to create practice and process, Baritz took steps to identify and create resources for learning. Baritz was a scholar in SUNY Albany's Department of History. A popular teacher and respected scholar, Baritz favored innovative approaches to curriculum, but insisted that the content and boundaries be moderated by professional academicians. "Responding to students as individuals did not mean going beyond meeting their intellectual needs," nor did it always mean "constructing individualized curricula," desirable as that might be for some students. (Bonnabeau, 1996, p.24)

Although he and Chickering shared the mission of creating student-centered alternatives to traditional education, Baritz questioned the readiness of many students to pursue an individualized study plan and whether "every curriculum had to be individually constructed through a contract with an individual student." (Bonnabeau, 1996, p.24). His proposed solution was to create structured independent study modules, often interdisciplinary in organization and designed by "some of the most high-powered intellectuals in the country" (Bonnabeau, 1996, p.24). Chickering, not unreasonably, saw this path of development as a slippery slope that would inevitably lead a regressive march to the traditional university patterns of behavior.

Baritz and Dodge were proponents of the second hereditary stream of increased student access through innovative distance learning, though Dodge recognized the value of individualized study plans anchored in student purposes. As an experimenting institution, over the years Empire State explored several models that promised to provide a sustainable source of sophisticated learning resources. The first, modules created by a visiting learning resources development faculty, was attempted well before personal computers and interactive telecommunications were available. Printed resources were still essential to distance learning. Staffed by visiting specialized scholars, they began to produce homegrown, highly flexible course modules. The expectation was that mentors would use these materials as creative sources for a student's individual program of study.

The conundrum for Hall was that he saw both of the hereditary streams as complementary and essential to ultimate success. And because the entire approach—from methods, to content, to processes—was uncharted, it was difficult for anyone to simply order conformity to a single approach. What was needed was openness to experimentation, trial, and student interaction and success. With strong leadership coming from three talented, committed individuals with differing means to common goals, the growing college faculty and staff were confused. Chickering sought to employ faculty recruited mostly from small colleges and "heavily invested in teaching and learning and sophisticated about such practices" as working one-on-one with students as a mentor (Chickering, 2011, 27 June, p. 10). Baritz, in contrast, saw his role in the hiring practice as "looking for bright experienced scholars who had done it all, and who were very dubious about the institution—hoping that they would drive it in the right direction" (Baritz, 1990, 20 March, p. 10). Hall and Dodge believed that Empire's mentors would need to balance both attributes, and adjust their interactions with the needs and interests of the students.

For many, Baritz and Chickering came to represent opposing pillars upon which to build the academic practices of the college. Hall allowed the natural tensions to grow beyond their productive life, frustrating not only several of his strongest leaders, but also confusing others in the organization. The tensions and misunderstandings that accompanied this creativity are not atypical of brave new institutions, and, indeed, many other institutions spawned during that period imploded from internal dissension and sometimes angry ideological battles. Empire's task was to prevent that while drawing the best ideas together for successful implementation. And so, the college forged ahead rapidly and pragmatically, some things working, and others not.

In the end, Chickering, Dodge, and Baritz did what they were supposed to do: create, structure, and experiment with and administer wholly nontraditional approaches to students and their studies; develop access to and applicability of extensive resources from among which students and faculty could devise flexible resources for learning; and extend the college to provide access for significant numbers of diverse and distant students.

Ultimately, the modules did not work. The faculty mentors, who had been experiencing the intellectual and personal excitement of freedom from the traditional boundaries of the academic curriculum, would not use them to the extent intended, understandably preferring to use their own sources. But mentors were also experiencing, with limited resources, intense personal workloads.

Yet the modules, though unsuccessful, were an impressive and valuable effort. The "development faculty" did create a number of remarkable materials, called colloquially "whatchamacallits." Highly interdisciplinary and flexible in their approach to an individual student's program of study, they seemed a reasonable answer to both individual study and high-level performance expectations. They also seemed to many to be the opposite!

But the modules did serve another critical purpose: they demonstrated to external observers that Empire State College had the intellectual capacity and standards in its faculty to fulfill its experimental mission. The modules were at times inspiring, providing significant amounts of credit for deep explorations of subject matter and new and flexible pathways of learning that covered every area of study offered by the college, including business and human services. The modules were written in welcoming narratives of conversation—much like the British Open University's course guides that were tutorials in print rather than the lectures of traditional correspondence courses—but with opportunities for focusing on what the student might find of interest; and, at times, they connected the student to other modules.

By July 1974, the college offered over one hundred modules in its catalog. Despite not igniting mentor enthusiasm, they were an effective means of demonstrating to the world of higher education, including adversarial colleagues at SUNY campuses, Empire's commitment to academic excellence. In fact, the following year, the New York State Education Department urged their further integration into the academic program, suggesting ways to improve them, and even emphasized the program's importance as expressed by students who used them. The praise for learning modules was contrasted with remarks about the shortcomings of individualized learning study plans (Carr, 1975, 24 March, p. 35).

The learning modules kept before the college community Hall's intention of creating alternatives, as anticipated by the framers of the prospectus; this provided flexibility for those students able to work individually and independently with a mentor, as well as those students who desired more direction, structure, and less introspection and self-discovery. The prospectus had clearly articulated a full spectrum of learning alternatives and even anticipated that "any individual student's program would probably be a blending of both options," combining "completely unstructured" to "fully structured" learning resources but recognizing at the same time that a student could "complete the entire requirement by following one or the other extreme" in its entirety (1971, 8 February, p. 16). The annual report of 1972, *Seeking Alternatives,* listed the possibile ways of learning at Empire State College:

1. Cooperative studies when several students share similar interest.
2. Tutorials in which a teacher helps a student pursue a particular competence.
3. Organized programs of self-contained resources including correspondence courses, programmed learning materials, and televised instruction.
4. Direct experiences, travel, field work, and the like, which become the object of examination and reflection by the student.
5. Independent studies, which usually call for a series of readings and writings, and which may also include direct experiences as described above.
6. Formal courses offered by colleges, agencies, and organizations other than Empire State (p. 50).

In taking the long view of ESC's evolution, Hall concluded that *"one of the things that explains the depth and complexity of Empire State is that there were these different major viewpoints which we tried to pull together into one institution—for the benefit of the student—so that we weren't a single mode institution. We weren't a monomodal craft that would have to fly only on that wing"* (Hall Interview, 1990, 13 June, p. 6).

Despite high hopes for a new approach to resources, the module program was terminated. Baritz went on to serve as executive director of SUNY's Commission on Purposes and Priorities. Chickering, beyond firmly establishing a progressive educational legacy, gained Danforth Foundation support to create the Center for Individualized Education (CIE), critical to sustaining the momentum of the developing mentor role. Also, he and Hall joined with a consortium of other new institutions, convened by Morris Keeton, to found, under another Carnegie grant, what later became the Council for Adult and Experiential Learning (CAEL). Thus Empire State became one of the first institutions to systematically incorporate Credit by Evaluation (now called Prior Learning Assessment) into its educational process for credit toward a university degree. Dodge moved to the center of a number of subsequent and increasingly effective strategies for providing learning resources to faculty and students, aided by many remarkable contributions from other faculty and administrative leaders.

ANOTHER SOURCE FOR LEARNING RESOURCES: THE BRITISH OPEN UNIVERSITY

The prospectus took special note of the British Open University inasmuch as Chancellor Boyer had sent several task force members to the BOU to discover what they might find of value. While the members of the planning panel were impressed with what they discovered, they generally agreed that it was unlikely to be relevant to the needs of the "new non-residential University College," neither as exemplar, nor as potential provider of course materials. The task force understood that a one-size-fits-all approach would not likely work well for an American clientele as BOU "required each student to go through the same general structure of learning" (*A Prospectus*, 1971, 8 February, p. 6). Nonetheless, the BOU model remained of potential interest, especially later as the demand for innovative instructional resources became more evident.

Having terminated the learning module program, the college turned to explore other potential possibilities for student learning resources. Eventually, a working connection with the British Open University, both with its correspondence courses and technical assistance in adapting their courses for ESC, would play an important role as part of a concerted effort to reach new populations, including students served by regional learning centers and their satellites. Of great significance was the fact that the BOU courses provided essential resources directly to students for study and validation.

The British Open University was established by Prime Minister Harold Wilson and his Labour Party in 1969 as a much needed alternative to the then elitist universities of the United Kingdom. The BOU's brand of correspondence study, combined with supplemental course materials produced by the British Broadcasting Company, rocketed BOU to worldwide acclaim. Soon the deep traditions of the classroom in the United Kingdom were challenged by a nationwide distribution system of independent study guides for adult learners, supported by regional study centers as well as by BBC radio and television broadcasts complete with audio and video tapes for further distribution and asynchronous utility.

By 1976, ESC's engagement with the BOU gained new force. As noted earlier, the New York State Education Department's review of ESC's academic program, though laudatory, focused on strengthening resources for learning. The reviewers expressed concern that the earlier learning modules had not become an integral part of ESC's academic program. They noted inconsistencies in the quality of the highly individualized learning contracts, as well as the insufficiency of liberal arts in programs of study. The BOU courses, given the universal praise of their broad general education, suggested value in making them available to ESC students. Moreover, they offered a significant means of responding to the need, originally voiced in the prospectus, for providing structured learning alternatives to students.

Empire worked with other SUNY campuses and BOU's North American Office to create ESC's Open University Review Panel. Beginning in January 1977, adapted BOU courses were tested with students and evaluated. An extensive report testified to the efficacy of ESC's academic program with independent study courses of exceptional quality (Lehmann & Thorsland, 1977, December). The college proceeded to adapt BOU courses for statewide use, offering students two options: either individual study at a distance by phone and mail, or face-to-face group studies, assuming that there would be sufficient enrollments at the regional learning centers.

In effect, there were now two programs offering directed independent study: Extended Programs, demonstrating the feasibility of providing degrees at a distance by employing a variety of structured learning resources, including popular learning modules as well as individualized contracts, and the Independent Study Program. The latter, which consisted primarily of correspondence courses—essentially lectures in print with assignments—had been transferred from SUNY to ESC in 1971. The program had success converting BOU yearlong courses equivalent to sixteen and thirty-two American Carnegie units, into more manageable four- and eight- credit courses. They were offered to students throughout the SUNY network of campuses as well as to any prospective student seeking independent study options.

In February 1978, Extended Programs and the Independent Study Program merged into a full-fledged center—the Center for Independent Study. Almost a year later, ESC reported these new resources to the SUNY vice chancellor, James Perdue, who commended the progress of the new center, making specific references to the use of BOU courses, and praised Empire for its "plans to revitalize the independent study thrust of [ESC's] campus mission" ((Perdue, 1979, 25 January). This endorsement led to additional resources going to the new center and a final name change—the Center for Distance Learning (CDL)—further strengthening Empire's association with the United Kingdom's Open University.

A FULL CENTER DEDICATED TO DISTANCE LEARNING

As was the case earlier with the module program, the Center for Distance Learning, infused with more resources, was not immediately welcomed across the college. Faculty mentors who supported the progressive spirit of individualized learning would have to be won over by CDL's efforts to incorporate progressive dimensions in its distance learning pedagogy and by demonstrating the center's practical potential for easing the heavy burden of student workloads carried by mentors around the college through the cross-registration of their students in CDL courses.

Center for Distance Learning faculty members taught courses and mentored study plans at a distance; they guided students in preparing prior learning portfolios for assessment; they oversaw discrete portions of the curricula within their academic expertise; they hired, trained, and supervised instructors; and they worked diligently at course creation, acquisition, adaptation, and maintenance. CDL students taking structured courses with faculty and adjuncts received narrative evaluations of their coursework and prepared degree programs that included rationale essays explaining their design in relation to educational purposes and career goals. Instead of face-to-face meetings, CDL advisors and instructors employed the telephone and mail as the primary modes of communication. Empire State College not only offered BOU courses and media-based courses developed by various national consortia, but added important student-centered features in courses developed by CDL. This individualized pattern was applauded by some BOU colleagues, for it began to describe the benefits of linking both educational strands upon which the college program was built.

CDL was reaching its majority and set on a path to become an integral part of the college, creating a distinctive branding of its distance learning programs. It began to expand rapidly in the 1990s, which continued into the new millennium and the decade that followed. Full-time CDL faculty ranks increased from twelve to forty. This expansion included much less dependence on the acquisition of ready-made mediated courses and much more on the continued development of student-centered courses with individualized assignments tailored to their interests. This focus emerged from a distinct model of relying more heavily on the development of a highly integrated adjunct community. It included not only an orientation to teaching at a distance, but also to the philosophies of mentoring embraced by the rest of the college.

THE TECHNOLOGY REVOLUTION AND ITS IMPACT ON RESOURCES FOR LEARNING

Key to CDL's pedagogical transformation was the initial effort to develop online learning courses in the 1980s which eventually completely replaced print-based courses in 2002. Daniel Granger led this early initiative, which was continued by Meg Benke in the 1990s when she became director and subsequently dean.

The use of technology in support of its faculty and students had figured prominently in the 1971 prospectus. The founders anticipated that over time, improvements in technology, as they became functionally available, would become fundamentally important to success. But from the earliest years, the available technologies were costly to buy and prohibitive to develop in house. For the first twenty years, faculty mentors relied almost entirely upon their own knowledge and skills, specialized tutors whom they could arrange to work with a single student, and a variety of aforementioned print resources, including, most importantly, books. Before the advent of the personal computer and the Internet, students were connected to their advisors and mentors only by phone and by mail. Face-to-face meetings, so prized by faculty colleagues, presented a troubling gap.

That raised nagging questions about quality assurance, especially for distance-learning students. But the emergence of the personal computer and facile, inexpensive use of an open Internet began to change things dramatically. These miraculous developments established a capacity that would revolutionize distance learning pedagogy.

In 1980, Empire State College purchased its first microcomputer, which was followed by a decade of activity to bring the college into the age of the personal computer. This included a heavy investment in desktop computers and modems, faculty training programs in the use of software, and instructional strategies for computer conferencing. CDL successfully tested these new technologies, which, unlike print-based courses, made it possible for students for the first time to work with their instructors in groups, communicating asynchronously rather than as isolated individuals. They were now joined in coherent communities of interactive learners. The cognitive and affective dimensions of this transformation were profound. Online learning, therefore, was a watershed for CDL, one that was propelled in the mid-1990s by dramatically less expensive and more powerful personal computers in the financial reach of a growing majority of adult students. This eventually facilitated the complete transition to online learning (Bonnabeau, 1996, pp.109-112). For Empire State College, it meant that the pedagogical divide between the progressive individual mentoring of the regional centers and the outreach and access capabilities of the Center for Distance Learning would begin to narrow. Both of the hereditary genomes of the college could thrive together for the benefit of students.

SUNY BY SATELLITE AND THE SUNY LEARNING NETWORK

The early efforts of the college to engage students in the use of emerging distance learning technologies were bolstered by support from the SUNY System. In 1989, Chancellor Bruce Johnstone provided funds to create a separate ESC center with a dual mandate: The Center for Learning and Technology would serve as a laboratory to test and evaluate telecommunications technologies for SUNY and for the Center for Distance Learning (Bonnbeau, 1996, pp. 118-119).

One result was the formation of a new course distribution system offering bachelor's degrees called SUNY By Satellite (SBS). The program connected SUNY community college graduates with one another and with their instructors via interactive televised lectures—in effect creating a statewide virtual classroom for each course. Eventually, the SBS network connected students in 20 locations across the state (Bonnabeau, 1996, pp. 119-120). A similar pilot program developed in cooperation with NYNEX (now part of Verizon) in 1994, provided interactive video conferencing courses for telephone employees encompassing four corporate sites, Albany, Buffalo, Syracuse, and Boston (Carnevale, Chandra, & Pauszek, 1998). These early, organizationally complex but technologically impressive ways of overcoming distance to create communities of learners were superseded after 1994. Their replacement was the flexible and inexpensive advent of the more accessible, interactive, and convenient technology of online learning courses via the World Wide Web.

In the process, Empire State College became part of a national community supporting the development of online programs across the country, funded by the Alfred Sloan Foundation through the Sloan Consortium (Sloan-C) that worked collaboratively with primarily strong online community colleges throughout New York State. ESC was an early leader by harnessing the learning from failed experiences with SUNY by Satellite to support high quality virtual services and full-online degree programs at a distance. These two early interventions allowed enrollment to grow rapidly. By spring 1996, this network of campuses offering online courses evolved into the SUNY Learning Network. Its growth was spectacular. Within five years, the SUNY consortium expanded from a handful of courses and students to one thousand courses and twelve thousand students (Lefor, Benke & Ting, 2001).

At the time, President Hall doubled as system vice chancellor for educational technology, promoting online learning as the next logical step in SUNY's pedagogical evolution. His two-year assignment (1993-95) included serving as chair for a task force of SUNY presidents on distance learning while ESC's Center for Learning and Technology played a leadership role in the coordination of SUNY's efforts. Hall, in speeches and conference presentations around the world, foresaw and promoted the emergence of a new kind of university. That university would evolve from a university of *convocation*— where all necessary resources for students need be assembled and held forever *in situ*—to a university of *convergence*. There the student, wherever he or she might be studying, could draw upon the best resources worldwide for study and reflection. The college prospectus, which had anticipated this eventuality, could finally begin to realize that promise. Now the student, not the campus, would be at the center—the ultimate in student centeredness.

Today, the Center for Distance Learning embeds strong, progressive educational practices in a huge array of discrete courses—once considered antithetical, even pedagogically immiscible, as when they were being fiercely debated in the early years of Empire's existence. Students are engaged with their peers—sometimes intensively—and with their instructors in ongoing course discussions, the very progressive method promoted by Royce Pitkin. They have regular opportunities to work collaboratively in online learning communities through presentations, projects, and other group-based activities, just as students do at the regional centers and their satellites who engage in face-to-face seminars, workshops, and group studies.

The Center for Distance Learning has successfully forged one of the most student centered online programs in the nation, aligning its program with those of the regional centers to combine both the progressive and distance learning streams of Empire State College's heredity. Moreover, the Center, during Benke's tenure as director and dean, engaged the faculty and staff in developing external partnerships with national unions and employers as well with the US military services. The Center now accounts for fifty percent of ESC's full-time enrollments.

OPEN SUNY AND THE FUTURE

In 2012, Empire State College submitted a proposal in support of SUNY Chancellor Nancy Zimpher's call for "systemness." Crafted by ESC President Alan Davis with leadership from ESC and other SUNY campuses, the vision called for increasing degree completion, revitalizing SUNY's leadership in online learning, sharing learning resources among campuses and recognizing ESC's expertise in prior learning assessment (PLA).

> SUNY has the capability of collectively offering the most extensive array of online courses and programs in the country. Open SUNY Online would build on the achievements of the SUNY Learning Network, which, in this proposal, would form the core of Open SUNY Online, and expand to include all of SUNY's online offerings, and be enhanced by the other dimensions of Open SUNY. In other words, to support the next generation of online teaching and learning (Davis, A. R. 2012, April, p. 5).

Two years later, Chancellor Zimpher launched Open SUNY, thereby creating the "world's largest consortium for online learning . . . comprising . . . 472 online programs and 20,000 course sections [for the academic year]. . . extending access to limitless numbers of people, anywhere in the world" (Zimpher, 1/18/2016).

These courses serve multiple needs. SUNY students enroll in online courses to reduce the amount of time to earn a degree from four to three years, a proposal first voiced by Ernest L. Boyer when he was chancellor, but long before the personal computer and web access. Moreover, students who have missed required classroom based courses at their own campuses can fulfill degree requirements online, another cost saving option. In both cases, the success of this option is the transferability of credits earned from one campus to another. Open SUNY online also serves the economic interests of New York State by providing courses that lead to credentialing and better articulation between the needs of business and education (Zimpher,

2016, 11 January). It also extends the reach of SUNY throughout the world, which gives new meaning to the word university. SUNY has become a university of both convocation and convergence, the latter, as noted earlier in the chapter, "where the student, wherever he or she might be studying, could draw upon the best resources worldwide for study and reflection."

Of particular importance to this revisioned and resource-enhanced dimension of the Power of SUNY is the central role of the Open SUNY Center for Online Teaching Excellence (COTE), which had its origins in the SUNY Learning Network. COTE has had remarkable success promoting faculty development in a broad-gauged continuum of online learning, from purely online to innovative support of bricks-and-mortar classrooms. COTE has supported over 5,000 faculty with training initiatives achieved through online instruction, as well as face-to-face workshops. In the process, a community of faculty online practitioners has emerged. They share their knowledge with the hundreds of faculty who join their ranks each year. COTE also conducts yearly conferences for online faculty and instructional designers (See COTE, Pedagogical Perspective). Finally, the center offers a peer-based mentoring program to develop competency in online course design and teaching. It is conducted by Open SUNY fellows who serve as volunteers. The program has expanded to include blended learning courses.

Since 2014, Open SUNY has enrolled over one quarter of a million students and has every expectation to accommodate the continued extraordinary growth of online learners (Zimpher, 2016, 11 January). In the process, the challenges Open SUNY faces—the massive student enrollments and maintenance of distance-learning pedagogy—are ongoing.

Empire State continues to experiment with educational technologies. Funded by the Gates and Lumina foundations, experimentation is underway with adaptive learning and competency-based education. But these experiences are still grounded in the philosophies of putting the student at the center and making sure that the technology is driven by connecting faculty and students where most appropriate.

In 2014, Empire entered a new era when the college search committee and the SUNY chancellor recommended the appointment of Dr. Merodie Hancock as its new leader. As president, she now provides critical leadership as the college enters an extraordinary time of change and growth.

Among the newest developments is the first concept approval for a doctoral level program in educational leadership, proposed within the Open SUNY. Joining programs at the master's level in adult learning and emerging technologies, these programs allow ESC to further model its educational approach and allow the institution to become a laboratory for continuing research and exploration.

Open SUNY campuses share with Empire State College the recognition that learning outcomes are directly related to the practices that bring students and their instructors together into learning communities (course sections) of manageable size to address the cognitive and affective benefits they engender. ESC, as it has for the past two decades of cooperation with the other campuses, will continue to address these system challenges.

QUESTIONS AND CONCLUSIONS

Mentoring individuals or groups of students, either face-to-face or at a distance, is still virtually unique to Empire State College. It embraces the principle that student purposes govern how ESC utilizes educational resources and their delivery. But these practices are not inexpensive in terms of talented specialized faculty, staff and effective technology. ESC's educational philosophy and practices stem from core values first articulated in 1971 in *Prospectus for a New University College*. SUNY is now preparing to accommodate many thousands of students in online courses. Finding a reasonable balance between costs while maintaining high quality services in Open SUNY will be critical in the current highly competitive environment for recruitment and retention.

Therefore, important questions remain: in this era of soaring higher education costs for institutions and students, will ESC and SUNY succumb to the call of economies-of-scale inherent in some approaches to online learning? Considerable numbers of institutions—public, independent, and especially for-profit—are using technology to forge a self-paced, lock-step, interchangeable parts system, a reborn industrial model that minimizes interaction with other students and faculty, cutting costs deeply. From our perspective, such a low cost, often profitable strategy, might surrender the powerful educational character that has separated Empire State College and Open SUNY from these approaches to postsecondary learning.

From this concern arises derivative questions: How might a reborn industrial model adversely transform the faculty role? Is there a tipping point for student-instructor ratios and student interaction that would make effective teaching impossible? Will student essays, term papers, team presentations, vibrant asynchronous exchanges among students, calls from their instructors, and other modes of interaction that personalize student experience in the virtual classroom succumb to standardized competency-based methods of instruction and evaluation? Ultimately, for good or for ill, the social and psychological dimensions of the educational journey students take with their peers and instructors is as important as the subject matter picked up along the way. There is, in effect, a noteworthy consequence of having 20,000 online courses offered during the academic year—with many duplicates among their numbers—and thousands of instructors across SUNY serving many more thousands of students: these inhibit the standardization of the curriculum; preserve the value of many scholarly voices opining about what is important and what is not; safeguard the independence and judgment of the professoriate in its instructional and curricular dimensions; and, most of all, perpetuate the human experience of being a student in an engaged community of learners.

The bold, forward-looking experiments initiated by the Gould/Boyer leadership within the remarkable environment of the 1970s, leading to the development and testing of new patterns of learning, are now coming full circle. Empire State College continues to share in modeling twenty-first century approaches to postsecondary education within the SUNY system, thereby fulfilling the original mandate for its creation.

REFERENCES

A Prospectus for a New University College: Objectives, process, structure and establishment. (1971, February 8). Draft. Office of the Chancellor. State University of New York. Empire State College Archives. Saratoga Springs, New York.

Benson, A. & Adams, F. (1987). *To know for real: Royce S. Pitkin and Goddard College.* Adamant, VT: Adamant Press.

Bonnabeau, R. (1996). *The promise continues: Empire State College, the first twenty-five years.* Virginia Beach, VA: The Donning Company Publishers.

Boyer, E. L. (1981, September 8). *The experimental college: Its heritage, its future.* [Draft of address given at Evergreen State College, Olympia, WA]. No. 1000 0000 0791. Ernest L. Boyer Center Archives, Messiah College. Grantham, PA.

Boyer, E. L. (1990, 31 August). *An oral history with Ernest L. Boyer/ Interviewer: R. Bonnabeau.* Oral History Project. Empire State College Archives. Saratoga Springs, New York.

Carnevale, C., Chandra B., & Pauszek, R. (1998, May). *Evolution of Instructional Technologies in Teaching Distance Learning Courses at Center for Distance Learning, Empire State College.* Paper presented at the SUNY Conference on Instructional Technologies. Cortland, NY.

Carr, E. (1975, 24 March). *Memorandum to J. Hall. Report of the New York State Education Department Evaluation Team.* Empire State College Archives. Saratoga Springs, New York.

Chickering, A. W. (1969). *Education and identity.* San Francisco, CA: Jossey-Bass.

Chickering, A. W. (1990, 16 August). *An oral history with Arthur W. Chickering/ Interviewer: R. Bonnabeau.* Oral History Project. Empire State College Archives. Saratoga Springs, New York.

Chickering, A. W. (2011, 27 June). *An oral history with Arthur W. Chickering/ Interviewer: R. Bonnabeau.* Oral History Project. Empire State College Archives. Saratoga Springs, New York.

Chickering, A. W. (2012, July 23). E-mail to R. Bonnabeau. Empire State College Archives. Saratoga Springs, New York.

Chickering, A. W. (2012, August 8). E-mail to R. Bonnabeau. Empire State College Archives. Saratoga Springs, New York.

COTE (Open SUNY Center for Online Teaching Excellence) (2015). Re: Mentoring Program. Retrieved from http://commons.suny.edu/cotehub/engage/open-suny-cote-mentoring program

COTE (Open SUNY Center for Online Teaching Excellence) (2015). Re: Pedagogical Perspective. Retrieved from http://commons.suny.edu/cotehub/pedagogical-perspective

Davis, A. R. (2012, April). *Open SUNY.* Office of the President. Empire State College Archives. Saratoga Springs, New York.

Davis, F. K. (1991, 16 March). *An oral history with Forest Davis. Interviewer: R. Bonnabeau.* Oral History Project. Empire State College Archives. Saratoga Springs, New York.

Davis, F. K. (1996). *Things were different in Royce's day: Royce S. Pitkin as progressive educator, A perspective from Goddard College, 1950–1967.* Adamant, VT: Adamant Press.

Empire State College Awards Honorary Degree to Lord Perry of Walton: British Open University Founder. (Summer 1982) ESC News, pp. 4-5. Empire State College Archives. Saratoga Springs, New York.

Gould, S. B. (Chairman, 1973). *Diversity by design: By the Commission on Non-traditional Study.* San Francisco: Jossey-Bass.

Hall, J. W. (1982). The social imperatives for curricular change. In J.W. Hall (Ed.) with B.L. Kevles, *In opposition to the core curriculum: Alternative models for undergraduate education* (pp. 13-38). Westport, CT: Greenwood Press.

Hall, J. W. (1990, April 8). *An oral history with James W. Hall. Interviewer: R. Bonnabeau. Oral History Project.* Empire State College Archives. Saratoga Springs, New York.

Hall, J. W. (1991). *Access through innovation: New colleges for new students.* American Council on Education Series/Macmillan Series in Higher Education. New York: Macmillan Publishing Company.

Jacobson, J. H. (1993, June 13). *An oral history with John Jacobson. Interviewer: R. Bonnabeau.* Oral History Project. Empire State College Archives. Saratoga Springs, New York.

Lefor, P., Benke, M., & Ting, E. (2001). Empire State College: The development of online learning. *IRRODL: The International Review of Research in Open and Distributed Learning. 2*(1), Retrieved from http: irrodl.org/index.php/irrodl/article/view/22/363.

Lehmann, T. & Thorsland, M. (1977, December). *Joint Report of ESC's Office of Research and Evaluation and the Office of Academic Development. Empire State College Field Test of British Open University Courses.* Unpublished Manuscript. Empire State College Archives. Saratoga Springs, New York.

Martin, J. (2003). *The education of John Dewey: A Biography.* New York City, NY: Columbia University Press.

Nolan, D. J. (1998). *Regents College: The early years.* Virginia Beach, VA: The Donning Company Publishers.

Perdue, J. (1979, January 25). Letter to James W. Hall. Empire State College, Archives. Saratoga Springs, New York.

Pierce, S. (1979, August) *Center for Distance Learning Fall Term Announcement. Workload Reduction Plan.* Empire State College Archives. Saratoga Springs, New York.

Pierce, S. (1979, June-July). *Center for Distance Learning Review and Prospectus.* Empire State College Archives, Saratoga Springs, New York.

Pifer, A. (1970, October 27). *Is it Time for an External Degree?* [Presentation by A. Pifer, President of the Carnegie Corporation of New York, at the Annual Meeting of the College Entrance Examination Board]

Seeking Alternatives. (1972). Annual Report. Empire State College Archives, Saratoga Springs, New York.

Weise, M. R. & Christensen, C. M. (2014). *Hire Education: Mastery, Modularization, and the Workforce Revolution.* Clayton Christensen Institute for Disruptive Innovation. Retrieved from https://www.christenseninstitute.org/wp-content/uploads/2014/07/Hire-Education.pdf

Worth, V. (1979, January 3). Memorandum to William R. Dodge. Empire State College Archives, Saratoga Springs, New York.

Zimpher, N. L. (2016, January 11). Re: 2016 State of the University Address. Retrieved from https://www.suny.edu/about/leadership/chancellor-nancy-Zimpher/speeches

IT TAKES A SYSTEM: THE HISTORY OF ONLINE LEARNING IN THE STATE UNIVERSITY OF NEW YORK

Eric E. Fredericksen

Associate Vice President, Online Learning and Associate Professor
University of Rochester

Developing an online course is not easy. Developing and offering an online course in the mid-1990's was not easy and certainly not as common as today. Starting a new online program in a new department or school is not easy. Creating an online program across multiple institutions of higher education is definitely not-so-easy. Consider trying to tackle all of those things at the same time. Sounds impossible, right? This chapter highlights the evolution of the SUNY Learning Network—the online program of the State University of New York—and how it accomplished all of those not so easy tasks with enrollments growing from fifty-six to more than 40,000 in just eight years and a number of national awards. This remarkable program was recognized across higher education as a model for other institutions and university systems, and the concerted effort to share best practices and research had a profound impact on the field of online education.

INTRODUCTION

The State University of New York is the largest comprehensive university system in the United States, with sixty-four institutions and more than 460,000 students. In 1994, a small project coordinated by the SUNY System Administration office, with two of the baccalaureate campuses and six of the community colleges, received a planning grant from the Alfred P. Sloan Foundation to support the creation of the Mid Hudson Regional Learning Network (MHRLN). Most of the initial planning effort and activity of this asynchronous learning network (ALN) was placed with the two state-operated schools, and in the fall of 1995, MHRLN opened with four courses offered to fifty-six students. While the author provided leadership to this program continuously from late fall in 1995 through fall of 2002, it might be beneficial to consider the design and development of this program in three phases: proof of concept, proof of scale, and proof of sustainability. As those phases are explored, we will consider the perspective of faculty, students, and the institutions.

PROOF OF CONCEPT (1995-1997)

The notion of a college offering an online course in 1995 was not as common and accepted as it is today. That is quite an understatement. So a very challenging aspect of the work at the beginning was for the staff to collaborate with the faculty on how to design an ALN, which was the original terminology used for what we think of as an online course today. Unfortunately, during 1995, the program experienced difficulties and a change of director occurred at the end of that year.

As the incoming director of the program at the end of the first semester, I found that there were many aspects that needed attention.

The first priority was the departure of the previous director, which impacted the relationships with the program staff, the schools, and the Sloan Foundation. The dedication and commitment of the program staff was unsurpassed, and they kept this program afloat during that year. They deserved more support and appreciation, and we tried to provide that to them, along with credit and recognition. A concerted effort to improve communication with our generous sponsor was vital to repairing that relationship. Regular trips to Manhattan with consistent updates were appreciated by our program officer. This was very important, because SUNY would not have done all that we did in the state without the Sloan Foundation. The Sloan Foundation support was essential to what we accomplished and the extent of our success. And related to the situation with the schools, as the new director, I made a point of meeting with the deans of the two schools offering courses on my third day on the job. I walked into the room with them and they conveyed a surprising message. Basically, they thought the best course of action was to separate. They would allocate the remainder of the grant funding to the two schools and do their own thing. (And that would be the end of the program.) Perhaps the benefit of only being in the director position for three days was my resulting response that we were not going to do that. We were going to regroup and get this program back on the right path. We needed to stick together and build a program. (And we did!)

The second area that needed attention was the vision and strategic direction of the program. At the time, there were other kinds of projects happening in the Office of Educational Technology (OET) in System Administration, and so it was initially viewed as just one of many. The original view of the MHRLN program was regional—in the mid-Hudson Valley. But given that an ALN enables the freedom of time and location constraints, that did not make a lot of sense. We needed to evolve the view that this was a SUNY-wide program, and this led to the renaming of MHRLN to the SUNY Learning Network or SLN. This name change was significant in that it positioned the program for the future. One other important dimensions to this expanded vision was to address the original thinking that this program was only for baccalaureate intuitions. It might be hard to believe today, but the original plan did not include community colleges offering courses. So this part of the program was adjusted, and a more inclusive vision enabled more engagement and enthusiasm from the initial group of community colleges.

At the beginning, most faculty were extremely skeptical. It was understandable, because no one had any experience with it. The initial approach was to have teams of faculty working together on a single course. You also had to have a dedicated instructional designer working on one course at a time. And at that moment in time, there was no faculty agreement and no position on intellectual property. Extra compensation for faculty was required, but that wasn't being dealt with consistently. New computers also had to be provided to faculty because we could not assume that they had something that was current. So the program benefitted from the efforts of the faculty pioneers who were open to exploring a new innovative approach to teaching and learning, and from their willingness to move forward despite a lack of clarity on many issues and practices. Basically, there was a one-to-one relationship between the number of faculty involved and the number of courses offered. We had a total of eight during the first year and that grew to thirty-four in the second year, as seen in the chart below. (A memorable moment in the spring of 1996 occurred at a Sloan grantees meeting at UIUC where, to the surprise and delight of our program officer and attendees, we announced that we were going to offer fourteen courses in a single semester! An impressive accomplishment at that early point in time.)

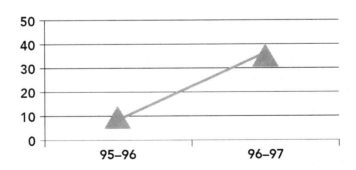

Figure 1.

In a similar way, the program also benefitted from the willingness of students who were open to trying something new. They also did not come into the program with any experience. But they were enthusiastic for the most part and appreciated the opportunity to complete college courses without the requirement of commuting to a campus. The enrollments totaled 119 the first year. and we knew the students by name. We spoke to many of them, as it was necessary to help them configure and setup their computers so they could access and participate in the courses. Enrollments in the second year grew to 460, as seen in the chart below.

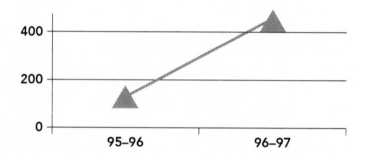

Figure 2.

From an institutional perspective, there was a lot to do. The basic platform for offering the courses had to be built. Commonly referred to as a learning management system (LMS) today, these systems were not commercially available when we started (e.g., Blackboard did not exist), so the program staff had to develop one from scratch. They did an exceptional job developing an LMS with thoughtful input from the faculty who were involved. And it worked across multiple campuses, which is still a phenomenal accomplishment. A major institutional shift was to move from the exclusive approach of baccalaureate schools only to a more inclusive model of involving community colleges. This led to a growth in the number of campuses offering courses from two during 1995-96 to seven in 1996-97, as shown in the chart below.

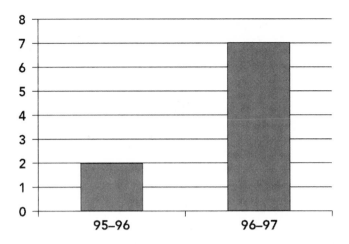

Figure 3.

Coordinating and operating an online program across more than one school is a unique aspect of the SLN program. Launching an online program at one school is challenging enough, but to do so with multiple schools leads to a lot more issues and questions that need to be addressed. Even though the schools were part of the same university system, there were tremendous differences in how they operated, including semester calendars, course coding, tuition rates, refund policies, course registration processes, and faculty contracts, to name a few. Consider a basic marketing question: how do you recruit students to the program when each campus has their own unique registration form? Initially we sent out a package for each of the two schools, but this quickly becomes impractical as new schools joined the program. So we collaborated with the registrars from the campuses, who were very helpful in the development of a common course registration form that would work across all campuses. It sounds like common sense and an easy thing to do, but it was very challenging in a very decentralized university system where each school has the latitude to make their own local decisions. So an important part of our endeavors was to explore the feasibility of addressing issues at a system level versus deferring to the local campus. This was a foundational element as we built upon our proof of concept (we can offer an online course and faculty can be satisfied and students can be satisfied and learn) and moved to proof of scale (we can offer lots of online courses across multiple institutions).

PROOF OF SCALE (1997-1999)

Despite the early success of the first phase of the SLN program, the SUNY System Administration office was faced with a hiring freeze and therefore less inclined to add significant staff resources to the effort. So in order to grow the program, we had to be creative and develop efficient and clever approaches to keep up with the demand. A fundamental and foundational effort that enabled this was the creation of the SLN faculty development process. Up to this point we assigned an instructional designer to work with each faculty member, and the work was somewhat unique and tailored to each one. In order to scale, a thoughtfully structured, four-stage process was created and put in place to guide faculty through the planning, preparation, design, and development of their online course, and the preparation to teach. The steps included (1) getting connected and online, (2) conceptualizing your course, (3) developing your course, and (4) piloting your course. This incorporated a series of three face-to-face hands-on workshops, which were complemented by access to a shared multimedia instructional designer (MID). Online resources and activities were also facilitated with the same course platform to enable the faculty to appreciate the experience of the online student. With a more organized approach, more faculty could participate and more courses could be developed. An instrumental aspect of the faculty development process was the enlistment of a faculty member to lead and facilitate the workshops. He had been teaching at his college for decades and was not only personable, amiable, hard working, and enthusiastic, but also well regarded, highly respected, and a delight to work with. There was great value in having a peer play a fundamental role in this faculty development experience.

The ability to support more faculty yielded a significant growth in the number of courses offered on SLN, as shown in the chart below (180 courses in 1997-98 and 460 in 1998-99).

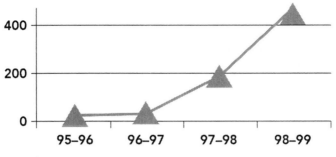

Figure 4.

In the first phase of the SLN program, students were provided a software application that enabled a connection and participation in their online courses. But distributing the software to students and supporting this application was no small endeavor. With our sights on growing, we needed to migrate the student experience to something they already had and that did not require support: a browser. This required a heroic effort on our program staff to migrate our platform to this model, but it was well worth it. We were able to keep up with the student demand for online courses, with enrollments in 1997-98 at 2009 and up to 6000 in 1998-99 as presented in the chart below.

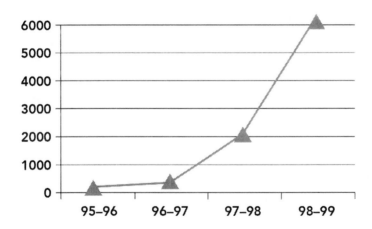

Figure 5.

In the 1997-98 academic year, the SLN program added twelve new SUNY campuses and another seventeen SUNY campuses in 1998-99, as noted in the chart below.

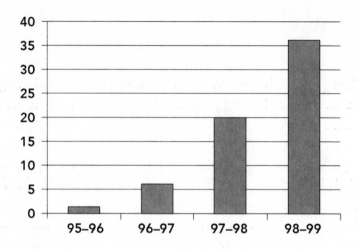

Figure 6.

The Sloan Foundation provided generous grant support to SLN, and this was used to promote campus expansion and support of specific online degree programs. This increase in campus participation required careful leadership. In our decentralized university system, the campuses valued their autonomy and local decision making. However, a system approach to the program required collaboration and some level of coordination. With advice and insight from many campus leaders, we articulated the roles and responsibilities for the system office and the local campus. We recognized and understood what was important to the campuses. Our organizational model respected their academic authority regarding what courses were offered and which faculty would teach them. It was also important that the campuses receive and manage the tuition revenue, state aid, and potential charge backs. On a related note, the campuses were responsible for enrollment management, advisement, and financial aid. All of this was consistent with how campuses operated for their face-to-face courses. So this was a fundamental guiding principle—that "a course is a course is a course." The fact that mode of instruction did not matter was very helpful as academic issues were considered. As a question was raised about a practice or potential policy, we would start by asking: how is this issue addressed in a face to face course? This was tremendously valuable, as some individuals thought there should be special rules for online courses. Our argument was that this was simply another mode of instruction, and the starting point should be that the same rules about face-to-face courses should be considered and applied. This also helped us sidestep arbitrary lines of what is and what is not an online course.

The responsibilities for the SLN program at the system office were focused on areas that the campuses might not want to do or create. In some sense, we helped the campuses avoid reinventing the wheel. SLN provided the faculty development program with training and instructional design support. SLN provided and managed all of the technology infrastructure, which operated in two distant locations and was managed 24/7. A help desk service was also created for faculty and students, operating late in the evenings and on the weekends. This was well received by the campuses. SLN provided overall program administration and marketing and promotion activities. In addition to building the multi campus learning management system, we also created a suite of applications that helped the program work with campuses and efficiently operate the program. The system approach made it possible to skip the implementation of what would have been redundant efforts and services at each local campus.

As we administered the SLN program, we used the Sloan funding to sponsor the creation of online degree programs. As more campuses joined, an interesting question came up: if Campus A has already offered a certain course online, would that prevent Campus B from offering the same course? We were able to skillfully navigate this question by deferring to our core principle of "a course is a course is a course." The campuses were already offering the same courses in face-to-face settings. So our view was that they should have the option of doing the same thing online. While we did not provide financial support for the second and third versions of a course, it was left to the local campus to decide if it was valuable to them. And it was, as the enrollments determined success.

There was another notable challenge for the SLN program to scale. The initial phase was contained in the mid-Hudson Valley. The twelve campuses that were part of the 1997-98 expansion were geographically distributed all over the State of New York. It was not practical to conduct faculty training only in Albany and ask faculty from all over the state to come to us. We had the pleasure of working with great people on the campuses and established partnerships with several of them across the state to host faculty workshops, and the SLN staff went on the road. This put a strain on our small team, but their dedication to this program was unrivaled. Their personal commitment to SLN was a primary driver in our success.

There is one part of this story that deserves a spotlight. As we began this phase, we recognized that it was critical to the long term prospects of SLN to integrate a research initiative into the program. We were extremely fortunate that our lead instructional designer had just completed his PhD in curriculum and instruction and had significant expertise in educational research. (His ability and skills were recognized further as he took on the role of director when the author departed SLN in the fall of 2002.) Combining the passion and enthusiasm of our associate director for faculty development and instructional design, with two highly regarded faculty members from two of our campuses (one from the Department of Educational Theory and Practice in the graduate school of education at one of our university centers and the other in the Department of Psychology at one of our community colleges), we created an impressive research team to guide and implement this research initiative. It was valuable to our program, as well as the field of online education in general, to collect and analyze data about the student and faculty experience. These research studies yielded multiple positive outcomes.

First, conducting research was aligned with the spirit of the academy and resonated with faculty. It was meaningful for some faculty that we were guiding educational research and sharing the results with them. One of the early faculty members involved with the SLN program often remarked that it was unfortunate that more innovations in higher education did not embrace the need for, and value of, educational research. It is not as common as it should be that new interventions are aligned with efforts to collect data about the program to help learn whether it is effective or not. So some faculty, members viewed the SLN program in a positive way, believing that we were doing this in the right way, and this impacted their willingness to participate. It was very enlightening for some faculty members to hear that those who that taught online courses through SLN were reporting higher levels of interaction—both in quantity and quality—than what they experienced in a traditional classroom (Fredericksen, Pickett, Shea, Pelz, & Swan, 2000).

Second, we thought of the research initiative in the spirit of continuous improvement. Given that we were constrained in our staffing and resources, we had to evolve the services, support, and overall operations on a semester-by-semester basis in order to keep up with the growth in faculty participation and student enrollment. The research initiative helped us to understand what was working and what areas needed to be improved. It helped us to learn about online pedagogy and what was effective for faculty satisfaction, student satisfaction, and student learning. It helped us to better understand the proper approach to the design of online courses. The research initiative not only helped us to survive, but also to thrive.

The third positive outcome of our research efforts related to raising visibility of the program within the university system and the sixty-four campuses. Press releases that highlighted growth and expansion also included research data and key findings. It helped to grab the attention of key institutional leaders, as well as the press, by pointing to very high levels of faculty and student satisfaction. We were able to share very kind and supportive stories, quotes, and testimonials from students and faculty. It was also significant and noteworthy that the SLN program was able to preserve and maintain that very high level of satisfaction while we doubled (or tripled) in size every year. And we accomplished that with the same level of staff and resources. It was beneficial to our program that we were viewed as efficient and effective, and it encouraged the leaders of the campuses that were not participating to explore the opportunity.

The fourth and final positive outcome of integrating a research initiative into our online learning program relates to the larger online learning community and higher education in general. We developed and managed one of the largest online learning program in the country, and so when we conducted a research study, we collected more data about the student and faculty experience than most every other online program in the United States. We were strongly encouraged by our program officer at the Sloan Foundation to do so. Sharing the positive results was beneficial to our relationship with our sponsor. We also shared our results with other Sloan Foundation grantees and anyone else in higher education that was interested. This included authoring book chapters, journal articles, press releases, and numerous conference presentations. We helped the broader online learning movement to understand what we were seeing in terms of what was effective. It helped to counter misperceptions about online learning being an isolated experience for students or online courses being only for technically savvy faculty and students. This provided an alternative to the opinion that online courses were diluted versions of their face-to-face counterparts, and created a more informed view that online courses could actually lead to higher levels of quality and possibly could be more effective than traditional classroom courses.

PROOF OF SUSTAINABILITY (1999–2002)

The third phase of SLN refers to the institutionalization of the program. Now that we had established that the SLN program could work with large numbers of faculty to offer significant numbers of courses to very large numbers of students, we needed to make one more step and finalize the financial model within the university system. While we operated SLN with resources from the System, there was a dependency on our grant support from the Sloan Foundation during the first two phases. We needed to develop a financial model where all of the resources needed to support SLN were within the state university system—both the system office and the campuses. Our wise and insightful program officer at the Sloan Foundation recognized the challenges of this transition and was supportive of a third major grant for this phase to help us create a bridge to the future. It might be amusing to consider the spirit of my message for this grant: "We need more funding so that we can figure out how to not ask for more funding." Given the success of the SLN program and the positive visibility for the Sloan Foundation, we received generous support one more time. Our program officer even acknowledged the good work of SLN in his testimony to the Kerry Commission in the US Congress in 2000, citing us as the second-largest online program in the country.

The shift to financial sustainability, to a large degree, depended on securing a financial commitment from the participating campuses. This was a difficult road to travel because the campuses had enjoyed the services and support from SLN for a number of years at no cost. In fact, SLN had even shared grant funding from the Sloan Foundation with the campuses during that time. So given that backdrop, initial campus feedback was that they would prefer to receive the services and support for free. That should not be surprising—who wouldn't want to continue with a free ride? But it was clear that was not a long-term option. We had to replace the grant funding component of our overall budget. With support from our SLN advisory board, comprised of campus presidents and other campus executives, we worked through a number of potential models. Our goals focused on the replacement of the grant funding as well as other objectives. The biggest factor in the SLN operational budget was related to the number of courses offered, so we thought our cost structure should center on that variable. This would mean that as the courses offered continued to grow, the resources for the SLN program would be in alignment. We also wanted to reward campuses that were doing a lot with SLN with some type of benefit for economy of scale. At the same time, we did not want to create any disincentives for a new campus that was just getting started with SLN with a very minimal point of entry. The financial model also needed to align with differences in course offerings by varying with the number of credit hours. Ultimately, we crafted a structure with a per-credit-hour fee that also included a reduced-credit-hour fee (plus a modest flat amount) if enrollments surpassed a certain threshold. It took a lot of time and effort to develop the model, and then more time and effort to shepherd it through an approval process. By the end of this phase of the program, the financial sustainability model was in place and SLN was positioned for the future without further financial sponsorship from the Sloan Foundation. It was also a moment to reflect on the importance of the Sloan Foundation. We would not have accomplished so much, or so fast, without their generous contributions.

As further evidence of the Sloan Foundation's recognition of SLN and our leadership in online education, we were selected to host not one, but three annual research workshops in 2001, 2002, and 2003 focused on online learning. These premiere, invitation-only events gathered the leading researchers from across higher education to collaborate and share ideas. The events led to three published books that captured leading research in the domain. The collection became a cornerstone of influential studies that had a great impact on the field of online learning, and it continues to be cited today. The effort of SLN with these workshops demonstrated our commitment to support the community and have a positive impact on online education in higher education.

During this sustainability phase, we continued our research initiative and explored the faculty and student experience at a deeper level. While we were happy to capture the very high levels of student and faculty satisfaction, we wanted to better understand what factors were contributing to the effectiveness of the online courses. This work underscored the important value of student interaction, both with the professor as well as with classmates. We felt that a new conceptual framework for computer-mediated communication, called the community of inquiry (COI; Garrison, Anderson, & Archer, 2000), which was presented by Randy Garrison at one of the national research workshops held great promise as a guide for us to explore online learning. COI is based on three fundamental elements, teaching presence, social presence, and cognitive presence, and it is one of the most referenced theories for explaining and predicting learning outcomes in online courses. SLN conducted one of the first studies to explore teaching presence in a large online program, and our findings were noteworthy. We found a correlation between student satisfaction and reported learning with all three components of teaching presence—design and organization, facilitating discourse, and direct instruction. This was important since it underscored the vital role of the faculty member in the online course and how prominent and visible they needed to be.

With increased visibility for the SLN program came additional expectations for a more prominent role it could play in the system. During this phase of the program, SUNY was developing a strategic plan for the SUNY system, and SLN became a top-ten strategic initiative for SUNY. In addition to playing a vital role in enhancing access for students, it also was viewed as a potentially valuable instructional resource. The enhanced role in the system was also a focal point for working with the New York State Education Department. We were able to collaborate with the good staff at NYSED to share our work and best practices. There was mutual emphasis on quality of the academic experience for students.

Another dimension of the evolution of the SLN program that is worth noting is the creation of campus MIDs (multimedia instructional designer). As some campuses grew in terms of faculty involvement and courses offered, it became clear that a staff member, with instructional designs expertise (not IT/technical support), resident on the local campus, was required. While the expanding campuses were happy to add this support, the SLN organization needed to adjust to ensure that these new instructional designers were functioning exactly as one of our own MIDs. We needed them to follow best practices and adhere to appropriate processes. So we developed a model of training and support for the campus MIDs and viewed them as part of our extended instructional design team. They participated in all SLN meetings and events, and we basically functioned and operated as a virtual team. The only difference was their geographic location. The way we evolved, SLN allowed for alignment with the growth in faculty participation in the program and helped mitigate hiring freezes that happened from time to time at system administration. In this phase, this organizational model of distributed staff across the state was also applied to additional, and very talented, IT staff resources who managed our technology infrastructure.

While we worked on the long term financial plan, the growth in course offerings and faculty did not slow down! There were 1000 courses offered in 1999-2000, 1500 in 2000-01, and 2500 in 2001-02, as presented in the chart below. Our studies about the faculty experience revealed some very interesting ideas. Beyond the 96 percent level of satisfaction, faculty were more likely to report that their online students performed better than their classroom students, rate their interaction with online students as higher than their classroom students, and rate interaction between online students as higher than their classroom students. Ninety-three percent of faculty thought the online environment was appropriate for their course, 96 percent of faculty viewed the design of their online course as an opportunity to consider alternative means of instruction, 93 percent of faculty saw it as an opportunity to consider alternative means of assessment. Faculty were ten times more likely to report more systematic design of instruction in their online courses. An interesting and significant finding was that more than four out of five faculty thought that developing and teaching an online course would improve the way they taught in the traditional classroom.

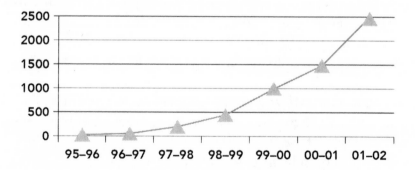

Figure 7.

With so many courses being offered, it is no surprise that we also experienced serious growth in complete degree programs. Certificates and degrees at all levels (associate, baccalaureate, and graduate) were available through SLN, as shown in the chart below.

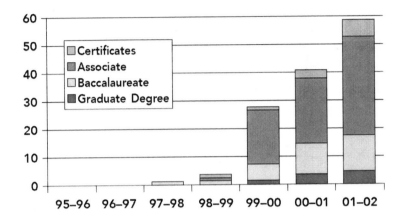

Figure 8.

Of course, student enrollments also continued to expand to 13,000 in 1999-2000, 25,000 in 2000-01 and 40,000 in 2001-02, as reflected in the chart below. We also collected interesting data about the student experience. Students providing feedback about their experience in a course on SLN noted more and higher quality interaction with faculty and with other students. In addition:

- 93 percent are more likely to ask questions.
- Twice as likely to actively participate in discussion.
- Twice as likely to ask for clarification.
- 83 percent improved their writing and communication skills.
- 80 percent put more thought into online discussion.
- 71 percent spent more time studying.
- 69 percent felt more comfortable asking an awkward question.
- 42 percent felt more comfortable disagreeing with instructor online, (Shea, Fredericksen, Pickett, & Pelz, 2002).

And when we asked students why they took a course on SLN, they reported a number of reasons related to schedule and convenience. Distance or proximity to the campus fell much farther down on the list of reasons, breaking or at least adjusting the presumptive notion of "distance learning." Online learning wasn't about distance—half of the students lived less than thirty minutes from the campus. The asynchronous aspect of online learning provided an instructional model that adapted to the schedule of the students.

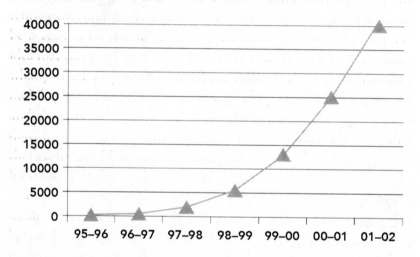

Figure 9.

Most of the remaining SUNY campuses joined the program during this last phase with, a total of forty-two campuses in 1999-2000, forty-seven campuses in 2000-01, and fifty-three campuses in 2001-02, as seen in Figure 10. It was an effective and helpful message to the new campuses joining the SLN program that we could help them skip starting from scratch as well as avoid some skinned knees along the way. We had become very effective at guiding a campus into online education.

The success of SLN was recognized by Educause, the nation's leading organization aimed at promoting the intelligent use of information technology. In 2001, Educause chose the SLN as the award recipient for Systemic Progress in Teaching and Learning, recognizing

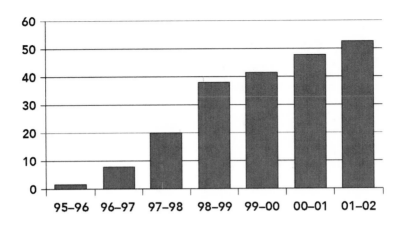

Figure 10.

the SLN's "transformative, sustainable, and replicable learner-centered teaching and learning" approaches. In addition, SLN also received the Sloan Consortium award for Excellence in Online Faculty Development in 2001 and the Sloan Consortium award for Institution Wide Online Programming in 2002. This was not too bad for a program that almost shut down during the first semester!

	Campuses	Courses	Enrollment	Sloan Funding
1995-1996	2	8	119	$1.4M Proof of Concept
1996-1997	8	34	460	
1997-1998	20	180	2060	$1.3M Proof of Scalability
1998-1999	37	460	6060	
1999-2000	42	1000+	13,000+	$1.3M Proof of Sustainability
2000-2001	47	1500+	25,000+	
2001-2002	53	2500+	40,000+	

Figure 11.

LESSONS LEARNED

We learned a lot during the development of SLN. And we accomplished a lot, as summarized in the following table.

We shared what we knew then, and it is a delight to return to this story and share lessons learned again. There is still valuable insight to be gleaned today.

The right organizational model is critical

A key factor in our success was the positioning of the SLN program in the university. We always felt that the online program needed to be integrated or woven into the academic fabric of the institution. This was counter to some other efforts at the time where other universities were spinning of separate entities—with substantial allocation of financial resources in some cases. We were frequently queried about these other approaches, but thankfully we persevered with our integrated model. There was a lot of media attention on virtual universities. But we used to say that we were *not* creating a virtual university, we were virtualizing our existing university."Culture and certain concepts in organizational theory in higher education (loosely coupled systems and organized anarchy) help explain some of the need for this positioning (Weick, 1976; Cohen & March, 1986). But the most salient part of this strategy was the essential role that faculty played in the development of the program. The primary role faculty plays in academic efforts aligns with the concept of professional bureaucracy (Mintzberg, 1986). We viewed this as a strength of SLN and a problem of other organizational models that created entities that were separated from the faculty.

Establishing a research initiative at the beginning of the program is vital

It won't surprise the reader of this chapter that we believe that establishing a research initiative at the beginning of a program is vital. As noted earlier, there are a number of benefits for this strategy. It will play a helpful and encouraging role with faculty, as it aligns with the spirit of the academy. Collecting and analyzing data about the faculty and student experience enables the program to capture what is working and what needs attention so that the endeavor can be continuously improved. And it can be advantageous for the institution to have this type of positive visibility.

It is important to publish, present, and contribute to the higher education community

Building on the importance of conducting research, it is important to share the results. They can be published and shared beyond the institution to the benefit of the field and the larger higher education community. Our ability to contribute to our colleagues at other institutions, as well as learn from them, was extremely valuable. We published numerous journal articles and book chapters and presented our work at state, national, and international conferences. Contributing to the larger higher education community helps us all.

Online learning is about pedagogyy, not technology

While new technologies are appealing, they are tools to support instruction. They are important, but they should be transparent, and the emphasis with online learning needs to be on pedagogy. Effective online learning programs center on supporting faculty members with the systematic design of instruction. A program needs to help faculty members with quality online course design through the consideration of alternative means of instruction and alternative means of assessment that align with the learning objectives of their courses. Leading with technology misses this essential and critical point and makes assumptions about the skills and experience of faculty members. While faculty members are experts and scholars in their field, our experience was that they might not have any background in designing and teaching online courses. This exact point was captured in the article *The Myth about Online Course Development* (Oblinger & Hawkins, 2006). This also tempers a view that only technically savvy faculty can teach online courses. This was not our experience. Our view was that good teaching is good teaching, and a professor who is a good instructor in a traditional classroom can also be a good instructor in an online classroom.

Establishing fundamental policies and practices are key
Building a program based on a solid foundation and fundamental policies can determine success or failure. The core principle of "a course is a course is a course" enabled us to appropriately address important issues as they arose. While some wanted online courses to be considered something different, we viewed them as the same. This approach leads to a common starting point. Rather than invent some new policy, we could begin analyzing issues from how they might be applied to a traditional classroom course, and then ask if the online nature of a course requires a different position or policy. If it helps, consider that we have consistent policies for traditional courses on our campuses, despite the variety. A large lecture hall course with hundreds of students is a different instructional experience than a small seminar class with fifteen students. This approach also helps determine who makes decisions about online courses. With our model, it is the same individuals who make decisions about traditional classroom courses. This also fits with the integration of online learning within the academy, rather than as a separated entity away from the faculty and academic leaders.

Address the questions that you understand at that moment in time
An interesting aspect of developing this program was that we were constantly solving problems and issues at every step. It should be noted that we could not have anticipated or understood every problem in advance. During the proof of concept phase, we would not have been able to conceive of the issues we needed to handle during the proof of scale or proof of sustainability phases. A program needed to deal with the problems directly in front of it and to know that there would be future ones to deal with. It was also important to not wait until we had the answer to every single question or issue to get started. If so, we would have never offered a single course.

Direct experience for your organization is valuable

There is a reason why they say experience is the best teacher. One's experience as a learner can really help one to understand. That is why we asked every member of the SLN organization to take at least one online course as a student so that they could comprehend the experience and be able to speak firsthand about it. Some people in SLN also developed and taught online courses so that they could appreciate the faculty experience. This enabled our entire group to break through misperceptions about online learning. As the leader of SLN, I even earned one of my graduate degrees completely online through SLN. This was a meaningful statement through all of the talks and conference presentations that were delivered. This knowledge and background was extremely valuable for our team overall, especially at that early point in time when online courses were not as common. It can be argued that this is a valuable strategy for today.

Individuals matter more than the size of the team

There is a saying that everyone is replaceable, but I don't agree with it. We had a very small core team, and every person was critical to the overall success of the program. I remain extremely grateful for all of their contributions, and for their passion and dedication to SLN. We benchmarked our program to other state systems and typically found much larger organizations with smaller results in terms of faculty and student enrollments. While we might have appreciated some additional resources, we would never trade any of our staff. *Who* you have on your team matters more than *how many* people you have on your team.

REFERENCES

Cohen, M., & March, J. (1986). Leadership in an organized anarchy. In M. C. Brown (Ed.), *Organization and governance in higher education* (5th ed., pp. 16-35). Boston, MA: Pearson.

Fredericksen, E., Pickett, A., Shea, P., Pelz, W., & Swan, K. (1999). Factors influencing faculty satisfaction with asynchronous teaching and learning in the SUNY Learning Network. In *Online education, Vol 1.* Retrieved from https://onlinelearningconsortium.org/book/online-education-volume-1-learning-effectiveness-and-faculty-satisfaction-1999/

Fredericksen, E., Pickett, A., Shea, P., Pelz, W., & Swan, K. (1999). Student satisfaction and perceived learning with online courses: Principles and examples from the SUNY Learning Network. In *Online education, Vol. 1.* Retrieved from https://onlinelearningconsortium.org/book/online-education-volume-1-learning-effectiveness-and-faculty-satisfaction-1999/

Garrison, D. R., Anderson, T., & Archer, W. (2000). Critical inquiry in a text-based environment: Computer conferencing in higher education. *The Internet and Higher Education, 2,* 2-3.

Mintzberg, H. (1979). The professional bureaucracy. In M. C. Brown (Ed.), *Organization and governance in higher education* (5th ed., pp. 50-70). Boston, MA: Pearson.

Oblinger, D. & Hawkins, B. (2006). The myth about online course development. *EDUCAUSE Review, 41,* 14-15.

Shea, P., Fredericksen, E., Pickett, A., & Pelz, W. (2003). A preliminary investigation of "teaching presence" in the SUNY learning network. *Journal of Asynchronous Learning Networks, 7*(2), 61-80.

Shea, P., Fredericksen, E., Pickett, A., Pelz, W. & Swan, K. (2001). Measures of learning effectiveness in the SUNY learning network. In *Online education, Vol 2.* Retrieved from https://onlinelearningconsortium.org/book/elements-of-quality-online-education-volume-3-in-the-sloan-c-series-2001/

Shea, P., Pelz, W., Fredericksen, E., & Pickett, A. (2002). Online teaching as a catalyst for classroom-based instructional transformation. In *Elements of quality online education.* (pp.103-126), Needham, MA: SCOLE.

Shea, P., Pelz, W., Fredericksen, E., & Pickett, A. (2004). Faculty development, student satisfaction, and reported learning in the SUNY Learning Network. In T. Duffy & J. Kirkley (Eds.), *Learner centered theory and practice in distance education* (pp. 343-377). Mahwah, NJ: Lawrence Earlbaum.

Shea, P., Swan, K., Fredericksen, E., & Pickett, A. (2001). Student satisfaction and reported learning in the SUNY learning network. In *Elements of quality online education, Vol 3.* Retrieved from https://onlinelearningconsortium.org/book/elements-of-quality-online-education-volume-3-in-the-sloan-c-series-2001/

Swan, K., Shea, P., Fredericksen, E., Pickett, A., Pelz, W. & Maher, G. (2000). Building knowledge building communities: Consistency, contact and communication in the virtual classroom. *Journal of Educational Computing Research, 23*(4), 389-413.

Weick, K. (1976). Educational organizations as loosely coupled systems. In M. C. Brown (Ed.), *Organization & governance in higher education* (5th ed., pp. 36-49). Boston, MA: Pearson.

THE CREATION OF SLOAN-C
History, Mission, and Evolution

John R. Bourne

Executive Director, Emeritus
The Sloan Consortium

INTRODUCTION

Over the years, from 1993 to 2012, the Alfred P. Sloan Foundation was one of the most important influencers in what has become known as online education. In this chapter about the creation and early years of the Sloan Consortium (Sloan-C), my recollections of will be used to describe what happened during the these years. I was first introduced to what the Sloan Foundation was planning in the area they called Learning Outside the Classroom in the early 1990s. Bourne met Burks Oakley at the Frontiers in Education conference in near Washington, DC in early November 1993. Oakley told me about the grant directions that Frank Mayadas, then newly appointed program officer at the Sloan Foundation, was pursuing. The introduction to Mayadas, and to the program he and Ralph

Gomory (then president of the Sloan Foundation) called Learning Outside the Classroom, would change what I would do for the next two decades. This chapter is the story of how the Sloan Consortium came to be, and what happened in the early years.

In the early 1990s, with grants from the Sloan Foundation, I had been conducting research about simulation of electronic circuits in laboratories. The meeting with Oakley precipitated an inquiry to Frank Mayadas about starting a group of universities that would collaborate to share information, what was later called a consortium—the Sloan Consortium, or Sloan-C. It was proposed to Mayadas that a journal be started to organize knowledge about what was going on among the grantees in the Learning Outside the Classroom program that Frank Mayadas and Gomory initiated.

A journal was started in 1997 with a grant made to Vanderbilt University, announced by the Sloan Foundation in October 1996. Authors were recruited to create articles for the first issue of the journal, which appeared in March 1997. Mayadas led off the issue with an article about the Sloan Foundation's perspective. The title of the journal was the *Journal of Asynchronous Learning Networks (JALN)*, so named to recognize the thinking at the time that online learning was mostly asynchronous and that learning occurred among networks of learners. The journal prospered and published about 400 articles in nearly fifteen years.

PURPOSE AND MISSION

The mission of the consortium was articulated in a 2009 edition of the Encyclopedia of Distance Learning as: "The purpose of the Sloan Consortium (Sloan-C) is to help learning organizations continually improve quality, scale, and breadth according to their own distinctive missions, so that education will become a part of everyday life, accessible and affordable for anyone, anywhere, at any time, in a wide variety of disciplines. Created with funding from the Alfred P. Sloan Foundation, Sloan-C encourages the collaborative sharing of knowledge and effective practices to improve online education in learning effectiveness, access, affordability for learners and providers, and student and faculty satisfaction." (Moore et al., 2009).

By 2016, the web page of the Online Learning Consortium (OLC, the successor organization of Sloan-C) stated, "OLC is the leading professional organization devoted to advancing quality online learning by providing professional development, instruction, best practice publications and guidance to educators, online learning professionals and organizations around the world.". From this quote, it seems clear that the original focus of Sloan-C in helping "learning organizations" shifted the focus to helping individuals in the field of online learning. This thinking is consistent with idea of shifting the organization to become a standalone institution funded by membership.

HISTORY AND FUNDING

Continuing the personal recollection paradigm for this chapter, the chronology of the evolution of Sloan-C is perhaps best understood by examining how the Sloan Foundation funded the operation of the central unit (headquarters) of what began as an informal organization and transitioned into a 501(c)(3) nonprofit organization. In the Learning Outside the Classroom initiative, the Sloan Foundation was in the business of making grants to promising areas to pursue research, development, and creation of applications. I was fortunate enough to receive grants that helped develop a central unit to organize building the headquarters of the consortium. The history of grants provided tells a story. The amounts and dates of grants provided by the Sloan Foundation and others demonstrate how thinking moved from one area to another as various aspect of the consortium were developed. The grants below are annotated with remarks that will help the reader understand the progression of how development occurred. Grants from the foundation are listed as well as grants from other sources that directly assisted in the growth of the consortium.

The initial grants from the Sloan Foundation were made to Vanderbilt University (Nashville, TN) in the years 1995 until 2000. I was a Professor at Vanderbilt until moving to the Franklin W. Olin College of Engineering (Needham, MA) in 2000.

Grants made to Vanderbilt University in support of the Sloan Consortium:

- **Sloan Foundation.** Study of asynchronous laboratory learning, $399,000, 1995-96.
  - *This was the first grant; it introduced me to the foundation and I began work organizing online learning in the area of laboratories online.

- **Sloan Foundation.** Study of ALN journal and newsletter, $30,000, 1996.
  - *I began to study how a journal and newsletter could help organize thinking about ALN (Asynchronous Learning Networks) among the community of universities that were beginning to become aware of the potential for online education. The first universities to become engaged were the Sloan Foundation grantees engaged in a variety of projects.

- **Sloan Foundation.** ALN journal and web, $185,500, 1996.
  - *The grant established the ALN journal (called the *Journal of Asynchronous Learning Networks (JALN)* and created the first website.

- **Sloan Foundation.** Management of technology online, $133,000, 1997.
  - *A first grant in a content area was made to Vanderbilt to create a management of technology program online.

- **Sloan Foundation.** ALN talk and conference, $60,000, 1997.
  - *The concept of creating a listserv was implemented and a first conference funded.

- **Microsoft Corporation.** Support of ALN conference and 200 copies of FrontPage software, $20,000, 1997.
  - *Workshops eventually became a mainstay of the to-be consortium. The grant of software from Microsoft paved the way for a successful implementation of a workshop to teach faculty how to create online courses.

- **Allaire Corporation.** Support of ALN workshop, ten copies of Allaire Forums, $10,000, 1997.
  - *Allaire Corporation provided a grant to implement forums for communication.

- **Hewlett Packard Corporation.** Donation of HP LH Server, $19,000, 1997.
  - *HP donated servers to implement the first web server for the informal consortium.

- **Sloan Foundation.** ALN web renewal, $270,000, 1998.
  - *The foundation continued and increased funding in 1998.

- **Hewlett Packard Foundation.** Donation of HP LX Server, $36,000, 1998.

- **Microsoft Corporation.** Continued Support, donation of 100 copies of FrontPage software, 1998.
  - *Workshops were doing well and Microsoft provided more copies of FrontPage, an early software system for developing websites.

- **Sloan Foundation.** ALN workshop on strategic planning, $26,000, July 1998.
  - * By 1998, it became time to plan strategies for the future.

- **Sloan Foundation.** Sloan online ALN reporting systems, $30,000, January 1999.
  - * In 1999, additional funding was provided to begin to put a system for reporting what work was going on in ALN.

- **Sloan Foundation.** ALN web renewal, $700,000, April 1999.
  - * By 1999, work was proceeding briskly with the journal, web and workshops and the foundation began to provide larger amounts of funding.

- **Hewlett Packard Corporation.** Donation of HP computer, $38,000, 1999.

- **Sloan Foundation.** Prototype of ALN program directory, $30,000, 1999.
  - * Also in 1999, a prototype of a directory of ALN programs was created to track how online programs were developing nationwide.

Grants made to Olin College in support of the Sloan Consortium:

The Sloan Foundation funding to Vanderbilt University ended in 1999, and the next grants were made to Olin College in Needham, MA. I moved to Olin in 2000 as a founding faculty member at the Franklin W. Olin College of Engineering.

- **Sloan Foundation.** Sloan Center at Olin and Babson Colleges, $350,000. Fall 2000.

*Olin College, in collaboration with Babson College, established a Sloan Center in 2000 located physically at Olin College in Needham, Ma.

- **Sloan Foundation.** Jumpstarting the Sloan speakers and consultants bureau, $45,000, Fall 2000.
  *Early work included building a speakers and consultants bureau and managing a quality initiative for the Army University.

- **Sloan Foundation.** Managing the Army University Quality Initiative Jumpstart, $45,000, Spring 2001.

From 2001 through 2013, grants from the Sloan Foundation continued on an annual basis to fund the operation of the consortium, as indicated below.

- **Sloan Foundation.** Sloan-C, $690,000, Summer 2001.

- **Sloan Foundation.** Sloan-C, $750,000, Summer 2002.

- **Sloan Foundation.** ASTD conference: $45,000 and $85,000.

- **Sloan Foundation.** Sloan-C, $720, 000, Summer 2003.

- **Sloan Foundation Sloan-C.** $900,000, Summer 2004.

- **Sloan Foundation.** Summer workshop, Victoria, CA, $105,000.

- **Sloan Foundation.** Core support proposal renewal, $1,000,000, July 1, 2005.

- **Sloan Foundation.** Summer workshop, Baltimore, MD, $101,000, 2005-06.

- **Sloan Foundation.** Sloan Semester grant for hurricane relief, $1,100,000.
    * Hurricane Katrina disrupted learning in New Orleans; the Foundation stepped up to fund an online effort for students who were displaced from learning activities.

- **Elluminate gift of services.** $184,000.
    * Elluminate (now part of Blackboard Collaborate) provided online synchronous services for meetings.

- **Sloan Foundation.** President's Initiative, $45,000.
    * The President's Initiative was a series of meetings to provide presidents of universities information about online learning.

- **Sloan Foundation.** Sloan-C renewal of grant 2006-07, $1,030,000, July, 2006.

- **Sloan Foundation.** Emerging technologies symposium, $100,000, 2008.

- **Sloan Foundation.** Start-up of Sloan Consortium Award, $4,000,000, 2008-13.
    * The final award made from the Sloan Foundation was dedicated to transitioning Sloan-C to a free standing, non-grant-supported non profit institution.

THE INFORMAL ORGANIZATION YEARS

From 1996 until incorporation in 2008, the Sloan Consortium was an informal group of individuals and colleges/universities. Originally drawing from the awardees of grants from the Sloan Foundation, the membership grew over the years. Starting from an online journal, workshops, and conferences, the consortium grew by providing inviting information and training largely for faculty. Vendors became interested and invested a bit in helping the consortium (see listing above). Screenshots of early work on the website are provided below so one can observe changes in the look and feel of the web, journal, and workshop presence.

Website

The first website for information consortium was hosted at Vanderbilt University on servers supplied by Hewlett Packard. The first URL utilized was http://www.aln.org. Figure 1 shows a screenshot from 1997.

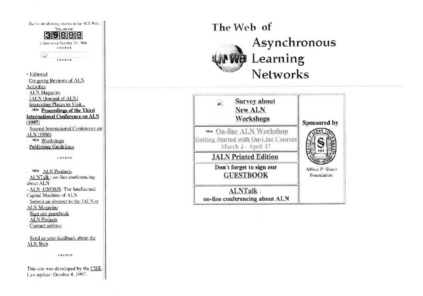

Figure 1: Website from 1997 featuring ALN. All figures used with permission of OLC.

The screen shot provides an idea of the things that were being tested in that early time period. The first issues of *JALN* had been published online. Figure 2 is a screenshot listing the contents of the first issue. Frank Mayadas authored the lead article for the first issue.

JALN

Journal of Asynchronous Learning Networks

Volume 1, Issue 1 - March 1997

ISSN 1092-8235

Go To JALN Discussion

TABLE OF CONTENTS

Asynchronous Learning Networks: A Sloan Foundation Perspective
Frank Mayadas
Program Officer, The Alfred P. Sloan Foundation

The Economics of ALN: Some Issues
Lanny Arvan
Associate Professor of Economics
Associate Director, Sloan Center for Asynchronous Learning Environments (SCALE)
University of Illinois at Urbana-Champaign

Costs for the Development of a Virtual University
Murray Turoff
Distinguished Professor of Computer and Information Science
New Jersey Institute of Technology

Gender Similarity in the Use of and Attitudes About ALN in a University Setting
John C. Ory
Cheryl Bullock
Kristine Burnaska
University of Illinois at Urbana-Champaign

Writing Across the Curriculum Encounters Asynchronous Learning Networks or WAC Meets Up With ALN
Gail E. Hawisher
Michael A. Pemberton
Department of English
University of Illinois, Urbana-Champaign

A Model for On-Line Learning Networks in Engineering Education
J. R. Bourne, Ph.D, Professor of Electrical and Computer Engineering, Professor of Management of Technology
A. J. Brodersen, Ph.D , Professor of Electrical and Computer Engineering
J. O. Campbell, Ph.D , Research Associate Professor of Engineering Education
M. M. Dawant, M.S., Research Instructor of Electrical Engineering
R. G. Shiavi, Ph.D, Professor of Biomedical Engineering,
Center for Innovation in Engineering Education, Vanderbilt University

"FREE TRADE" IN HIGHER EDUCATION
The Meta University
William H. Graves
University of North Carolina at Chapel Hill

Figure 2: Issue 1, JALN, *1997.*

A variety of changes in the look and feel of the website occurred as the work evolved. Figures 3 through 7 show several incarnations of the front pages—continually reflecting improvements in the way web pages could be presented. The name changed for a short while to netlearning.org and finally to www.sloanconsortium.org with an alias of www.sloan-c.org (2000). After the organization became self-sufficient, the name changed to www.onlinelearningconsortium.org (2014).

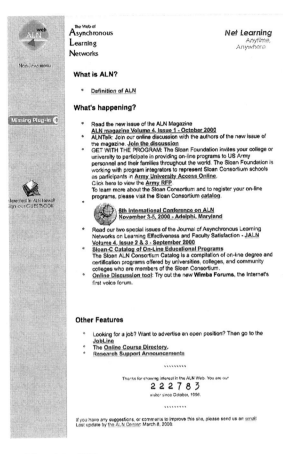

Figure 3: Evolution of the website, 1999.

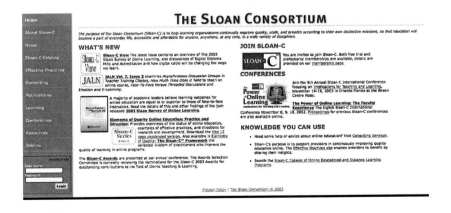

Figure 4: Evolution of the website, 2003.

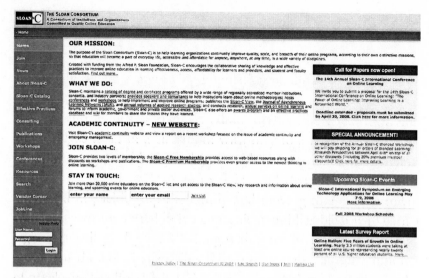

Figure 5: Evolution of the website, 2007.

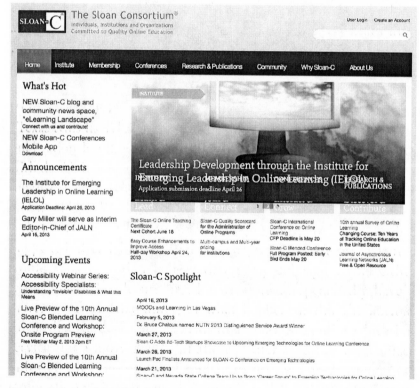

Figure 6: Evolution of the website, 2013.

Figure 7: Evolution of the website, 2016.

Journal

The Journal of Asynchronous Learning Networks followed the mantra from the outset that authors should have actually done something—collected data, demonstrated advancements—in short, made a real contribution to the literature in the papers published. For the first issues, articles were all recruited. The journal was then opened for contributions, and articles submitted were reviewed by an editorial panel. In the early years, it was difficult to secure articles that fit the criterion above. However, as time progressed, more and more articles were submitted, associate editors appointed, and a robust flow of articles became available.

Workshops

As early as 1997 and 1998, the first workshop—"Getting Started with Online Courses"—was offered by the emerging consortium. Created at Vanderbilt University, the course offered the following topics online:

- Reviewing and exploring existing ALN courses
- Learning the basics of HTML language
- Creating web pages using the Microsoft FrontPage
- Building a syllabus and assignment pages for your own course
- Creating course materials
- Using Multimedia for course materials
- Adding discussion tools to your course

At the time, the staff at the headquarters unit of the consortium felt that the workshop was a huge success. Microsoft provided copies of FrontPage (a now-discontinued editing and website administration tool) for participants, and many faculty were off and running, creating their courses in these pre-course-management-systems days. This workshop was the jumpstart for the highly successful series of workshops created in the late 2000s and persists today at OLC.

Communication Among Members

An early objective on the work of the consortium was to provide a means for people in the Asynchronous Learning Network world to communicate with each other, sharing knowledge about what they were learning about what was then called ALN. A listserv was started along with a website called ALNTalk. Over the following decades, communication with the listserv increased, and became a stable communication vehicle. A content management system was implemented in later years to provide segmented topic areas. As technology progressed, discussions were moved to LinkedIn, Facebook, and other social media outlets.

Conferences

The first International Conference on Asynchronous Learning Networks was held in Philadelphia, PA, in October 1995. Conferences over the next three years were held in New York at the Marriott, World Trade Center. The University of Maryland University College hosted the 1999 and 2000 conferences. In 2001 the conference moved to Orlando, FL, hosted by the University of Central Florida, and has remained there ever since.

During the same period, a conference on blended learning was initiated and a conference on technology created. These conferences proved to be a mainstay of the Sloan Consortium and attracted many attendees with papers, workshops, and vendor displays. The program of vendor support proved to be a vital source of income for the consortium.

Books, Effective Practices, Awards, Membership, Surveys

A variety of means for engaging Sloan-C participants' interests were tried during the early years of organization, and many have continued. Books that captured knowledge at conferences (proceedings) and stand-alone books were produced, both in print form and as downloadable files. Members' effective practices were reported and awards given at the annual conference to recognize them. A full slate of awards was implemented for individuals and institutions. A survey was implemented in collaboration with the Babson Survey Research group, which became very popular and widely cited. Membership both for institutions and individuals was introduced, offering discounts on conferences, workshops, and publications and other materials.

Fellows

In late 2009, the fellows program of Sloan-C was established to recognize individuals who had shown the following:

- Outstanding and extraordinary qualifications in the field of online learning
- Significant experience in online learning or an allied field
- A record of distinguished service to OLC or the field
- Extraordinary contributions or leadership in the field of online learning

Since that time, thirty-eight individuals have been recognized in six classes (including 2015). Recognized each year at the annual meeting of the consortium, these fellows have contributed greatly to the success of the consortium.

What Worked to Make Sloan-C Viable?

Overall, conferences seem to provide the most valuable feature of Sloan-C. Conferences provided the best learning experience for membership by including workshops, paper presentations, and contact with vendors. Of course, the latter helped fuel the ability to become self-sustaining. Awards seemedd to bolster conferences, as members and non-members could attend conferences to be recognized by their peers. Likewise, recognition as a fellow or as the purveyor of effective practices proved popular. In short, to learn, to talk, to meet new people, and to be recognized were, not surprisingly, among the things people in the new organization perceived as most important.

In terms of external recognition, the *JALN* (now the *Online Learning Journal*) successfully cast the Sloan Consortium in the light of being a leader in purveying knowledge about online learning. Likewise, workshops garnered attention from faculty wanting to learn about online learning, and the surveys provided needed information for chief academic officers, the press, and others.

The combination of these offerings propelled Sloan-C to the position of becoming a stand-alone organization, operating with funding from memberships, conference registrations, publications, workshop income, grants, gifts, and sponsors.

LEADERSHIP

The leadership of the Alfred P. Sloan Foundation was responsible, through its grants, programs, and insightful management, for the creation of what has to become known as online learning. While other groups contributed, in my opinion, the large investments in grants made by the foundation in the Learning Outside the Classroom programs had a very major impact on how online learning progressed. As early as 2001, the Sloan Foundation website (www. sloan.org) provided information about asynchronous learning.

"LEARNING OUTSIDE THE CLASSROOM"

The Sloan Program in Asynchronous Learning: Anytime, Anywhere, Online

The goal here was to make available quality higher education and training anytime and anywhere for anyone who was motivated to seek it. Grants had gone to institutions of higher education to encourage their use of Asynchronous Learning Networks (ALNs), which made possible electronic access at any time to remote learning resources such as instructors, fellow students, text, and software. Sixty institutions, ranging from elite universities to community colleges, had directly received grants from the Sloan Foundation, constituting the Sloan Consortium.

Ralph Gomory, President, Alfred P. Sloan Foundation, 1989-2007

Ralph Gomory became president of the foundation after a distinguished career at IBM. He was instrumental in the conception of the Learning Outside the Classroom program and supported the growth of the program during the formative years of the consortium. He remains senior advisor to the consortium.

Frank Mayadas, Program Director, Alfred P. Sloan Foundation, 1992-2012

Mayadas was recruited from IBM by Gomory to lead various initiatives at the foundation, including the Learning Outside the Classroom program. He vigorously pursued excellence in this program and is responsible for the success of the program. He was the founding president of the consortium and remains on the board.

The Sloan-C Board of Directors

The early board of directors for the consortium consisted of individuals selected because of their involvement in the grants program of the foundation. Mayadas became the first president. An early listing (July 2003) of board members showed a very small number: Anthony Picciano (CUNY), Burks Oakley (University of Illinois) and Gary Miller (Penn State University). Since that time, the board of the organization has grown considerably. As of 2016, the board has eighteen members.

The Executive Directors

I was the founding executive director, retired in late 2011, and was recognized by the board of directors on Nov 11, 2011. A search of the next executive director occurred, and Bruce Chaloux was selected, along with the addition of a new title—chief executive officer. Bruce Chaloux died an untimely death on September 28, 2013, and after an extensive search, Kathleen Ives was selected as the new CEO and executive director. She remains in this post as of 2017.

TRANSITION FROM INFORMAL TO FORMAL STATUS

Formalization

For the time period from the late 1990s until 2008, the consortium was an information organization. A final four-year grant was provided by the Sloan Foundation in 2008 to enable transition to a self-sustaining organization. In 2008, incorporation as a non profit 501(c)(3) was obtained in the state of Massachusetts, and the transition to being a formal organization began. Anticipated income to the incorporated non profit was envisioned as being generated primarily by conferences, membership dues, and workshop income. Six years later, at the request of the foundation, on July 7, 2014, the name of the organization was changed to the Online Learning Consortium (OLC).

OBSERVATIONS

The Sloan Foundation model was highly successful. It started with exploratory grants to many institutions, then created a centralized organization that would consolidate activities benefitting both higher education institutions and faculty. Identifying what worked and what didn't and then providing a means for transition from the grants programs to a fully self-sustaining nonprofit organization worked very well. Basically, starting slowly and building out carefully was the model. Did it work? Yes, we think so—given that OLC is now a viable non-profit and is working well to provide knowledge about online learning to the world.

REFERENCES

Moore, J. C., Bourne, J. R., & Mayadas, A. F. (2009). The Sloan Consortium. In P. Rogers, G. Berg, J. Boettcher, C. Howard, L. Justice, & K. Schenk (Eds.) *Encyclopedia of Distance Learning, Second Edition* (pp. 1884-1893). Hershey, PA: Information Science Reference. doi:10.4018/978-1-60566-198-8.ch278

NOTES

Many of the dates listed in this article have been verified with the "Wayback Machine" https://archive.org/web/ which maintains an Internet archive. Not all information is available but a sufficient amount was secured to enable feeling fairly accurate about the dates listed.

AN INTERVIEW WITH DARCY HARDY
A Profile in Institutional Innovation

Associate Vice President, Enterprise Consulting
Blackboard

WILLIAM PATRICK: Let's start at the beginning. How did you get started in online learning? I know you've been involved with it for over twenty-five years.

DARCY HARDY: I started in distance learning in the late '80s and, through that, evolved into audio conferencing and video conferencing when I was at the University of Texas at Austin, at the time when the University of Texas System was rethinking how they looked at distance learning. This was around 1996, and that was the time when we were all starting to get excited about the Internet for learning. I was asked to lead a strategic planning group on how the University of Texas System could think about meeting the needs of students at a distance in a better way. That led to us establishing what was called the UT TeleCampus, and that was in 1997. I ended up moving over to the System offices and leaving the UT Austin campus, which is about

226

eight blocks, but I went down to the System offices, where I helped to build and then ran the TeleCampus for the next thirteen years.

WP: I know this was all a long time ago, but can you remember how you felt near the beginning of this? What was your attitude, your motivation? Why distance education?

DH: Couple of things. When I got into distance learning, I was working on my doctorate. This was around 1988. And I have a colleague who is here at Texas State University, used to be called Southwest Texas State, here in San Marcos, Texas, and she is still a faculty member there. At the time, we were at a dinner club and I was all excited, talking about this new thing that I was getting involved with around distance learning—using technology, taking correspondence study to the next level, and taking education to the students through technology. And she said very clearly that she thought the whole thing was a flash in the pan, this whole distance learning thing, and that it was never going to take off. Even when we got to the point where the Internet was taking off, she would always tell me I was going to waste my career on this stuff. I run into her all the time—as a matter of fact, I saw her a month ago, when she was here at our house. Every time I see her, she says, "Don't say it. I know, you were right. Don't say it."

WP: Let's talk more about Texas. You've been there most of your career, right?

DH: I have been. I started at what is now Texas State as a grad student and a junior faculty member. Then I went to the University of Texas at Austin in 1988. I was in the middle of my doctoral program, and I did an internship at a curriculum center at UT Austin. It was very serendipitous. I was there to do my internship around curriculum development and while I was there, this fellow—who was running a fledgling audio conference/distance learning program for high school students to take health occupations courses across the state—he left, for various reasons. And someone came up to me at that office and said, "You're an Instructional Technology major. Have you taken any courses on instructional telecommunications?" Well, I had taken one course. There was only one course at the time. And so they said, "Since you've taken that course, why don't you take this program over?"

I knew nothing. I had taken the course but it was so archaic, even outdated at that time. But I took over this fledgling distance learning program that was for students who lived in rural parts of Texas. We connected them by telephone through an audio conference bridge. I mean, literally, this is where you were pulling the wires out and plugging them in to the bridge. We had a teacher outside of Dallas who was a certified health occupations teacher, and she would teach students across the state because they came from very small school districts that couldn't afford to have health occupations teachers. But yet these students wanted to go into these areas.

I did that for a few years and we started expanding it. We added Spanish, 1, 2, and 3. We added the program I'm probably still most proud of: we added an algebra course. We called it algebra across the Wire, and it was designed for migrant students—students of migrant workers who had left school early, before the school year was over, and usually returned late. All of them struggled with math. They usually failed algebra or high school math. So we built this program, and we built it to be taught by telephone. So we were teaching algebra-by-telephone to kids of migrant parents who were scattered around the US It was wildly successful, and I think that was when my thinking actually started changing around what's possible using technology, because everyone told us it was not possible to teach math by telephone. What we ended up with was a methodology that ultimately, although they didn't know anything about us, the Math Teaching Association agreed with. Around that time is when they started talking about the need for students to explain how they came up with their responses, instead of just walking up to a chalkboard and showing how they did a problem. They actually had to talk it through and explain how they came up with their solutions. It all happened about this same time, so we were really successful.

I didn't become a zealot—and I am not now a zealot—around distance learning, thinking that it's all things for all people and that everything can be taught at a distance and you don't need any face-to-face time and you never need to have an instructor with you, holding your hand, to walk you through something. I'm not like that. But I also don't buy it when somebody says, "Well, that's great for that discipline, but we could never teach that for our discipline." That's when I cry, Foul, and start thinking, "*Well, yes, things can be done here.*" The only reason I mention all that is because I think that sort of framed my thinking going into the '90s, and into online, when people again said that we couldn't deliver something online for X, Y, and Z reasons. It has to be face-to-face.

Anyway, fast forward to when I started working at the UT System and we started building out the TeleCampus. At the time there was, and there still are, fifteen University of Texas campuses. UT Austin is the flagship, but there are nine total academic institutions, and six medical, or health, institutions, and a handful of those had already been dabbling with the idea of using the Internet to teach. They were already starting to do some things with online. Every school in the System was already doing video conferencing—it was there, and we all used it, but it didn't explode like online learning did. So we had some schools that were already doing it.

The idea behind the TeleCampus was to centralize some of the activities that are necessary for a successful online program, so that every institution in the UT System didn't have to do it themselves and reinvent the wheel each time. So we started out by building sort of a virtual campus, though it was never degree-granting and never intended to be degree-granting but it was a service-oriented unit that would support online learning for all of the campuses in the UT System. It was really focused around three major areas: one was course development and technology; another one was around marketing and communications; and the last but not least one was around student services. The TeleCampus built out these three areas and then worked with the institutions in coordinating programs and pushing for collaborative programs, multicampus programs where two or more campuses would work on a particular degree program so no one set of faculty had to bear the burden of creating all of the courses. We'd split it up and offer a collaborative degree that ran through the TeleCampus but where the enrollments actually belonged to the institutions so they benefited from the tuition fees.

WP: Right. While they may not have been degree-granting, students still got their credits.

DH: They got all their credits from the institutions. But we facilitated it, and we wrapped things around the programs that the institutions themselves couldn't do. For example, marketing: it's changed a little bit now, but back then, and even for the most part now, most institutions don't have a huge marketing unit, and if they do they're marketing the institution as a whole. Well, back then, it was really important for there to be a marketing effort for the programs these campuses were offering online. And so we coordinated that effort. We branded the institutions through the TeleCampus, and we marketed the TeleCampus in places where students were looking for online programming. So the students may not be looking at UT Tyler in Midland/Odessa for a particular program, but they're looking for a kinesiology master's degree that may be online and it's through the TeleCampus, but it just so happens that six universities, including UT Tyler, are the ones that are offering the program. So the marketing efforts were a great service that we centralized.

We also centralized things like 24/7 help desk support. Most of the campuses in the UT System are not the size of UT Austin, and they don't have the funding or the resources that a UT Austin might have. Same is true with some of the medical schools. The medical schools have more funding to do these kinds of things, but they don't do a lot of online. So 24/7 support was coordinated through the TeleCampus.

Back in those early days, digital libraries were fairly new. Only the larger schools would have really a good level of digital resources for students. We piggybacked on licenses at UT Austin and others and we built out the UT TeleCampus digital library, which every student who was enrolled in any of the programs offered through the TeleCampus would be able to access. So we could level the playing ground.

One example is that we had an MBA that was collaborative. It involved eight institutions. Out of those eight institutions, I think one or two could access LexisNexis, which was the digital resource critical for MBA students. Now they all do, but at the time, most of our schools only had it face-to-face. They couldn't afford to offer the digital version. But we could offer that through the TeleCampus by piggybacking on UT Austin's license, at the time, and we could make it available for the students enrolled in the program regardless of whether or not they were enrolled in a course offered by UT Austin or not. They were in the MBA online program even if the course credit was coming from UT Brownsville, for instance. So they could get to those resources.

WP: Yeah, that sounds really important.

DH: It was at the time. Now every campus has a digital library. Every campus has access to those. But it was groundbreaking at that time to bring the services together. Our mantra for the TeleCampus was always around the following: make whatever is available to students on campus available to students online. If you're going to get in the space, you can't tell a student that they have to come to campus for anything. And that may seem kind of . . . People would say, "Why would you even think that?" Well, back then, we were going uphill in trying to convince campuses that you couldn't play in this space of online learning if you expected the students to come to campus to get an ID card. Or if you were going to charge them parking fees. There were certain things that these learners would never need and they didn't need to pay for. Now student services fees around libraries, and costs like that, absolutely.

I think we were groundbreaking in the sense that we developed a centralized/decentralized model. We sat at the system level; we recognized ourselves as a service unit—to serve the faculty and the students at those campuses, at our campuses—but we drew a line between what should logically remain on a campus and what logically could be centralized. And among the things that remained under the purview of the campus was, first of all, the faculty. We didn't take the faculty. They were teaching courses for their institutions. They were teaching them in-load, but the credit for their teaching and the credit for the courses—and the students for those courses—belonged to that institution for that course.

We also made sure that instructional designers were on the campuses while we coordinated and oversaw and mandated quality standards for these courses. We worked with all of those designers, and we actually provided funding for all the campuses to pay for an instructional designer if they didn't already have one. But those designers needed to be on the campuses to hold the hands of those faculty, and to sit down with them face-to-face, to help move them in a new direction. So we saw that as important.

What we did, we would supplement, if a campus needed help to do some high-end course development that they didn't have anyone to do, and our team also built all kinds of technology things for the campuses: we built flash templates; we built an online evaluation system, so that we wouldn't have to mail a course evaluation to students who were enrolled online; we designed things like a simulation engine that was still open source. So while we didn't actually build all of the courses, we were that course development and technology shop that built and designed things that made course development and faculty teaching and student learning better, for not only the courses and the faculty and the students, but also for the institutions themselves.

WP: Why did they hold onto the UT TeleCampus name, because the word "TeleCampus" connotes television distance learning from the '80s?

DH: Well, the TeleCampus is gone. The TeleCampus was "sunsetted," to use the chancellor's word at the time, in 2010. The decision was made in 2010 that there was no longer a need for this centralized unit because the campuses could do all of it themselves. They were all advanced enough to do this on their own and there was no longer a need to have anything centralized.

WP: Did that turn out to be true?

DH: Well, that's not really my place to say at this point.. But once that decision was made, they let go all twenty-six members of the staff, all of whom are in great positions now. I went to DC and worked with the Obama administration for three years. So we all landed well. But then the System turned around and invested fifty million dollars in building another unit, called the Institute for Transformational Learning, which is doing some really neat things, especially now around competency-based education (CBE), but they're still doing some of the same things that we did for the campuses. It's just under a new chancellor. However, the dissolution of the TeleCampus sent shock waves—it was in *Inside Higher Ed*; it was in *The Chronicle*; there were a lot of people who voiced opinions about how this shouldn't have happened, because we were also a kind of R&D group. Our colleagues, who were at other institutions and in other systems across the state, they would look to us to help them think through what they were doing with their online programs and looked at us as examples. We won every award you could win as an organization, but the decision to dissolve it was one that we had to respect. While we weren't happy about it, we all moved on.

WP: Well, as you said, you certainly landed on your feet if you moved to Washington and worked with the Obama administration.

DH: Well, I did that as an IPA (Intergovernmental Personnel Act) employee for three years, and then I came to Blackboard in January of 2014. I helped build out what is now called Enterprise Consulting. I have a team of eight former academics who have been doing this kind of work for a long time and now we consult with institutions—colleges and universities, and organizations like The Nuclear Regulatory Commission, in building out their online presence and all aspects of what it takes to get there.

WP: Can we talk about those two separately? Could you talk about your three years in government, and then move on to your time with Blackboard?

DH: Sure. Again, weird things have happened. The announcement to close the TeleCampus was made on April 8 in 2010, and in June of 2010 I got an e-mail from the Deputy Director of the Office of Science and Technology Planning (OSTP) at the White House. This is where NASA is housed, along with Technology Policy. I got an e-mail from this guy named Tom Kalil and he said, "My name is Tom Kalil. I'm wondering if you have the time to visit tomorrow about a position in the Obama administration. I'd like to visit with you."

So we talked, and as it turned out, what they needed help with was that there was a two billion dollar grant program that was spread out over four years, with 500 million dollars each year, starting in 2011. It had just gotten off the ground. The president had just announced it. Congress had just approved it. The grant was coming through the Department of Labor, and one of the things that needed to be embedded in this grant program was a requirement for any school that received funds to engage in some type of technology-enabled online learning in order to reach the workforce people that this grant was targeting. So at first, the grant was all about helping displaced workers get back into the job market, or to elevate their positions in the workforce.

My job was to go to DC, work at the Department of Labor for a year, and help in the office that was facilitating the Trade Adjustment Assistance Community College and Career Training Grants Program (TAACCCT), and really help guide their requirements and the knowledge-base at the department around online learning and technology-enabled learning and the different aspects of that. That's a quick summary of what my role was.

So I went to DC, got an apartment there, and went back and forth between home in Texas and Washington. Then I was asked to stay a second year with the Department of Labor, and I did that, and I was planning to end my time there at the end of 2012. But the under secretary of the Department of Education, Martha Kanter, asked me if I would come over to the Department of Education for a year and work with their unit that dealt with adult literacy and how to use technology to extend the reach of adult literacy programs across the country. I learned so much while I was there, but one thing I learned was that there are 37 million adults who fall below literacy levels in this country, and our federal programs are only reaching two million of those. So you've got a pretty huge gap.

While not all people who are below literacy levels would necessarily do well in an online environment, many of them could. And so the idea of putting some of the programming online, in order to make it more accessible and available for people who need literacy-skills training, would be helpful. So I worked on that for a year. And then, at the end of 2013, I said, "I'm done."

WP: Why did you feel that way?

DH: Well, I had been away from home for three years and, even though our children are grown, I mean my husband was here in Texas—and the dogs and the cat and my home. I lived in a little apartment in DC, which I loved. Actually, I loved my time there. I made some fabulous friends, and I lived within walking distance to the Mall. I went all over DC. I even got to go to the Rose Garden when the president was signing a bill. There were experiences there that pretty much shaped me for the next wave of whatever I was going to do, so I was ready. I did the project I needed to do at the Department of Education. I had done what I needed to do at the Department of Labor, and I was ready to come home.

WP: How different was that experience—working in government—than working in academia for you?

DH: It's so funny. I tell people, when I was at the University of Texas at Austin, every college and every school—whether it was the College of Engineering or the School of Education—they all work in a silo. I don't care how hard you try. They generally don't work across schools and colleges. They do their own things, and sometimes they have faculty meetings, or faculty senates where there are representatives from every school and college and department, but they don't work together unless there is a reason to collaborate. And when I was at the University of Texas System, with the TeleCampus, I witnessed that at an institutional level. The University of Texas at Austin didn't necessarily work with the University of Texas at Brownsville or the University of Texas at Permian Basin or Tyler or San Antonio. They didn't really work together, so when we came forward with the TeleCampus, it was one of the first times when there was actually a system-wide—I mean in recent times—a system-wide initiative where the System put this service entity together. We really worked to get them to work across campuses and to work in teams and in multicampus degree programs and things like that.

When I went to DC, and worked at the Department of Education and the Department of Labor it was no different. They work in silos, even though there are all these secretaries, of labor or health or education or whatever, who were appointed by the same guy. They're all appointed by the president. At the University of Texas System, there is one chancellor. At the University of Texas at Austin, there is one president. But yet all of the leaders in all of these places work for their own organizations, primarily, and to the point where they don't necessarily cross-pollinate and collaborate. It's not the federal government's fault; it's not the university system's fault; it's not the fault of the universities themselves. It's the way people work, unless there is something out there that gets them to work together.

With the TAACCCT Grant Program, even though the Department of Labor received the funding, that program was developed and delivered in conjunction and in partnership with the Department of Education. There was a forced partnership there and, while it wasn't always pretty, they worked together. But that's not the norm—not the norm there, and not the norm in a university system, and not the norm at an institution. That was a huge eye-opener for me—to realize it doesn't matter at what level you're working. There are going to be silos, and somebody has got to take steps forward to get people to work together or they never will.

WP: Bear with me: this is a half-baked thought that just occurred to me. I know you've done a lot of work with the International Forum for Women. Do you think any of this lack of collaboration is gender-based or do you think it's just institutional?

DH: You know, that's a really good question. In 2003, I co-edited a book called *Dancing on the Glass Ceiling*, and it was about women leadership in technology. Don Olcott, Jr., was really the lead editor and I was involved as a co-editor with him. It was a series of interviews and first-person chapters by men and women in the field of technology and online learning, and the status and the state of women in the field. As a result of that, the year I was president of the US Distance Learning Association, I put forward the idea of having a women's conference. The goal of the conference was based on the book, and it was about celebrating the glass ceiling—dancing on the glass ceiling. That was the name of the book; that was the name of the first or the second International Forum for Women in eLearning (IFWE) conference. The whole idea was not about bashing men. Some people thought that was what it was about. But it was about celebrating women in leadership positions, particularly in distance learning and technology and online learning. And the phenomenon of how many women are in leadership positions in this field.

Now there are still problems. There is still a glass ceiling for a whole lot of women. There are still issues of equality. When you hear Hillary, and Bernie—you hear them talk about it a lot. But the idea of having equal pay for doing the same job still doesn't happen. In several positions in my career, there were other people who had my same title and I was not making near what they did and I was doing the same kind of work. So it still exists, and those are things we do talk about at IFWE, but it's not about wringing our hands and being so upset that we aren't at the table when we should be, or not in the corner office when we should be. It's more about, how did other people get there? What did they do to get there? What did they learn about being a leader to get to that point? And it also is about, how do you make yourself visible at the table? So it's kind of a twist. It's an acknowledgement in many cases that there are and continue to be challenges for women, but the point of IFWE is around celebration of women and gaining knowledge from women who are in those positions of leadership.

WP: Interesting. But back to my original question, which was, do you think the notion of siloing was gender-based in any way? Do you think women adapt when they get into those settings and develop the same tendencies as the men who work there?

DH: Yeah, I think the siloing has nothing to do with gender. I think it's more culture. If you look at a campus, those colleges and schools are extremely protective of themselves. Many of them think they're the best college or school on the campus. The same thing is true when you get to a university system: they're very protective of their brand and their space and their reputation, what people think of them, and the same thing is true in the federal government.

WP: It may just be human nature.

DH: I think it is. But it's to the detriment, sometimes, of being able to have progress, of moving forward. If we're all going to sit in our own little playhouse and do our thing and not be willing to make some changes, make some adjustments, in order to work together for the betterment of the whole, that's a problem.

WP: So after your three years in Washington, in January 2014, you went to Blackboard. How did that happen?

DH: There were a couple of reasons why that happened. One was I have known Blackboard since the early days. I still have a good friend who was there pretty much from the beginning. I became a client of Blackboard in, I think, 2001 or 2002. They were our third LMS (learning management system). I was very engaged, I guess is the way I would say it. Some of the people at Blackboard back then might not say "engaged" was the right word, but I was very engaged in how they were serving us as a company. But in the process, I began to really respect the company and what they were doing as far as the technology was concerned.

So all the years that we had them as a client at the TeleCampus—by the time the TeleCampus closed, we didn't have any real complaints about the products. What brought me to them as an employee was the fact that, with Blackboard, there is a whole side of the company that most people are not aware of, and that's the services and consulting side. The software is great. That's our bread and butter. The LMS, Collaborate—whatever kind of product or software you may associate with us—but on the services and consulting side, by 2014, the company was really working hard to fulfill a need of institutions that went well beyond the technology. It was more around the kinds of services they needed, whether those were marketing and enrollment, or support desks or, in the case of my side of that services and consulting group, the consulting itself. There is one whole group of consulting that deals with helping institutions with the technology and how to use it the best way.

My part, and why I really got excited about coming over, is about the strategic consulting that is critical to being successful in online learning, which most institutions do not have when it comes to building out online programs. My team, and I often refer to this team as a group of recovering academics, as opposed to former academics, because we all come from academia. I have people on my team who come out of . . . for example, I have somebody who was the deputy director of IT at the University of Chicago for fifteen or twenty years, but he dealt with the teaching and learning side of IT. I have people who came out of educational technology and faculty development. I've got people who ran collaborative e-learning organizations, or worked in online learning as a director. I've got people who dealt with outcomes and assessment and now CBE. I have people who dealt with retention issues around online learning, and I've got people who dealt with accessibility issues in online learning. So this team, which cross-trains each other—these are all people who came from leadership positions and who now work together to build collaborative engagements for, and consulting engagements for, institutions. And so we meet institutions wherever they need us.

One thing I tell people is that we are a consultancy inside of a software company. We are technology-agnostic. We are LMS-agnostic. It makes no difference to us where a school is, or what technology they're using in regard to their online learning projects. We're helping them with everything from their vision, mission, goals, accreditation, state authorization, faculty development, program development, and course development, all the way through the evaluation of their outcomes, and building out how they make their decisions on how they keep students, how they make decisions on what to change in order to improve their programs. That's what my team does.

WP: Well, you're right. I had no idea that Blackboard contained all of that.

DH: Most people don't. And that's okay. When I came on board, I had conversations with people for a good six months before I took the position. But I came on with just three people, and one of them ended up leaving. Now, though, I have eight. There are eight of us, and I try to make sure that we have all areas represented, so that when people hire us, they're not just hiring a person to come and consult. They're hiring the team. They may communicate primarily with one person but we bring in each other, as needed, for different parts of the engagement so we have the experts at the table at the right time.

WP: Sounds like a great service.

DH: I'm loving it. I'm going into my third year, just starting my third year. If you had told me ten years ago that I would be working for Blackboard, and/or that I would be loving it, I would have never been convinced, because I had a different conception of the company back then. A lot has changed with the company. We just got a new CEO, who is providing excellent leadership. The perception of the company has been starting to change, that we're not just an LMS— that we're actually a more powerful partner beyond the LMS. We just have to help make sure people know that.

WP: Now how different is it working with Blackboard than it was working in academia? How is your life different?

DH: There are several things that are different. Probably the biggest one is that if we want to move on something, we move. We don't have to have a report or a study conducted by a committee to make something happen. That's probably the biggest change, because in academia if you want to revolutionize something or make a drastic change in how something is done, you're going to have a committee that will study it and work on it and make a recommendation. And then somebody else has to approve it, and then you might do it.

I always tell people that what we do in academia unfortunately becomes like *Raiders of the Lost Ark*: you do a report, you spend a year on it, you make a recommendation, and somebody puts it on a shelf and says, "Thank you very much. Check that off."

WP: Academia in general is so risk-averse.

DH: That's true. While we at Blackboard are very clear on risks, we bring those up at the very beginning. We start talking about that right away, but we can pivot, make adjustments, and move on them really at the drop of a hat. We don't have to wait for somebody to make some long-term commitment to a committee or a study to determine whether we should go that way.

WP: You've been very generous with your time, Darcy. Let me just ask you a final question that I'm sure you know is coming. Where do you think online learning is headed in the future?

DH: You know, a lot of people would say that online learning is going to move to mobile. I don't believe that. Online learning, as it currently exists and where it may be in the next five years or so, should be accessible on mobile devices, particularly tablets and iPads. The idea that this is going to go to a phone, I don't think is realistic unless what you're trying to do is reach the millions of people who have a mobile phone but are not online. If you're going after that group—and there are adults who are below literacy who have phones but don't have access to the Internet except through their phones—then that's different. Now will that same audience use their mobile phones for online learning? I think that's highly unlikely.

So the mobile, in the sense of taking what's available primarily in an online version and being able to access it 24/7, as long as you have a device—yes. Building programs that are specifically targeting mobile only? I know that people will disagree with me, but I don't necessarily see that. Of course, I could be wrong. I do think that within the next ten years there is going to be something else. I don't know what it is. But it's just about time for something to come about, from a technology standpoint, that disrupts.

I think the MOOC (Massive Open Online Course), which is already dying, will completely die. That will no longer be something we consider. It may turn into something else to make things open. I'm all for open. I also am a strong supporter of the open educational resources (OER) movement, and I really believe that that is going to take off and that it's going to impact how we offer programs through whatever technology we're using—by using more and more OER, by making college more affordable, so there aren't these gigantic, ridiculous checkbook expenses that are way overpriced. The more we see that, the more affordable these programs will be. My focus would be more on the OER and on building assessments around OER. It's not the MOOC but its educational resources that didn't have assessments tied to them that institutions will honor and that would all be online and you could get credit for it.

WP: Now that you're talking about mobile, there's an interesting correlation with the algebra=over=the=phone program you ran. Let's think about all those immigrants, legal and/or illegal, who are out there and may not have laptops or tablets.

DH: These are mostly legal immigrants whose kids are going to public schools legitimately. In some ways, as you were saying that, I thought, "Well, I just contradicted myself." I just got through saying an hour ago that the program I was most proud of was when we took algebra to the telephone, and now here I am saying that I don't think mobile will be the primary delivery method for online learning, thinking of the cell phone. So I stand to correct myself. Maybe, if you're targeting the audience who are only able to access anything by phone, which includes some of our very poor citizens and people below literacy levels, as well as many people in third-world countries—if all they have is a phone, then I'm all for designing things for mobile. But if it's for average students who think they're going to access all this content on their phones, I don't buy it. Most of them carry tablets and have other means to get online.

WP: Well, it's interesting that one size doesn't fit all in our culture. You might think that it would, but it clearly doesn't.

DH: Right. And that's why, if you were to look back at Robert Gagne, who was a leader in educational theory, and others, when they talked about learning . . . you know, all of these methodologies are just tools in the toolbox. There's a guy, Richard Clark, who is a professor in California and probably retired now, and his book was one of the books that I read when I was in my doctoral program. When I actually met him a few years ago, I said, "Oh, my God, you're that guy." He was the one who said that when you're using delivery methods, and I'm paraphrasing here, but when you're using different delivery methods, it's just like the vegetable truck that's delivering the vegetables. The vegetables are the main thing. That's what people want. The delivery truck is just the delivery tool, and you could say the same thing about every single technology that we use to deliver instruction—from face-to-face to video to audio to audio conferencing to online to mobile. All of that is just a way to deliver content, and that will continue to evolve. But if you don't stay focused on the design, the instructional design behind the content itself, it isn't going to matter what delivery method you have.

BEFORE THE FALL
Breaking Rules and Changing Minds

Darcy W. Hardy

Associate Vice President, Enterprise Consulting
Blackboard

> "Hi, Dr. Hardy? This is John Doe from ABC University and
> I just read a story about the UT TeleCampus. We think it's
> a great idea and we want to build one, and I wondered if you
> have a moment to tell us how."

Ummm, okay.

The following chapter and postscript look back to 2009, when the UT
TeleCampus was at the height of its success, and 2010, when the decision
was made to disband and decentralize the services of the TeleCam-
pus. It describes the thirteen-year process of designing and building a
multi-campus, service-and-delivery unit for one of the largest university

systems in the US. While the establishment of the TeleCampus was questioned at first, it rose to prominence nationally, and would become a model collaborative program. The UT System benefited greatly from the groundwork our team laid; we arguably paved the way for its future success in the online learning space. As of 2017, the team—although we have moved on to new professions—is still in touch. It was a profound experience for all.

The idea of someone contacting me to ask how to build a multicampus. collaborative distance-learning organization in "a moment" is typical. Most people, administrators included, have no idea what it takes to develop and nurture a unit such as the University of Texas TeleCampus. Those who do understand have probably built one themselves. The TeleCampus is part of the University of Texas System (www.utsystem.edu), which includes nine academic universities and six health institutions, with a total of approximately 195,000 students. In our case, the concept of "system" refers to a grouping of institutions with an umbrella administrative unit that has broad oversight of the system as a whole. While each campus has its own administrative infrastructure, the administration unit coordinates many system-wide functions, such as group health insurance, legal affairs, and facilities and construction planning. The UT TeleCampus is a centralized utility that was created in 1998 to help further the development of distance—and specifically online—education for the UT System as a whole. But this chapter is not about how the UT System is organized or even how the UT TeleCampus functions as an aggregator. It's about the many challenges faced when flexibility is established for a System through a centralized virtual university project.

While this is not a case study on the building of the UT Tele-Campus, most of what will be covered is a result of that effort to move multiple campuses into a flexible-learning environment. I will tell you some stories about how administrators' perceptions can be more influential than reality on a flexible-learning project, how massaging egos can bring about buy-in for a new movement, and how alarming it can be to find out how little many people care about the nuts and bolts of collaboration. I also try to relate how gratifying it is when "Aha!" moments become a daily circumstance, when everyone starts to "get it," and I suggest ways to sustain the momentum and keep the idea of flexibility moving forward. And, finally, I discuss the part that economics and politics play in building these types of flexible-learning (i.e., online) systems and how they can influence the role of these systems once established. Think of it as a walk down memory lane during a time in the 1990s when online education was new, funding was flush, and everyone was excited about how this new delivery mode could increase the flexibility of the institutions—even if they didn't realize it themselves at the time. And then fast forward to 2009, when online education has indeed forced more flexibility but funding is now an issue across the board. As we often say in our office, "Everyone loves what we do but no one wants to pay for it." Intrigued? Read on—I'm just getting started.

IN THE BEGINNING

Twelve years ago, I didn't think that creating a multicampus "virtual university" had anything to do with promoting flexibility in our institutions. To me, this concept of flexibility was (and continues to be) all about access. But not access in a way that just means making something available—it's more about a deliberate attempt to think about students' circumstances, about how, when, and why they learn. It's about truly taking educational opportunities to a level that implies that the institution is willing to do whatever it takes to make these opportunities available to students. I also had no idea how challenging it would be to work with so many institutions at once—and I was completely naïve about various university processes. I felt from the start that because this was a good thing to do, everything would just fall into place and all of our campuses would sing my praises for heading up the initiative. This was the first of many errors in my thinking.

Faculty, for one, responded quite differently than I expected. Those of us who were developing the UT TeleCampus (the vice chancellor, various staff, and me) thought that the faculty would embrace the opportunity to develop and teach courses online. What could be wrong with being able to extend the reach of your courses, provide a more flexible learning environment, and even provide flexibility for yourself? Apparently, a lot. I remember my boss at the time, Vice Chancellor Mario Gonzalez, catching considerable criticism from faculty members across the UT System as he tried to explain the concept of the virtual university. They were certain that the System's administration offices were simply trying to cut costs by putting thousands of students in each online course and at the same time getting rid of the faculty and their salaries, or significantly reducing their numbers. We were shocked! There was very little trust in the whole idea of a UT TeleCampus, partly because of fear of the unknown and partly because we in TeleCampus were from UT System administration offices and were perceived as carrying agendas of unfunded mandates for others in the UT System. You know the old saying, "We're from System, and we're here to help." I'm not sure our colleagues believed that at first.

So what did we do? The first thing was to get a handle on, or fully analyze, our place in the process. By that I mean we recognized, accepted, and actually embraced the idea that we were going to be a service entity, and we decided from the beginning that we would provide the best services possible. That mantra continues to be a driving force in the UT TeleCampus, and in my opinion—which counts, since I'm the author of this chapter—it is one of the primary reasons for our success and possibly the reason why others who did not embrace this concept failed. We help our institutions to look good. That is our goal. I tell presidents and provosts, deans and faculty members the same thing. The TeleCampus is designed to make the faculty look good by helping them to develop and deliver high-quality courses, and to make the institution look good by ensuring that the courses and programs are meeting the expectations of our state's higher education governing board as well as regional and discipline-specific accreditation associations. If you think about it, my assurance to a chief academic officer that what his or her institution offers online through a centralized unit is of high quality and meets accreditation standards can be a pretty powerful promise.

But acceptance did not come overnight. There were meetings with faculty senates and the system-wide faculty council, discussions among executive officers on the campuses, and conversations with distance education staff on the various campuses. There were turf issues where one campus was overly concerned that another campus would steal its students if the other campus offered courses online that the first campus did not, or that if they both offered the course or program online, one campus might draw in potential students from another campus. There was fear of losing jobs. Many reasons could be cited for the resistance we encountered in those early years, but I think the biggest reason was fear of the unknown and the perception that this new form of delivering instruction was growing exponentially right before their traditional eyes. Scary stuff indeed.

For me, the key was to find the most skeptical but influential people on each campus and build relationships with them. It's really all about relationships. Once established, they open the door for honest and respectful discussions. They build trust. Truth be told, some of these skeptical and influential people found me instead of me finding them, because they wanted to get to the bottom of what we were trying to do—they didn't want to wait for a meeting; they wanted to know right then. Sometimes the conversations were tense and challenging, but in the long run, I not only won over most of those skeptics, I went on to have great friendships with them. I can look back at those beginnings and say with all sincerity that building those relationships has had a major influence on the success of the TeleCampus.

One of my favorite books is *The Power of Nice—How to Conquer the Business World with Kindness,* by Linda Thaler and Robin Koval. I happened to catch Thaler and Koval talking about the book on the *Nightline* television program several years ago. They caught my attention because everything they were saying was exactly how I attempt to live my life, both personally and professionally. Although the title of the book references the business world, the "Power of Nice Principles" (there are six) can be applied to education, any workplace, or life in general quite easily. With chapters entitled "Tell the Truth" and "Shut Up and Listen," you learn quickly that by being honest with colleagues, by acknowledging their own level of understanding and expertise in addition to your own, and by actually listening to their ideas instead of formulating what you plan to say next while they are still talking, you massage their egos in a way that is sincere. I don't use the idea of massaging egos in a negative way. What I have learned, however, is that everyone needs positive strokes. When you are attempting to do something revolutionary (which is how I view what we did in building the TeleCampus in the late 1990s) and you don't provide those strokes, or you don't appreciate the thoughts expressed by those you plan to serve, you'll end up going nowhere before you ever get started. I highly recommend the book (it's a short read) for anyone planning to jump into a lion's den.

Another major driver to our initial success was our relationship with the UT System Board of Regents, particularly Regent Tony Sanchez. We met regularly with the board back then, so the members understood well what we were doing, and having a regent who was excited about distance and online education at such an early stage was truly an advantage. Combine that with having an innovative chancellor like William Cunningham, and things happen. We could have had all the great ideas in the world about how to move the initiative forward and become change agents, but without having access to people with power, we wouldn't have been successful.

The bottom line is that the establishment of strong relationships helped to break through the barrier of mistrust we were bound to experience, and they helped to change the minds of many a skeptic. And when some of those relationships are with influential administrators, they can open doors across an entire campus—or a system, for that matter.

"COLLABORATE? ARE YOU KIDDING?"

One of the reasons behind the establishment of the UT TeleCampus was to facilitate collaboration among our campuses. Our first program, in 1999, was highly collaborative—an MBA that involved eight schools of business at eight institutions. I know what you're thinking. Yes, looking back, we probably were crazy, but at the time, it seemed like the right thing to do. And in the long run, it worked well to get a lot of people on board quickly and to jump-start the online initiative.

The challenges were many. We needed the schools to agree upon a curriculum, agree upon who would develop and deliver what courses, agree to accept each other's courses as their own, and agree to offer the degree even though the student would take only two courses from the home institution. And if that wasn't enough, we had to figure out how to allow these students to take courses from multiple institutions without being admitted in a traditional manner so they could avoid applying for admission to each campus separately, paying application fees, and so on. Oh, and let's just throw in the fact that the UT System institutions do not share a common student information system, nor do they all use the same brand (e.g., PeopleSoft, Banner, etc.). Moving them to a flexible-learning environment all at once was not going to be easy, but once we decided to develop the program, there was no turning back.

Like most university systems, the institutions in our System were not used to collaborating on many things in 1997. All of our campuses are standalone institutions, with UT Austin being our flagship research campus. The remaining eight academic campuses are not satellite versions of UT Austin; they each have their own mission and direction. And most of them are located several hours from each other, so the idea of working on projects, much less academic programs, in a collaborative fashion was foreign to most faculty. But we were determined to bring this new model forward and help our campuses to work together.

It should be noted that UT Austin was not one of the eight campuses involved in the collaborative MBA. Remember that online education was brand new and did not have the reputation for quality that it has today. The dean of the business school at that time probably had legitimate concerns about how it would look for his business school to be involved in a collaborative program like this. He was paid to worry about the business school, not to worry about a UT System initiative. I don't think it's a secret that flagship institutions will generally push back on collaboration if they do not consider the potential collaborators to be peer institutions.

So how did we get the eight participating schools of business to agree to this whole collaboration thing in the first place? Easy: it was cash. Chancellor Cunningham, who, as I've mentioned, was very innovative and believed in having the campuses work together, had the foresight to recognize that, in order to get the campuses excited about an initiative from the UT System offices, he needed to provide financial support to help offset course development costs. After all, even though we were facilitating the collaboration and wrapping a suite of faculty (training, course development) and student (digital library, access to key staff on campuses) support services around the program, the courses and the faculty members belonged to the institutions. And while it of course helped that the push for the MBA was coming from a chancellor who also happened to be a former dean of the UT Austin school of business as well as a former president of that institution (and some of the deans probably went along with the idea for those reasons), in the long run, I think the deans would all agree that it was indeed the right thing to do at the time and that by working together, we built an extremely successful program.

I think one of the biggest mistakes that people in senior leadership roles like mine make is to not bring the right people to the table at the right time. It's almost as if we want to avoid the pain and misery so much that we skip certain steps in the process. For example, once we decided to build collaborative programs, it became clear that we couldn't expect students to formally apply for admission to every campus involved in a program and then ask them to register separately at each campus each semester. At the same time, we knew that making changes to any administrative process was going to cause great distress for our admissions officers and registrars. But pushing forward the concept of flexible learning is not just about developing programs or changing viewpoints; it involves serious consideration of how our administrative processes must change to accommodate new ways to deliver higher education.

We chose to bring admissions officers and registrars to the table early, and, as you might imagine, we definitely rattled their cages and provoked some mental anxieties: "What? Allow students to take courses from the institution without filling out the traditional forms and then not register in the typical manner?" But do you know what happened? After all of the discussions about why this wouldn't work or how it couldn't be done, it was the people at the table themselves—yes, the very people who pushed back at the beginning—who came up with the solution. This is how you make changes that stick. You don't mandate and you don't try to create the solution yourself. Instead, you let the people who understand the issues make the changes. My role as the leader of this new organization was to provide a space where solutions could be discovered and to encourage the process with positive reinforcement. As a result, we ended up with a process that would allow students, once admitted to a UT institution, to enroll in courses across the System, and the process was developed by the very people who would be administering it. It was a win-win for every one, and it put us one step further down the road to creating that flexible learning environment.

So, as you can see, what happened during the process of creating the MBA as a highly collaborative program is that we accidentally stumbled into transforming policies and processes that forced what we are now calling flexible learning. We had no idea at the time that we were actually providing the stimulus for systemic change on our campuses. I am not implying that our campuses had not already been delivering distance education—many had been doing so for years— or even that we were the first organization in the UT System to put forward ideas about online education. But by stepping way out of the comfort zone of so many people to build highly collaborative programs, we were able to break through barriers and change points of view in a broad way. And, as a result of the experience developing the MBA, the TeleCampus became known as a "collaboration engine," which opened doors for other projects that would come in our future.

STAKEHOLDERS AND THEIR INFLUENCE

I wish I could say that all of our stakeholders have understood the TeleCampus and what we do and that they have been our champions. Unfortunately, and realistically, I can't do that—but please know that we had a lot of stakeholders, from our boards of regents to UT System executive officers, to campus presidents and provosts, to the deans and faculty members on those campuses. We are a very large system, so it's not necessary for everyone to be in favor of what we do. However, it does make a difference when the stakeholders decide to take a stand one way or the other. I'll never forget the year we were just starting to develop the TeleCampus. In a meeting, Regent Sanchez asked me, "Dr. [he always just called me Dr.], why can't we just film every professor at UT Austin and send it over the Internet to our campuses?"

This was 1997, mind you, so my first response was of course related to the technology and how we hadn't reached the point of sending full motion video across the ether. But the second part of my response really got to the heart of the matter. In order to build buy-in for a multicampus initiative, it's important that no one campus (especially the flagship campus) be seen as superior. Whether or not the campus is ranked higher than the other campuses in the System is irrelevant for a project like this. We needed all of our campuses to feel that the TeleCampus was a service entity for them, individually and collectively. Fortunately, Regent Sanchez understood exactly what I was talking about on both fronts, and the suggestion was never made again.

There are other stakeholders who have had a huge influence on what we do but who still don't quite understand us, or understand why online education has become so popular. It's a little disheartening when I give a presentation about all the students we reach and how high our course completion rates are and I get a comment about the value of running tracks and trees on a college campus and a question about how we can possibly replicate those online. That's when I wish I could scream, "The students we serve don't care about the track or the trees on a campus!" But of course I do not, or at least I don't scream it. I mean, I'm passionate, but I'm not crazy. And is it flexibility or convenience, and does it matter? I was once told that we don't need to make it easier for these "time shifters," referring to students who choose to supplement their face-to-face course schedule with an online course here or there because they work, or they have family needs, or they simply do not want to get up early on Tuesdays and Thursdays to sit in a four-hundred-person auditorium and listen to a teaching assistant lecture. Regardless of how people look at online education, whether they like it or not, or if it bothers them because it makes access too easy, the online train is rolling full blast and it's not going back to the station now.

Generally speaking, some of our most influential stakeholders see us as only a technology shop. It's not their fault since most of them have not been on the development and delivery side of an online course. They may think that it's simply a matter of a professor making class notes into a pdf and/or posting PowerPoint slides (and even adding audio!), requiring a reading assignment or maybe a post or two in the discussion forum, and then providing some type of assessment. Some may stop at the posting of the slides. At any rate, we all know that developing a quality online course takes much more effort than that. Without experiencing it themselves, it's probably unfair to expect them to really understand. So our endless job is to help them see that technology is only one part of what we do. UT TeleCampus and its staff are about teaching and learning, technology, marketing, and student services, and about making our suite of services available for our fifteen institutions and the students we serve together.

I have worked hard to build positive relationships with our various stakeholders over the years. Chancellors have come and gone, regents have come and gone, campus presidents, deans, and faculty members have come and gone. But the students keep coming, and they are coming in larger and larger numbers. By far the majority of our stakeholders do understand what we do and understand the need to meet this growing population. Furthermore, they embrace this innovative way to reach new students. We continue to have innovative members on our board of regents, as well as chancellors and presidents. I have found that those who are the most innovative seek to know more about the online world, and whenever possible, I try to deliver. As a result, I now have a strong set of mentors who help to guide me in challenging situations. As I said previously—it's really all about relationships.

To date, my success rate in educating and convincing stakeholders that what we do is a benefit to our university System is about 70/30. Some can see the systemic changes that have taken place across the campuses to benefit a flexible-learning environment, and they think it is good. Others don't think it's important, and still others don't notice at all. Some don't understand what we do simply because we don't see or meet with them face-to-face. Face time with stakeholders is critical, and when you don't have it—for whatever reason—life can become quite interesting. But does the 70/30 split worry or depress me? No, not most of the time, because I am sustained by the lessons I've learned over the past twelve years, and I am confident that what we are doing is good for students who want access to high-quality online courses and degree programs. Where better to get those programs than from the University of Texas System?

LESSONS LEARNED

As you might expect, and as a result of my twenty years in distance education, I have learned many lessons. Some were easy, others more difficult. Some of them shouldn't have had to be learned in the first place, but I think they helped me to understand how to bring flexible online learning into the mainstream across my institutions. I share a few of them with you in no particular order of importance.

1. It is important that a change agent have access to people who have the power to help make the change agent

successful. If you are going to do something revolutionary, you have to find champions in high places. Once you find them, hang on to them as long as you can and build your program as well as you can, because the day will undoubtedly come when you have some in power who are definitely not your champions. Having established a solid organization might just carry you through any hard times you may end up facing.

2. You have to prove yourself as someone who can provide assistance and add value—and you must show that you really do know what you are doing. As I mentioned, I work at the administrative level of a large university system. When we started designing the UT TeleCampus, it wasn't as though the campuses were just sitting there waiting for us with open arms. In a situation like this, or one where you are trying to convince a skeptical audience that flexible learning is the way to go and that your group in particular is the one to go with, proving your value and having a *healthy* level of confidence may be the best way to gain the trust you need to be successful.

3. Don't worry about who gets credit. If the bottom line is that you need something to work, find a way to get there. Work with the people who can make it happen. If necessary, guide them through the problem you are facing and, even when you think you already know how to solve it, allow them to reach the same conclusion on their own. So what if they think it's their idea? You end up getting what you need and they feel a sense of partnership—which is exactly what you want.

4. Understand that you are not a faculty member and therefore will never have the clout to speak to faculty

members as a peer. Find champions in that audience and help them to reach out to others. Sometimes faculty members are hesitant about putting courses online because they don't want to make a mistake and look bad in front of the students or their colleagues. Your champions can go a long way in making hesitant faculty more comfortable in the online learning environment.

5. I don't think I can say enough about the importance of keeping your cool and remembering the principles of being nice. It almost sounds too easy, but in the ever-changing world of online education, just reaching out and being collegial—as opposed to mandating and/or demanding change—can move an initiative forward much faster. Honest and respectful communication is critical. When I was younger, I didn't know how to bite my tongue very well. When I felt that someone was treating me, my staff, or my organization unfairly, I would defend in a way that made me feel good at the time but that got me nowhere—and certainly didn't change the opinion of the offender. Today, I defend in a way that is much more strategic and much more focused on getting the most positive outcome possible. Rule #1: Write the first e-mail while you are upset to get it out of your system, read it, delete it, wait twelve hours and then write the one you should send. Rule #2: Never pick up the phone when you are upset. See Rule #1.

6. Know which rules to break and ask for forgiveness later, which ones to bend, and which ones to leave alone. The editors of this book asked me to give some examples here. I am of course hesitant because I am still breaking and bending rules (in a good way), but here's one. As mentioned previously, our first program

was the collaborative MBA. We announced that we would be developing it, we received a proposal from the eight schools of business that outlined how it would be designed, and we even started course development *before* we realized we had a serious problem. Since the students would be taking only two courses from each campus including the home campus, we were going to be in direct violation of an accreditation rule regarding a residency requirement. We didn't want to stop the development, so we contacted the accrediting agency, worked with them, and ended up becoming an example of how to do collaborative programs. The newest principles for accreditation from the agency include a statement that allows for collaborative programs—by breaking a rule, we were able to pave the way for others.

CONCLUSION

If you have dark and stressful moments about working on flexible online learning within *one* institution, add fourteen to it and welcome yourself to my world. Overall, I would have to say that I love my job, I love the people I work with—okay, most of them—and I love the fact that I've been a part of this learning revolution. Have there been moments when I thought I should have gone into a different field? Honestly, no. Even with all of the frustrations and challenges that come with doing something new and different, even when people don't really understand what we do, even when I'm wrong, I can't think of anything more exciting than being able to provide vision and ideas about the way to design things like the UT TeleCampus. Anyone who knows me well knows that I'm at my best during the building phase of things and am not one to enjoy the maintenance phase. I'm not always strategic in my planning, but I know enough to surround myself with people who are. I suppose that is another lesson. The TeleCampus is about to embark on a new project that excites me greatly. There is a growing population of adults who have some college credit but who have not received a credential—a diploma or degree. For the most part, these adults are not interested in driving to a campus to sit in a classroom with fifty to a hundred eighteen- and nineteen-year-olds three days a week. They are not interested in taking time off of work to go to class. And they are definitely not interested in packing up the family and moving to a college town. What they *are* interested in is a convenient and flexible way to earn a legitimate college degree. Working with some very innovative institutions in the UT System, the TeleCampus will roll out a number of accelerated online bachelor's degree completion programs in the fall of 2010. This is what it's all about: providing a flexible learning environment to meet the needs of a target population. Just thinking about how many adults we are going to help in the very near future reminds me that no matter what anyone thinks, what I do is worth it.

POSTSCRIPT

"Texas Kills Its TeleCampus"—such was the *Inside Higher Ed* online publication headline on April 9, 2010. The day before, I had met with the University of Texas System chancellor, and he had informed me that the UT TeleCampus (UTTC) had accomplished its mission and would be closed on August 31, 2010.

When I was asked to write this postscript to explain what happened after I had written the chapter, I wasn't sure where I would start or end. I believe that many colleagues who either wrote about the closure or who wrote to me personally have a pretty good understanding of what happened. But the bottom line is that the decision was made to decentralize online education services for a move that "will allow greater access to UT courses online, leading to improved student success and graduation rates" (from the UT System press release, April 8, 2010). Operationally, each campus in the UT System is now responsible for all things related to distance and online learning on that campus. There are no longer any centralized services like a common course management system (CMS), marketing services, or a 24/7 help desk, or even a consistent quality control system, although there are still some common activities among those campuses involved in collaborative degree programs.

It is true that most of the UT campuses are prepared, to some extent, to handle online education. They each already have a CMS and several have robust support centers with strong and experienced leadership. To the inexperienced administrator, it might have looked as though the TeleCampus was a duplication of effort. In truth, however, eliminating the TeleCampus operation means that the UT System campuses now have to duplicate all of the services that were centrally offered through the UT TeleCampus—or not offer them at all. And if they do offer the services, they are now duplicating effort. As for whether this decision will increase or decrease flexibility in the operations and user interfaces of the UT System, that remains to be seen. Clearly, those making the decision to decentralize felt that by doing so, the campuses would experience greater flexibility via a smaller, less-coordinated operation. As many colleagues have pointed out, only time will tell if the decision was indeed the right one.

Today, the UT TeleCampus is closed. The entire staff has moved on to other things. For me, the bright side is that staff members of the TeleCampus—from its beginning in 1997 to its end in 2010—are able to take the good work we did and the incredible things we learned, developed, and accomplished, and spread that knowledge and expertise out across the state, our country, and indeed, the entire online education world. When we recall all the accolades we received during those thirteen years, it feels pretty powerful: we can say that there are approximately fifty-plus people now doing great things based on what we did at the TeleCampus. Even if those fifty-plus colleagues are not in the field right now, I know that they are using things they learned from our teamwork at UT TeleCampus.

Personally, I learned more in the past three years about professional relationships and trust than in all the other years of my career combined. Call it my coming of age, if you will. My innocent belief that good things happen when you work hard and show success has been shattered. I have become a more hardened individual. And, regrettably, I'm less emotionally charged than I once was. It was a rough time for me personally, and I still carry some guilt over what happened. What could I have done differently to prevent this? And it doesn't matter when people tell me that the decision was not my fault—if you are a good leader, you take responsibility for what happens to your staff. That's what I believe, anyway.

RECOMMENDED READING

Banyai, Istvan. 1995. *Zoom*. New York, NY: Puffin Books.

Barash, Susan S. 2006. *Tripping the Prom Queen*. New York, NY: St. Martin's Press.

Benfari, Robert C. 1999. *Understanding and Changing Your Management Style*. San Francisco, CA: Jossey-Bass.

Gladwell, Malcolm. 2000. *The Tipping Point*. New York, NY: Little, Brown.

Hardy, Darcy W. 2007. *Leadership Counts . . . and Adds More Than Numbers*. Keynote address at the Annual Conference on Distance Teaching and Learning, Madison, WI, August. Retrieved from http://www.uwex.edu/disted/conference/Resource_library/search_detail.cfm?presid=53 29

Olcott, D. & Darcy Hardy, Eds. 2006. *Dancing on the Glass Ceiling: Women, Leadership and Technology*. Madison, WI: Atwood Publishing.

Thaler, Linda K., and Robin Koval. 2006. *The Power of Nice: How to Conquer the Business World with Kindness*. New York, NY: Currency Doubleday.

ONLINE AND OPEN EDUCATION
Parallels and Perspectives

Gary W. Matkin

Dean, Continuing Education, Distance Learning, and Summer Session
University of California, Irvine

The Online Report Card issued by the Online Learning Consortium in February 2016 was based on a study by the Babson Survey Research Group (the Babson Report) and indicates that in fall 2014 over 20.5 million college and university students were enrolled in online courses in the US Almost half of these students were taking all of their courses online, with the remaining half taking at least one course online (Allen & Seaman, 2016). Considering that in 2015 there were about 20.4 million higher education students in the US, it is clear that online education has become a permanent feature of US higher education (Almanac of Higher Education, 2015-16).

Another indication that online education has "arrived" is the fact that the 2016 Online Report Card is the last (of thirteen) that will be issued. Online education will now be tracked in the regular course of national data gathering. While this conclusion is hardly surprising, it has taken over twenty-two years for us to reach this point of general acceptance of online education.

1994 might well be termed "the year of online education." At that time, the awareness of online education by the general public and members of the higher education community expanded sharply. As efforts to exploit Internet technology for learning began in earnest, online education's promises and threats drew increased attention.

Now, we can look back on the twenty-two years that it took online education to transform higher education, to understand the dynamics of the transformation, and to draw conclusions from what we have observed. We can also begin to assess one of online education's most important ripple effects—the rise of open educational resources (OER) and the promise of universal education.

PERSPECTIVES

This chapter is written from the perspective of a participant/observer, someone who had the opportunity to, within the period of one working lifetime, see, hear, feel, and document the second major transformation in higher education—a transformation created by Internet technology with an impact to rival that of the invention of the printing press. I served as associate dean for Extension at the University of California, Berkeley, during the mid-1990s when extension's Center for Media and Independent Learning (CMIL) first gained funding from the Alfred P. Sloan Foundation to mount online courses. I was, and remain, a research associate at the Center for Studies in Higher Education at UC Berkeley, which, in 1994, was headed by Professor Martin Trow. He, Dr. Diane Harley, I, and several other members of the center began an informal observation of the online education phenomenon that continued until Trow's death in 2007.

Then, in March 2000 I became dean of continuing education at the University of California, Irvine (UCI) and in that role, with the help of many colleagues and UCI administrators, had the opportunity to build an online learning center from the ground up. Early in my tenure at UCI, we formed a relationship with Marshall Smith and Cathy Casserly of the William and Flora Hewlett Foundation and received some of that foundation's first funding to examine open education. That association continued until eight years later when Smith and Casserly stepped down from the Foundation. By that time, UCI had become a leader in open education. UCI is a charter member of the OpenCourseWare Consortium (now the Open Education Consortium), and I became its founding treasurer. UCI's open website has been judged in the top five in the world. In September 2012, UCI became associated with Coursera, the MOOC (Massive Open Online Course) start-up, and today (early 2016 and 2017) UCI is one of the top five course offerors on the Coursera platform, with over 2.5 million enrolled learners to date. This chapter is based, then, in part on specific experiences I have had, and on an overall awareness of the major events that shaped the history of the transformation. I will relate specific events of my own experience to the general trends as examples of what was happening along the path toward acceptance of online education and the continuing story of open education.

UNIVERSAL EDUCATION AS IMPERATIVE

Fortunately, a very powerful lens through which to view the many aspects of the online education transformation was and still is available to us—universal education. Today, universal education can be described as the idea that anyone should be able to learn anything, anytime, anywhere, for free. Remarkably, Professor Martin Trow of UC Berkeley provided us that view as early as 1974. He stated that the problems and trends in higher education at that time "can be understood better as different manifestations of a related cluster of problems, and that they arise out of the transition from one phase to another in a broad pattern of development of higher education, a transition—underway in every advanced society—from elite to mass higher education and subsequently universal access" (Trow, 1974). While this early essay concentrated on the problems of the day, the transition from elite education (less than 10 percent of the population enrolled in higher education) to mass education (more than 30 percent), the third phase, universal access, was not well articulated.

Universal access (education) advocates clearly contemplated extending educational access to the whole population through institutions, extending the notion of the community college (easy and inexpensive access) and leveraging new computer technologies. Through the '70s and '80s, universal education was a concept that became a kind of catchall for each new advance in the use of technologies from the fax machine, to teleconferencing, to, ultimately, the Internet. As these new enabling technologies emerged, Trow's conception of universal education focused first on those who had been systematically excluded from higher education as a means for them to gain access. But, as a sociologist, Trow expanded on the theme, projecting universal education's impact on higher education and on society at large. He foresaw, in 1988 (Trow, 2000) and again more comprehensively in 2006 (Trow, 2006) that universal education was emerging as an obligation of the middle class and had become a means of adapting the whole population to rapid social and technological change. Not only was universal education breaking down the boundaries between life and learning, it introduced the concepts of "term-time" (just in time) learning, diversity in learning populations, the understanding that large populations of learners never had to visit a campus, and the idea of openness and the shift from (academic) standards to "value added."

It is through universal education that we can see more clearly both the distinction between online and open education and their close relationship. Online education has clearly improved access to students in higher education by removing both time and place constraints. But it is open education that pushes into the concept of universal education by removing (or considerably reducing) the cost barrier and expanding the subject matter offerings exponentially, to subjects and subject levels beyond or outside of those subjects traditionally offered by higher education institutions. Universal education has shifted from being an unattainable ideal or goal, to an imperative.

Many millions of people around the world continue to face frustration over not being able to reach their potential because of a lack of access to higher education. This frustration spans all educational levels, from the poor of developing countries to the unemployed technical worker in the US This imperative is so compelling that it invades almost every aspect of higher education in the world today and will be called upon in this chapter to explain many of the events of the transformation chronicled here.

FOUNDATIONS LEAD THE WAY

Sloan/Berkeley. In late 1994, Frank Mayadas of the Alfred P. Sloan Foundation approached the UC Berkeley administration with an offer to fund some online courses. Knowing that the faculty and academic senate of the Berkeley campus were not ready to engage in online instruction, the administration referred Mayadas to Mary Metz, dean of University Extension, who administered the Center for Media and Independent Learning (CMIL), then under the direction of Mary Beth Almeda. In 1991, the Extension Media Center, a film rental and sales library serving California schools (previously, since 1916, the Department of Visual Instruction) and Independent Study (previously the Division of Correspondence Instruction) were combined into CMIL. CMIL, not part of what was considered mainstream instruction at UC, had the historical mandate to serve the whole university as its distance learning provider and so had no policy barriers in adopting Internet learning as yet another way to fulfill its mission. No exceptional review procedures from the faculty were considered necessary. Thus, an impediment commonly experienced by top-ranked institutions was not present in the case of UC Berkeley.

In 1995, the CMIL received its first funding from the Sloan Foundation as part of its program to foster online education, known as the Asynchronous Learning Network (ALN) initiative. Created in 1992 by Sloan's president, Ralph Gomory, the ALN was launched just before the Internet became generally available to people, "to make quality online education widely available as an ordinary form of higher education through grants to institutions and by building a community of practice." (Mayadas, 2013). Further, the foundation wanted to "explore education alternatives for people who cannot easily attend regularly scheduled classes." (Piccicano, 2017). The Sloan funding came to CMIL with the condition that the money received should not be used to fund either hardware or software and that the learning platform should be an existing, widely available utility that everyone could use. By January 1996, the CMIL had launched nine courses ranging from hazardous materials management to critical thinking on America Online (AOL). The success of these courses led CMIL to launch its own online website in March 1998, which had enrolled over 4,000 students by 2000. The 1996 courses were certainly the first publicly available online courses offered by the UC system. Sloan funding of online education at UC Berkeley ultimately exceeded $1 million, and the Sloan Foundation went on to fund over 100 more universities for online learning efforts. To fulfill its mission of "building a community of practice" the Foundation funded the Sloan Consortium, now called the Online Learning Consortium, which helped institutions establish online education on many campuses and fostered the sharing of best practices (McGuire, 2014).

While online education surely would have been developed anyway, it is clear that the Sloan Foundation played a huge part in achieving its goal for the acceptance of online education in higher education in the US and across the world.

UC IRVINE FUNDS ITSELF

At UCI in 2001 the executive vice chancellor, Michael Gottfredson allocated $500,000 to University Extension and the School of Social Ecology to produce what became the first, and for many years thereafter, the only online degree in the UC system—a master of advanced study in criminology, law, and society (CLS). The CLS department had been offering both an undergraduate major and a PhD. But despite being very close to its professional counterparts across the state, the department did not offer a master's degree. Understanding the audience for such a degree—hardworking, engaged professionals in the criminal justice system—the faculty of CLS sought and worked hard for approval of an online delivery method, eventually gaining approval of the academic senate, as an experiment.

The experiment has proven successful. The CLS degree is in its fourteenth year and regularly attracts sixty-five or more students each year. Creating the degree launched UCI's Distance Learning Center, headed by Jia Frydenburg, with instructional design accomplished by Larry Cooperman. Thus, a strategic need by one department launched UCI into online degree education.

Hewlett/Irvine

In late 2000, Marshall Smith and Cathy Casserly of the William and Flora Hewlett Foundation visited UCI Extension. Smith had recently been appointed program officer for education at the foundation and was in the process of shaping an initiative in open online education resources. An immediate issue presented itself: where should OER reside? How would OER be stored, found, used, reused, and transformed? The answer seemed to lie in the creation of one or more repositories of OER. But how would the resources in the repository be identified so that potential users could find them? How would intellectual property issues be handled? To address these issues and others, UCI received funding from Hewlett foundation for a national seminar on open learning repositories, one of the first grants made by the Hewlett fzoundation in its new initiative. This UCI grant was followed by several more, totaling about $1 million, devoted to producing or exploring OpenCourseWare. This included the funding of an open resource for public school teachers who study for the California Subject Examinations for Teachers (CSET), the passing of which qualifies them to teach math and science in California public high schools.

One of Hewlett's major grants was to the Massachusetts Institute of Technology (MIT), which, in 2001 announced that it would put its entire undergraduate program in an open format.

With this announcement, suddenly open education became a focus of attention, with many other universities joining in. The Hewlett Foundation, with MIT in the lead, created the OpenCourseWare Consortium (now the Open Education Consortium), which, within a few years, had over 300 institutional members offering over 30,000 open courses. UCI followed Hewlett's lead and in 2007 established its own open education website, which, by September 2012, had over seventy open online courses posted to it.

Smith, Casserly, and the Hewlett Foundation played a huge role in initiating and creating a world wide sustainable infrastructure for open education. Today open education is growing and serving more people every day. Any major institution, to maintain its reputation, will have to both produce and use open education as part of its day-to-day operations. The Hewlett Foundation initiated and created a sustainable infrastructure for open education. The returns on Hewlett's investment will be felt around the world for decades to come as it advances Trow's ideal of universal education.

Several lessons can be drawn from these three examples, which present many parallels. First, as illustrated in the UC Berkeley-related examples, the foundations approached major universities for the experiments, recognizing that the acceptance of the innovation was more likely if institutions of unquestioned quality endorsed the innovation. Second, each foundation sought to sustain the movements through the creation of institution-based consortia composed first of early adopters that then helped guide newcomers. But the most important lesson from this examination is that in each case (online and open education), the instigator of the innovation was not higher education or its institutions but an external ideator with significant funding that saw universities as the logical place to invest. Several major universities, motivated in part by the available funding and also by a complex of motives, quickly responded to the challenges posed by the foundations.

The UCI example illustrates the path many universities took to seize for themselves strategic advantages. For some universities, online education offered opportunities to expand the market for their existing programs, and these local decisions dominated the marketplace, edging out, as we will see, the "big players."

UP AND DOWN THE GARTNER CURVE

Online Comes to UC Berkeley. As CMIL's online education efforts proved successful, University Extension, under the leadership of John Ebersole (at that time, director of business programs), began to create online programs for delivery through Extension to its traditional continuing education audience. The UC Berkeley Academic Senate asserted its review policy and extension began its efforts to gain approval for extension-offered online education. After a very lengthy consideration, the Senate Committee on Courses approved the first online extension course in December 1998. This was most likely the first official approval of online courses in the UC system.

This approval came in time for a new experiment at Berkeley. In late 1999, Stuart Skorman, president and founder of HungryMinds. com, approached UC Berkeley Extension with a proposal to produce online education courses in the field of e-commerce. Skorman had founded HungryMinds on September 9, 1999 with $4.5 million of his own money and funding from other investors. A self-described "serial entrepreneur," Skorman's idea was to create online courses that would cater to a wide variety of learning styles, including students with dyslexia, a condition Skorman himself suffered from as a child.

In very short order, Berkeley was producing three courses per quarter with funding of $75,000 per quarter from HungryMinds, an arrangement that lasted about three quarters. UC Berkeley Extension offered the e-commerce courses, but, after an initial success, the succeeding enrollments dropped off dramatically. E-commerce, while a hot topic, did not have an established place in the workforce.

The HungryMinds business model changed several times, finally focusing on trying to be the "Amazon.com of online education." The hope was that HungryMinds could become a portal to the hundreds of thousands of people who were looking for the right kind of online education. Many obstacles immediately presented themselves. Most prominent was that online education courses came and went so quickly that by the time they were entered into the huge database, the information about them (start times, format, etc.) was obsolete. HungryMinds closed its doors on August 11, 2000, just short of a year after its founding, with a sale to IDG Books (terms not disclosed).

The HungryMinds experience at UC Berkeley Extension was echoed many times during this period, which spanned the first two stages of the Gartner Hype Cycle, a graphic representation of the maturity and adoption of technologies. The cycle predicts the typical progression of attraction and development of innovation, starting with the "trigger of technology," rising to the "peak of inflated expectations," and then proceeding through the "trough of disillusionment" to the "slope of enlightenment" and the "plateau of productivity." HungryMinds was founded just at the inflection point of Gartner's "peak of inflated expectations" and closed as the curve began sloping downward into the "trough of disillusionment."

While UC Berkeley Extension benefited financially from its short association with HungryMinds, other universities were not so lucky. Columbia, for instance, invested heavily ($40 million) in Fathom, a consortium of fourteen major universities, libraries, and museums, each pledging to contribute their brands and intellectual resources to create and offer high-quality online courses. While Fathom eventually enrolled over 45,000 students in its courses, it closed its doors in January 2003, having generated just $700,000 in student income and investments from other universities (Kirp, 2004). A very similar story was repeated over and over again in the early 2000s. Unext/Cardean, a conglomerate of universities similar to Fathom but mostly funded by outside (venture capitalist) interests, persisted for a while and then disappeared. The same happened at Pensare (Duke), NYU Online, Caliber (Wharton), University Access (Harvard, University of North Carolina, and USC), and for-profit spin-offs at Temple and University of Maryland (Kirp, 2004).

ONLINE EDUCATION'S GARTNER CURVE

All of these ventures tipped into the trough of disillusionment because of common reasons. First, despite the hype about online education in the press and in higher education in general, the public was really not ready for it. Each venture vastly overestimated the demand for online education—the income streams generated were just too slim to sustain the huge investments that were pumped into the ventures. Second, the first investors saw a business model that required an initially large capital investment in hardware and software, the acquiring of talent (high priced professorial "stars"), the development of high-end media-rich courses, and marketing. It seemed that heavy capitalization could grab large segments of market share so that highly capitalized first movers would command the market. The idea was that a "Death Star alliance" of universities with high brand recognition (such as Harvard and Columbia) could partner with large telecommunications companies to keep out smaller players.

In fact, just the opposite happened. Low cost, proprietary turnkey course management systems (CMS) became readily available. Using local talent (professors from the offering institution) and low-cost course development and authoring techniques allowed second, and third-tier colleges and universities to enter the online marketplace, attracting their traditional local students through low-cost marketing efforts. The online learning industry maintained the cottage industry nature that had characterized higher education in the US since its beginnings. Today, as outlined in the first paragraph of this chapter, most US universities are offering online education—the Death Star alliance has been defeated. We have clearly entered Gartner's plateau of productivity.

MOOCS COME TO UCI

In July 2012 MOOCs (Massive Open Online Courses) gained their first public awareness when two Stanford professors offered two courses in artificial intelligence, for free, on the Internet. Over 160,000 students signed up for these two courses. Within a couple of months, the Silicon Valley venture capitalists had created several start-up firms to capture the financial rewards of this phenomenon. Udacity and Coursera were formed as for-profit corporations.

In an eerie parallel with the online experience, Harvard and MIT put up $30 million to start EdX, a non profit MOOC provider. Seed capitalists formed Coursera, which was initially formed with sixteen universities. By July 2012, Coursera was looking to increase that number. Coursera approached UC Irvine for membership. On September 19, 2012, UC Irvine Extension (now called the Division of Continuing Education), using already existing open or online courses, joined Coursera and committed to offer six MOOCs starting in early 2013. Because UC Irvine Extension was already deeply involved in open education, MOOCs did not precipitate any extraordinary institution-wide conversation or approval process. Coursera seemed to be just another open channel through which the academic excellence of its courses and faculty could be distributed. Since the cost of generating MOOCs was relatively low ($10,000 to $15,000 per course) and because of the existence of online assets, no significant up-front investment was required. So in 2013, UCI was in at the start of the "year of the MOOCs." The partnership has proven valuable to both parties. Today, UCI is one of Coursera's top five income producers and usually doubles its development costs in income.

THE OPEN EDUCATION GARTNER CURVE

The classic Gartner curve for open education probably does not quite fit, particularly if open education and MOOCs are considered together (as they should be). The peak of inflated expectations for early open education was probably in the 2003-04 period, just as MIT was completing its open courses and as the MIT-based OCW Consortium was attracting members and mounting open courses. There was a small trough of disillusionment in the following years as open education did not seem to attract the numbers of users, particularly institutional users, that was expected. The main problem was that it was difficult for people to find the open resources when and in a form that was useful to them. And, with the proliferation of open resources, there was an understandably wide variance in quality.

However, during this trough, open education in the form of broad-scale utilities such as YouTube and iTunesU grew dramatically. If there was a trough, a new drive toward a peak of inflated expectations began in 2013 as MOOCs came on the scene. Now, in early 2016, we are probably in the trough of disillusionment for MOOCs. The previously mentioned Online Report Card indicates that "most institutions have decided against MOOCs or remain undecided (58 percent and 28 percent respectively). However, the number of institutions that currently have MOOCs increased from 8 percent in 2014 to 11 percent in 2015, and the number of MOOCs and the number of people signing up for MOOCs is increasing all the time (Allen & Seaman, 2016). "Massive" is still very much the right descriptor: UCI's 50 MOOCs have attracted over 1.6 million engaged learners (those who actively engage in a learning activity), since inception in January 2013.

PARALLELS AND PREDICTIONS

The concepts of universal education and the Gartner curve provide us with lenses to look at online education. Now well-developed and mature, open education is still early in its development and draws some parallels that may help us predict the future.

Overestimated Market. The first parallel is obvious: that early hype about the numbers of the general public who would take advantage of the innovation was, in both cases, wildly overstated. The public simply did not understand what online education was in its early days, so the fact that online education could reach thousands and thousands of people did not mean much when the market was approached. Similarly, at least until the advent of MOOCs, the potential of the open education audience (essentially the Internet-served world) was just not able to take advantage of the thousands of OER available.

Open education is clearly beyond the early stage of public awareness and is now deeply penetrating all aspects of education, including continuing education and corporate training. The advantages of anytime, anyplace, low-cost learning are a large incentive for people with busy lives and corporations with restricted training budgets. It is clear that MOOCs have stimulated the public awareness of the value of open education although there are large segments of the population that still have not heard of MOOCs. But the imperative of universal access will carry the day for open education as it enters the slope of enlightenment.

Lost Investments. The second and related parallel is that the new innovation attracted major investors, both by higher education institutions themselves, and from the for-profit sector. In the case of online education, virtually all of these major investments failed to generate any significant return resulting in the failure of the organizations created to exploit the new technology. The open education parallel in the early days of the initiative did not see such an investment except by foundations; it was not until MOOCs came along that the real parallel with online education occurred.

Certainly the jury is still out on whether Coursera, EdX, and Udacity will survive, but their futures are shaky at best. The very large investments already sunk into these ventures will be hard to monetize. So far, only low-cost certifications of learning have generated any significant income and it is uncertain whether this stream of income will increase or be joined by others. It is likely that the MOOC providers will shift into full-fledged, for-fee online continuing education organizations, first using university-generated content and slowly adding their own content in an effort to capture more direct income from course fees. We are already seeing forays by MOOC providers into corporate training markets, with or without university partnerships. In general, we are also seeing a retreat from the free offerings, with only the basic content now being provided for free and "enhanced" versions of courses coming with higher fees. For these MOOC organizations, the challenge will be how to keep their current supply chain for courses (universities) operating at the same time they begin to compete with it.

Use of University Brands. A third parallel is the leadership of major research universities. The Sloan Foundation sought out UC Berkeley and other institutions of high repute for its early online experiments, understanding that those institutions could generate the credibility and the press coverage needed to get the online movement to lift-off stage. As online education gained momentum, for reasons cited earlier, major universities became deeply involved both financially and pedagogically in online education. Similarly, the Hewlett Foundation funded MIT and got a very large amount of credibility for the open movement from the commitment of MIT's faculty to open education. MOOCs also started with major institutions such as Stanford, Harvard, MIT, Yale, UC San Francisco, and others. The leaders of the two innovative movements tried to piggyback on the brand and reputations of these institutions to get others involved. This created a "missing the train" psychology with a commitment to MOOCs somehow equaling a commitment to the new technologies that were forecast as transforming higher education. The firing and rehiring of President Theresa Sullivan at the University of Virginia is highly illustrative of this phenomena. While some of the early big names in MOOCs are retreating a bit, others are pressing forward, gaining advantages in brand recognition, and, indeed, financial returns. As the business of open education becomes clearer, major universities will realize that to be competitive in the marketplace they will have to both produce and use open education.

THE FUTURE

While the short-term future of online and open education is a bit clouded, the long-term future seems more certain and predictable, especially if we see universal education and the imperative of open education as givens. What are the long-term implications of what we have just examined?

Lifelong Learning. It is clear that higher education will have to embrace the sixty-year curriculum and will have to become more serious about serving, throughout their lives, those who they graduate. Continuing education will have to take a more central place in the life of universities as they seek to maintain relationships with graduates and to engage in regional and national workforce development efforts. Universities will have to address the nationally recognized skills gap not only through curricular reform within the degrees they produce but also as they seek to keep the knowledge gained in those degrees current. The barriers for universities to become more engaged in continuing education are steadily being answered through online and open education technology. It is now possible to reach hundreds of thousands of students with high quality education. Universities cannot afford to miss the chance at such impact.

Two Markets. The "two markets" for undergraduate degree education will simultaneously more completely differentiate themselves and blur along pedagogical grounds. It will not transpire that online education will be the main form of delivery to traditional-aged college and university students. The sociological place of college as a repository for developing minds and preparation for adulthood will not go away. The lecture method is not dead and never will die. It will remain an important and cost-effective way for teachers to convey to students their passion for a subject and its importance.

However, for those more mature students already in the workforce with formed personalities and already shouldering adult responsibilities, online and open education will continue to create new opportunities for access, for inspiration, and for community. The two markets will merge to some extent as technologicaly-mediated learning objects are available to both audiences. Classroom-based education will be supported by technology in increasing ways, from immediately available video capture of lectures to complex simulations and adaptive learning techniques developed first for online delivery. This simultaneous differentiation and merger will continue to confuse discussions about online and open education into the future.

Target Audiences. Online and particularly open education will shift from serving a very general, broad audience, to more targeted audiences, particularly those most deserving of education and least able to afford it. Here we might have in mind clinicians on Indian reservations in the US, third-world rural farmers needing efficient irrigation systems, local specialists in ocean reef preservation, and water quality maintenance workers in major third-world cities. Virtually any world problem, physical or social, has education as part of it solution. Now education can be delivered cheaply and directly to those who need it, when they need it. This kind of impact is not lost on foundations and on international organizations such as the World Bank and UNESCO.

Life/Learning Balance. As we move more closely to universal education, people will experience the life/learning balance problem. Just as now most of us face the work/life balance problem, exacerbated by 24/7 access to our cell phones and the Internet, with work demands competing in real time with family and other responsibilities, so the instant access to learning possibilities will create a similar problem. Martin Trow (2000), in fact, predicted this, saying that the boundaries between learning and life would blur. "Just in time" learning will become available, requiring work or personal time to accommodate it. The concept of the "learning junkie" will emerge, as some individuals are not able to manage the life/learning balance well. Fortunately there will be OER on how to cope with this new demand on our conscious existence.

Universal Education. As we contemplate the stage of the Gartner curve where both online and open education have reached the plateau of productivity, the distinctions between face-to-face, classroom-based, online, and open education will completely merge into "education." Modes of education will be so intermixed and transparent that they will no longer be meaningful distinguishing features of what we know and experience as learning. Even as the challenges of achieving universal access seem insurmountable, it marches steadily toward us, filling up the horizon. We must begin to look beyond the horizon to the consequences of a more highly-informed and educated world, a world where expertise acquired over many years can be challenged in an informed manner by laypeople, where ignorance takes new forms, where "niche knowledge" challenges wider vision.

Importantly for higher education, what does universal access mean for teaching and learning? Teachers will increasingly become architects for learning, or concert masters, selecting learning assets that lead to knowledge, curators of the learning experience and context. A world where everyone can learn anything, anywhere, anytime, for free is now unimaginable, but its consequences are beyond any ability to predict. I'm looking forward to the next twenty-two years.

REFERENCES

Allen, I.E. & Seaman, J. (2016, February). *Online report card: Tracking online education in the United States.* Babson Survey Research Group. Retrieved from http://onlinelearningconsortium.org/read/online-report-card-tracking-online-education-united-states-2015

Almanac of Higher Education 2015-16. (2015, August 22). *The Chronicle of Higher Education. Pg33.* Retrieved from http://chronicle.com/specialreport/The-Almanac-of-Higher/4

Kirp, D.L. (2004, September). Shakespeare, Einstein, and the Bottom Line. Cambridge: Harvard University Press. Retrieved from http://www.hup.harvard.edu/catalog.php?isbn=9780674016347

Mayadas, A. F. (2013, March 11.) Online education: A quick overview. [PowerPoint presentation]. Alfred P. Sloan Foundation. Retrieved from https://www.regents.nysed.gov/common/regents/files/OHESloan%5B1%5D.pdf

McGuire, R. (2014, May 29). Sloan's Frank Mayadas on the early history of online education. *SkilledUp.* Retrieved from http://www.skilledup.com/insights/sloan-frank-mayadas-early-history-of-online-ed

Piccicano, A. G. (2017). Online Education Policy and Practice: The Past, Present, and Future of the Digital University. New York, NY. Routledge Taylor and Francis Group.

Trow, M. (2000, Spring). From mass higher education to universal access: The American Advantage. Retrieved from http://www.cshe.berkeley.edu/sites/default/files/shared/publications/docs/PP.Trow.MassHE.1.00.pdf

Trow, M. (2006). Reflections on the transition from elite to mass to universal access: Forms and phases of higher education in modern societies in WWII. *International Handbook on Higher Education,* edited by J.F. Forest and Philip G. Altbach (Eds.), (243-80). New York. Springer.

Trow, M. (1973). Problems in the Transition from Elite to Mass Education. Paper prepared for a conference on mass education held by the Organization for Economic Development (OECD), Paris, June 1973, pages 55-101. Retrieved from files.eric. edu/gov/fulltext/D091983.pdf

BUILDING AN INDUSTRY
WITH AN INDUSTRY
Perspectives from an Online Learning Innovator

Carol Vallone

Chief Executive Officer
Meteor Learning

My first job right out of college was at Merrill Lynch in New York City, where I researched new market opportunities for financial products. I was there for a short time then moved to Boston, and that's where my career really began. I worked for a number of organizations that developed and sold software to Fortune 500 companies—defining new markets, launching new products, building out new customer segments, and supporting the sales teams in building their territories.

As my career progressed, I became president and chief operating officer of a corporate training organization that utilized a proprietary method for analyzing, organizing, and presenting complex information to improve productivity and reduce risk for major corporations. My transition to the online education market occurred in the late

1990s when I decided to sell my interest in the corporate training company and launch a new business.

Soon after, I met a non profit organization that was focused on Universal Design for Learning (UDL), a research-based set of principles to guide the design of technology-based learning environments that are accessible and effective for all learners, including those with learning and physical disabilities. Together we formed a company called Universal Learning Technology and developed a learning management system (LMS) that integrated the UDL principles, and allowed faculty and students to interact over the internet.

Over the years in the corporate market, I saw that back-office systems were developed first, followed by "front-worker" productivity tools. In the late 1990s, most college and university campuses had network infrastructure supporting back-office systems such as registration and financial aid, but there weren't any front-worker productivity tools. Drawing parallels to the corporate market, moving beyond the back-office administrative systems and building a new online teaching and learning application looked like a huge opportunity to leverage the network infrastructure already in place.

The first version of the LMS was called Bravo (and was actually a "course management system or CMS, to reflect individual course usage). Bravo was implemented as a supplement for face-to-face instruction for traditional on-campus students in an asynchronous mode. It was very instructor-centric and was positioned to improve faculty productivity. Initial usage was with individual faculty members who were putting their courses online—a bottom-up adoption model driven by early innovators.

As Universal Learning Technology launched Bravo, we were met in the market by an online learning technology platform called WebCT (Web Course Tools). It had been developed by a computer science faculty member at the University of British Columbia and made commercially available. WebCT had developed solid reference accounts and had a great academic reputation. Given that both companies were focused on the same market with a similar offering, I approached the founder and offered to acquire the company for a 1 +

1 = 3 win! We completed the acquisition and decided to build from the WebCT brand name.

As we built out a global customer base, WebCT also developed a global customer advisory board. It was comprised of academic and technology leaders from post secondary institutions who would inform the ongoing strategic and product direction. We collaboratively built the "industry with the industry." Adoptions grew from individual faculty to enterprise-wide, but the LMS was mostly used for supplemental materials. Major educational publishers developed their content in WebCT-ready cartridges so students could easily acquire their materials online. And many companies integrated their technologies with WebCT to extend capabilities requested by the advisory group. Not only did individual campuses adopt it enterprise-wide, but WebCT was also designed to serve the needs of entire college and university systems.

By 2005, WebCT was adopted in almost 2000 post secondary institutions in seventy countries and fourteen languages. Our major competitor approached us to acquire the company, and I completed the transaction in 2006.

After a brief retirement, I joined a company called Wimba as the CEO. This was a next-generation synchronous technology designed for live learning where traditional as well as nontraditional students could attend classes online from convenient locations. Still instructor-led, the online learning market was transitioning from a "faculty productivity" model to a "student engagement" focus. Core curriculum was being redesigned utilizing the advanced features of online technologies, including adaptive learning for personalized pathways and analytics to track and monitor student outcomes. Live classrooms could be launched from within asynchronous learning management systems to extend the learning experience and included the capability to record sessions for later review. In 2010, I sold Wimba to an LMS company, and the live classroom continued to function within that environment as value-add capabilities to the core LMS solution.

After another brief retirement, I became, in 2012, the CEO of a company that focused on competency-based education (CBE) and is known today as Meteor Learning. The core offering was assessing student learning gaps and providing online instruction focused on mastering skills to fill those gaps. The idea of progressing based on personal skill mastery as opposed to progressing based on "time in seats" was evolving as the next-generation learning model.

The company formed two advisory boards—one comprised of college presidents to brainstorm on market strategy and another comprised of academic and technology experts to brainstorm on specific products and services.

Our advisory boards delivered a clear strategic message. With workforce skills gaps growing, higher education is challenged to close the gaps. Further, the profile of students has changed and colleges and universities need to focus on the nontraditional learner. Future growth would come from new student segments, primarily working professionals seeking degrees aligned with their career objectives.

Delivering traditional online degrees to the nontraditional learner, however, was not the answer for closing workforce skills gaps. In order to truly serve employers' requirements, skills needed to be defined by employers, assessments to demonstrate skill mastery needed to be developed, and learners needed to progress along personalized pathways in a flexible and convenient online model. As with the early days of the LMS, however, it was difficult for institutions to internally develop expertise to design, launch and market online CBE programs, and to provide appropriate services for new student segments. Our advisors suggested that we offer a full suite of services and technology that would support an institution in developing and launching online CBE degrees.

The company's legacy CBE expertise was well suited to leverage into a new business that would address the workforce skills gaps with personalized and flexible online degrees that build job-ready skills and meet employers' requirements. Today, Meteor Learning's mission is to enable our higher education partners to close workforce skill gaps by delivering high-quality, workforce-aligned degrees for working professionals.

In the late 1990s and into the early 2000s, online learning grew from the adoption of LMS platforms. As the market evolved, online learning growth was fueled by the introduction of online program management companies that provided outsourced services to support the development of on-ground to online programs.

Today, given the early and fast-growing nature of CBE, post secondary institutions are looking for both technology *and* enabling services to secure a rapid market position. As the industry leader, Meteor Learning designed our offerings to serve the market needs. We invest upfront capital and provide services and technology that include strategic market assessments to identify large and growing markets with critical skills gaps; competency-based program design and development that aligns degrees with workforce and licensure requirements; marketing, recruitment, and enrollment services to attract highly qualified candidates to degree programs; enabling technology to support student learning, develop competency profiles, and provide critical learning analytics; and executive coaching focused on academic and non academic support throughout the entire student lifecycle. The following white paper, entitled "Framework for Developing and Implementing a CBE Portfolio Strategy that Closes Workforce Skills Gaps," which I authored in 2016, provides a detailed look at Meteor Learning's approach.

Over the past fifteen years, the role of online learning and the strategic motivation for delivering online content has evolved dramatically. In the late 1990s, individual faculty adopted the LMS platform to improve their productivity and deliver individual courses online. Technology platforms were not mission critical and were line-item expenses. Today, college and university presidents are focused on solving skills gaps through comprehensive online CBE programs. The next-generation CBE learning model is viewed as a strategic imperative to attract new student segments, generate incremental enrollments, and create new revenue streams. Importantly, the future sustainability and viability of higher education is dependent on the ability to close workforce skills gaps by delivering programs that meet employers' needs.

FRAMEWORK FOR DEVELOPING AND IMPLEMENTING A CBE PORTFOLIO STRATEGY THAT CLOSES WORKFORCE SKILLS GAPS

Introduction

Our nation is faced with large and growing workforce skills gaps, and higher education is challenged to close the gaps. As reported in the 2013 Lumina report covering America's opinion on higher education, "Just 11 percent of business leaders *strongly agree* that higher education institutions in this country are graduating students with the skills and competencies that their businesses need." (p.25).

Competency-based education (CBE) programs can directly address the workforce skills gaps with personalized and flexible degree options that build job-ready skills and meet workforce requirements. To fully capture the potential of CBE programs, however, institutions need to develop a CBE portfolio strategy that aligns institutional strengths with market needs and focuses on closing workforce skills gaps. In a world being reshaped by adult learners, accelerated pathways to degrees, and massive demand for affordable, high-quality education, it is not enough to just be online. Institutions must demonstrate learning outcomes and align degree programs with employers' hiring needs. CBE presents a compelling solution to drive enrollments, differentiate academic programs, and serve working professionals who require flexibility and seek to graduate job-ready.

Meteor Learning has developed a framework to help institutions develop and implement a CBE portfolio strategy that brings together administrators, faculty, staff, and industry in generative conversations that catalyze new programs.

This paper provides an overview of the promise of CBE and where it is headed; it also presents Meteor Learning's framework for a CBE portfolio strategy. We highlight strategic questions that institutions should ask as well as some lessons we've learned from working with a number of higher education institutions.

The Promise of CBE

Competency-based education provides strategic, financial, and academic opportunities for colleges and universities. With CBE degrees, institutions can do the following:

- Drive enrollment growth from new student segments
- Generate incremental revenue
- Create stronger ties to employers' requirements
- Lower the total cost of program completion

Competency-based education, which can take many forms, promises to address some of higher education's most serious challenges. For example:

- Educational opportunity: Approximately 45 million Americans over age twenty-four have some college but no degree. CBE may represent the best opportunity these individuals have to advance their education and career.
- Employer/workforce connection: Employers consistently report skills gaps in current workers and the inability to find enough qualified personnel. College graduates may be unemployed or under-employed. By involving employers in defining competencies for CBE programs, institutions can increase hiring of graduates, improve competencies of current workers, and ultimately improve economic vitality in their areas.
- New revenue generation: It is difficult for colleges and universities to identify alternative student segments that can be targeted for incremental revenue generation. Online CBE programs attract working professionals seeking degrees that align with workforce requirements, thus allowing institutions to leverage their brands and generate new sources of revenue.
- Cost control: Cost is the number one concern around higher education. Institutional leaders want to find cost savings for their institutions and, importantly, for

individual learners. Online CBE degrees can incorporate assessments for prior learning and experience, thus saving the students the time and money associated with unnecessary courses.

- Innovation: Institutions are being pressured by lawmakers and the public to change the way they do business. With the rapidly aging workforce and the need to fill the looming skills gap in our economy, institutions can offer CBE degrees that provide flexible ways to engage and skill up working professionals.

Growth in CBE is primarily driven by working professionals who are seeking online programs they can attend while working. CBE is attractive to adult and nontraditional learners because of efficiency and flexibility but also because students graduate job-ready. Employers are interested in CBE to help alleviate the skills gap and better align education with their needs.

CBE addresses the significant need for increased post secondary and graduate education through flexible course and degree options for adult and nontraditional students. Thirty-eight percent of those enrolled in colleges and universities are over the age of twenty-five, and 25 percent of those students are over thirty. Today's large nontraditional audience encompasses talented and mature students between ages of twenty-five and forty-five, who will form the heart of the US economy for the next three decades.

Because CBE is heavily dependent on online learning, attitudes towards online education are important. Sixty-six percent of chief academic officers believe that online education is critical to their institution's long-term strategy. In addition, 74 percent of academic leaders rate the learning outcomes from online education as the same or superior to those in face-to-face courses.

Record numbers of college and university presidents are interested in CBE, with the majority of presidents believing strongly in key elements of CBE. For example, 62 percent of presidents surveyed believe that credit should be given for prior learning. Further, 88 percent support awarding academic credit for demonstrated competencies. In a recent survey, one quarter of presidents say they currently offer CBE. Another 10 percent say they have CBE programs under development. Almost 20 percent say they are very likely or extremely likely to develop CBE programs in the next five years.

Market data further highlights that over 600 institutions currently offer or are developing CBE programs, up from just twenty-five only a couple of years ago. Four factors are driving market growth:

- Alignment with national attainment goals, both for increasing the number of Americans who complete college, but also for workforce development.
- Engagement with state and regional workforce development initiatives. For example, fifteen states have policies that support the development of CBE programs in the belief that CBE will strengthen economic growth.
- Innovations in educational technology. New tools and services are being designed for instruction and student support that range from adaptive learning platforms to integrated planning and advising systems as well as outcomes reporting.
- Responsiveness to consumer demand. Adult and nontraditional learners want the flexibility and job-readiness of CBE in their degree and certificate programs.

METEOR LEARNING'S FRAMEWORK

Meteor Learning has developed a framework it deploys with its post secondary partners to identify, develop, and implement a CBE portfolio strategy. Institutions should consider these critical elements whether "going it alone" or in partnership with a commercial company.

The framework includes:

- **Comprehensive market assessment**. Meteor Learning determines which programs and which student segments have the highest growth potential for CBE. We conduct primary and secondary research to evaluate external factors such as employment trends, industry and discipline growth, and competitive positioning. We also analyze internal factors, such as areas of academic expertise, employer partnerships, and enrollment trends by degrees conferred.

- **Effective CBE program design.** The core of Meteor Learning's CBE program design is defining competencies/learning outcomes based on industry and licensure requirements, and then developing the CBE curriculum to tie activities and assessments to the desired outcomes.

- **Customized marketing and enrollment services.** It is important to develop customized marketing and enrollment services to meet the unique needs of the student segments identified in the market assessment. Meteor Learning develops and delivers services that reflect the brand, culture, and mission of the institution and are focused on attracting the most qualified applicants.

- **Unique technology designed for CBE Programs.** CBE is a customized and formative approach to education that requires new technology designed around a competency vs. a course structure. While Meteor Learning's technology is an indispensable tool for online program delivery, we also provide CBE program design and instructional models that leverage the technology to optimize student outcomes.

- **Robust student services.** Once students are admitted to a CBE program, it is critical that they have access to a range of services designed to support their unique needs. Meteor Learning's retention services include financial aid assistance, academic advising, tutoring and executive coaching.

Below is the description for each element and the critical questions to consider:

Market Assessment

CBE is not a one-size-fits-all approach to education. Designing and implementing CBE programs should begin with market research, employer input, and business projections to ensure that graduates are job-ready and that there is sufficient need to justify the investment in the program, both in the short and long term. The research will help validate program choices, such as by estimating demand and assessing competitive differentiators. It may also reduce risk by modeling program viability and evaluating long term growth potential.

The questions you seek to answer in your strategy will determine the type of data you need. Strategic questions institutions may want to ask include:

- Does CBE represent an incremental opportunity—for example, can we improve curriculum alignment creating stronger ties to employers?
- Can we quantify large and growing market segments that have large skills gaps?
- Does the institution have the ability to create a strong student value proposition that is differentiated from others?
- Does the program fit with the institutional brand and mission?

While there are many possible approaches to market assessment, elements should include the following:

- Market analysis: A high level analysis of the graduate supply vs. the job demand to determine areas of opportunity for developing programs. Key areas to consider are market, employer, and job mix; mix of job openings vs. the employer mix; and degrees conferred vs. job openings to determine areas of under-supply.

- Program relevance: A detailed analysis of the jobs in the program areas of opportunity. Factors to consider include area employer base dynamics, job-level forecasting, and changing market requirements for education and job skills.
- Program competitiveness: An assessment of offerings from competitive institutions, both online and traditional. Areas to consider include tuition levels, competitor program profiles, and current student trends.
- Program alignment: Alignment of proposed programs with the institution's brand and mission. Areas to evaluate include student segmentation, brand perception, institution mission, and organizational readiness.

Our work with colleges and universities leads us to three key observations linked to our belief that opportunity analysis is potentially the most important step in the CBE framework.

- Competency-based education represents a different value proposition compared to traditional higher education. There is tremendous opportunity for CBE in adult learner markets. Institutions must have a clear understanding of the size of the market segments and their value proposition within each segment if they are to be more successful than their competitors.
- Few institutions conduct detailed market assessments. Without the assessment, institutions cannot make strategic decisions about market gaps, competitive posture, or market growth. Without data, strategic directions may only be wishful thinking.
- Today, most of higher education serves a stagnant eighteen-to-twenty-two year-old market. CBE is the new opportunity area for market expansion with working professionals, just as online learning was twenty years ago. A savvy market assessment is key to

institutional decisions to optimize investments in new market opportunities.

CBE Program Design

Designing and developing the academic program begins with key decisions such as whether the program is credit-based CBE, direct assessment, or a hybrid. Other facets include curriculum design, activity design, resource development, and creation of assessments and scoring rubrics. Putting content online does not necessarily improve learning or performance, so academic program design goes beyond content to focus on learning objectives and activities that engage learners and help them develop complex skills.

As part of program design and development, institutions may want to ask strategic questions such as the following:

- What should the model be designed to achieve? Are the competencies flexible enough to serve entry-level practitioners as well as those more advanced in their careers?
- What changes should we make to better align our curriculum with employer needs? How do we evaluate whether those changes are effective?
- Based on the intended audience, what features need to be embedded in the academic design (e.g., length of terms, start dates, prior learning assessment strategies, etc.)?
- Do we have the internal expertise and time to design/redesign our program? What other resources might accelerate the timeline and improve program success?
- What is our vision for the learner experience?

Although the academic program is considered to be under the control of the institution and the faculty, it is critical to remember that CBE is closely tied to the workplace and employer needs. As a result, competencies are usually determined by groups of academic and industry experts. External stakeholders might include employers, professional associations, unions, or others. Employer roundtables or councils may be ongoing to keep competencies up to date with changes in the industry.

Note that assessment is an essential part of program development. Employers are particularly interested in critical skills such as the ability to solve complex problems that are ill-defined and require knowledge of multiple disciplines. Solutions to these problems require learners to use both analytical and creative skills, often integrating mathematical, scientific, social, and cultural elements. Because twenty-first-century skills are so complex, developing assessments may require the expertise of industry and academic subject-matter experts.

Three observations based on our work with colleges and universities may be helpful to others as they develop the academic program.

- Developing competencies and doing the instructional modeling necessary to align learning objectives and activities requires expertise that is not always well represented at colleges and universities, either in faculty or staff. Institutions can develop programs, as well as their internal expertise, by partnering with an experienced provider. Lessons learned from developing the first CBE program readily transfer to other parts of the institution.
- Faculty are highly motived to transform programs to CBE when they understand the major benefits of transparency to students (e.g., using the dashboard). As students see where they are, where they need to go, and how to get there, their success is enhanced. Faculty also have powerful tools to help them see where students are having difficulty, saving them time. Rather than searching for the problem, faculty can spend more time supporting student comprehension.
- Credentialing, certification, and training are melding with college and university degrees. Since

postsecondary education is so closely linked to corporate training, with CBE programs institutions may want to work even more closely with employers to ensure that they understand future needs of the industry as well as how to build degrees with stackable credentials.

Marketing and Enrollment Services

As the program is being designed, the institution can prepare its marketing strategy and enrollment process. Student success is often closely linked to the fit between students' experience/expectations and the program. Considering the great diversity of adult learners and increasing number of online programs available, careful market segmentation is a critical first step.

There are several distinct segments to the adult learner market. A recent study indicates 57 percent of students fall into one of three segments that align well with competency-based learning.

- *Career accelerators* are learners who choose a program to improve their earning and career potential. Most likely they are in the workforce. They comprise approximately 21 percent of the adult learner market.
- *Career starters* are learners who choose a program that will allow them to complete a degree as quickly as possible. This segment accounts for 18 percent of the adult learner market.
- *Industry switchers* are learners who are seeking a new direction for their career, often looking to leave their current job. They place high value on job placement and account for 18 percent of the adult learner market.

The steps in marketing and enrollment include target profiling, brand alignment, developing a marketing plan, lead generation, and enrollment management. As the institution moves through this part of the framework, strategic questions include:

- What is the profile of our intended audience?
- What key differentiators and values of our institution must we convey to prospective students?
- In a digital, social, and mobile world, how do we engage prospective students rather than just push messages at them? What is the formula for building trust with them?
- What partnerships will support program enrollments, provide employment to our graduates, and generate further interest in the program?

Market channels will encompass online, social, face-to-face, and business-to-business. Choose marketing channels based on students' behaviors and needs. For example, the program may want to leverage websites frequented by degree seekers. E-mail campaigns might target alumni or use purchased mailing lists for outreach. Developing social marketing channels (e.g., Facebook) is important as well. Consider virtual open houses or webinars. More traditional approaches, such as featuring the program in the institution's alumni newsletter or in ads, should not be forgotten.

Employers and partners are critical channels. If employer roundtables were used to solicit input for the program, those same employers are likely to share information with their employees, such as through career fairs or internal communication. Many institutions have partnerships with area community colleges as well. All should be considered as possible channels for marketing and recruitment.

Our experience suggests you also consider process, technology, and targets.

- Be sure you have mapped processes such as recruitment, enrollment, and financial aid and be sure to take a student-centered perspective. Your prospective students will want clear guidance on how to start— and complete—their program. Learners look for a clear pathway to completion.

- Leverage technology for robust, real-time data and analytics, and custom workflows, to keep prospective students engaged throughout the enrollment lifecycle. It is critical to manage prospective students from inquiry through application and enrollment.
- Set targets. For example, what is your intended inquiry to conversion ratio? How quickly should a prospect move from inquiry to registration?

Technology for CBE programs
While technology is an indispensable tool in CBE programs, technology alone delivers no value. It is the combination of strategy, the right technology, data, skills, and processes that deliver value.

Faculty and advisors alone cannot customize each student's experience; technology can help. Advising and coaching systems can help identify the support that students need and link them to information, intervention, and coaching. Tools can help students develop personal action plans, along with sending reminders and setting up tracking mechanisms. Case-management tools can help advisors, faculty, and others share necessary actions and observations. Planning tools, which typically track students' progress, can improve the use of advisor time and can reduce errors.

Most existing technologies were not designed for the development and delivery of CBE degree programs, instead being conceptualized around courses and credit hours. CBE technology solutions may integrate with existing systems, such as the LMS, extending and integrating with other campus technologies to provide the following:

- Defined competencies aligned with employer and licensure requirements
- Self-paced and live instruction
- Rich dashboards for performance monitoring and tracking
- Competency profiles with demonstrated skills

A CBE application can make the student's program and progress visible at all times, beginning with credit received for prior learning. Dashboards can highlight the student's progress as well as provide a mastery report. Dashboards customized for faculty and success coaches allow them to monitor student progress; at-risk students are flagged for follow up. Detailed reporting can pinpoint specific issues, allowing faculty, students, and coaches to spend time addressing challenges rather than finding them.

As institutions work on program delivery and technology, strategic questions to ask include the following:

- How can we use technology to move beyond automation to enhancing the student experience?
- Can we use technology to change the basis of competition, such as an ultra-convenient experience that is personalized in real time?
- Are we using administrative and academic systems data to feed analytics tools and improve decision making?
- How can we use technology to enable process improvements, such as creating mechanisms for early interventions, tracking student progress, or making scheduling of appointments easier?

Institutions must maintain their core IT systems and implement new ones, such as analytic tools for student success, competency tracking systems, and dashboards. Since learning is online and competencies are being tracked, a great deal of data is generated. Institutions will need to have robust data capabilities and policies.

Observations that may be helpful to others include the following:

- Data collection, reporting, and visualization tools are critical so that students, instructors, and coaches have access to timely information about the state of learning. CBE faculty cannot rely only on experience and instinct. Students need information about where they are having difficulties and their progress on a personal learning path.

- Comprehensive and ongoing training and communication is essential to program delivery and technology. Staff may need training in how to apply analytics to their area. A culture of data-informed decision making must be communicated throughout the organization. The investment in staff training may be as important as funding for the technology.
- Program delivery and technology require working across boundaries. A team structure and specific targets can lead to the shared commitment that allows units to transcend turf and focus on problem solving.

Student Services

Adult learners, particularly those new to CBE, may need academic and non academic support to be successful. Since most students are balancing work, family, and education, time management and tracking of competencies are particularly important. Student success systems often integrate traditional campus support elements (e.g., tutoring) with personalized program plans, dashboards, and coaching.

Questions institutions should ask include:

- How are students supported in their CBE journey? Academically? Personally? How can we best help them navigate the curriculum, financial aid, and other trouble spots?
- Are we leveraging technology to empower students, advisors, and faculty? For example, can data-driven interactions between faculty and students lead to richer teaching or advising moments?
- How can "pathway thinking" lead to greater student success and increased completion rates?
- How do we support students' career goals, career placement, and career advancement?

Part of developing a strong student success program is defining tasks as well as roles and responsibilities, both for individuals and the technology. Examples include tracking student progress through the program, ensuring faculty have access to academic records, or scheduling appointments with faculty or coaches. Self-service tools may improve efficiency; dashboards may improve communication.

Many CBE programs utilize coaches, absorbing some of the advising and routine academic activities normally assigned to faculty. Coaches can fill multiple roles. For example, students meet regularly with coaches to review their dashboard and plot next steps. Coaches learn where students are having difficulty (or success) and follow up as needed. Many interactions are proactive, directing students to material, reminding them of study skills, reinforcing goals, etc. If it is an administrative bump in the road, the coach can connect the student with the institutional unit that can help resolve the problem.

Students often need a range of non-academic support, as well, such as enrollment assistance or help with financial aid paperwork and employer reimbursement. Others need help acquiring books or digital subscriptions, or identifying counseling or other institutional resources.

Our experience suggests that institutions remember the following:

- Student success puts the student at the center. Shift from the idea of students navigating an often complex and fragmented higher education system to the idea of the system being integrated and aligned to deliver the best experience for the student.
- Student success is a combination of cognitive and non cognitive factors. Engagement and persistence are critical. Success coaches as well as the personalized and formative approach of CBE support both non cognitive factors and the core academic development of students. Frequent, positive reinforcements are key.

- The student experience is a critical element in student success. Remember that experiences include human-to-human and human-to-technology interfaces.
- Adult and nontraditional learners want the flexibility and job-readiness of CBE in their degree and certificate programs.

CBE as a Catalyst for Institutional Strategy

Competency-based education is much more than just presenting content online or modifying existing degree programs—it is a different context for most institutions. The audience is different. The assumptions are different (for example, time is allowed to vary but not mastery). Organizational processes must be redesigned. Institutions that develop CBE programs are not just opting for a new degree program, they are moving into a new context where conventional notions of student, curriculum, support, timeline, and outcomes are reconceptualized.

While CBE may be an element of an institution's strategy, CBE has the potential to reshape many parts of the institution's approach. Elements of CBE that can be applied more broadly across the institution include the following:

- Growing enrollments by attracting new student segments
- Generating new revenue streams to fuel strategic initiatives
- Individualizing a student's path to mastery
- Shortening the time to mastery as a result of faster diagnosis of learning needs or course trouble spots
- Improving student success through targeted interventions
- Deepening learning and improving transfer of knowledge through digital engagement and assessment of skills such as systems thinking, collaboration, and problem solving in the context of subject-area knowledge

- Creating a new credentialing paradigm, integrating formal and informal learning in ways that serve the individual and employers
- Improving academic resource efficiency and reducing overall costs to students and institutions through better analysis and decision making
- Addressing today's skills gaps and improving employment opportunity

As the institution develops its CBE portfolio strategy, it may transform the entire institution's strategy. An exploration of the business model for a CBE program, for example, may catalyze a different view of business models and processes for other programs. The use of technology to support student success may change notions about personalization. Broad questions may arise from CBE explorations such as the following:

- What exactly is a course?
- How do we rebalance capacity with changing student demand?
- Can we achieve better learning through better use of data?
- Is there an opportunity to self-fund new initiatives as a result of CBE revenues?
- How do we design programs that fill workforce skills gaps?

CBE clearly delivers cost effective, flexible learning opportunities for working professionals seeking degrees aligned with workforce requirements. CBE should also be at the core of traditional on-campus education—that is, defining desired learning outcomes (competencies), specifying the learning objectives and related activities to reach the desired outcomes (competencies), and having a way to measure and demonstrate mastery.

WORKS CONSULTED

Babson Survey Research Group. (2013). *Grade change: Tracking online education in the United States*. Retrieved from https://onlinelearningconsortium.org/survey_report/2013-survey-online-learning-report/

Chronicle of Higher Education (2015). *A new measure for collegiate learning: What presidents think about the promises and pitfalls of competency-based education*. White paper. Subscription only.

EDUCAUSE Review (2014). *Using technology to engage the nontraditional student*. Retrieved from http://er.educause.edu/articles/2014/9/using-technology-to-engage-the-nontraditional-student

EDUCAUSE Review (2014). *Designed to engage*. Retrieved from https://er.educause.edu/articles/2014/9/designed-to-engage

Eduventures. *Ready for primetime: The competency-based market opportunity*. Retrieved from http://www.eduventures.com/about-eduventures/membership/ Subscription only.

Johnstone, S., & Soares, L. (2014). *Principles for developing competency-based education programs*. The Parthenon Group.

Klein-Collins, R., & Baylor, E. (2013). *Meeting students where they are: Profiles of students in competency-based degree programs*. Center for American Progress. Retrieved from https://www.americanprogress.org/wp-content/uploads/2013/11/CAEL-student-report-corrected.pdf

Lumina Foundation Study, with Gallup. (2014). *What America needs to know about higher education redesign*. Retrieved from https://www.luminafoundation.org/files/resources/2013-gallup-lumina-foundation-report.pdf

Oblinger, D., Ho, A., Mitos, P., & O'Reilly, U. (2015). In C. Dede (Ed.), *Data-intensive research in education: Current work and next steps*. Retrieved from http://cra.org/wp-content/uploads/2015/10/CRAEducationReport2015.pdf

National Student Clearinghouse. (2012). Press release. National Center for Education Statistics. Retrieved from http://www.studentclearinghouse.org/about/media_center/press_releases/files/release_2012-04-19.pdf

LEARNING FROM SCREENS
Two Decades of Online Education

Stephen J. Andriole

Thomas G. Labrecque Professor of Business Technology
Villanova School of Business
Villanova University

INTRODUCTION
This chapter looks at online learning technology, pedagogy, workload and outcomes, and the inter-relationships among them. It offers a set of best practices that have emerged after twenty years of learning from screens.

In 1994, technology was limited and stationary. In 2015, it was flexible and ubiquitous. In 1994, pedagogy was constrained by technology and the learning "best practices" of the nineteenth and twentieth centuries. In 2015, pedagogy included all varieties of delivery and engagement. In 1994, very little was known about the workload required to design, develop, deliver, and measure online learning for individual courses or whole academic programs. In

2015, metrics existed to help faculty, students, and administrators understand what it takes to successfully design, develop, deliver, and measure online course and master's degree outcomes.

Figure 1 presents the focus of this chapter, which examines the twenty-year journey and attempts to predict the future along the dimensions of technology, pedagogy, workload, and outcomes from emerging and expected best practices. This is deliberately done as two points in time, which is the result of my direct participation in the design, development, delivery and measurement of online courses.

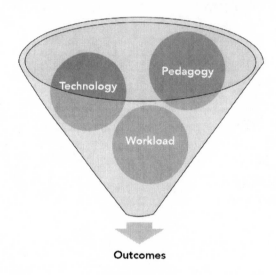

Figure 1: The challenges of online learning.

ONLINE LEARNING IN 1994

In the fall of 1994, Drexel University began offering courses over an Asynchronous Learning Network. While unconventional course and curriculum design and delivery was by no means new to Drexel, this was its first foray into interactive network-based *anytime, anyplace* education. The project was supported by the Alfred P. Sloan Foundation, which had an ongoing research program in Asynchronous Learning Networks (ALNs)—and the masters of science in information systems (MSIS) was the first completely online MSIS program in the country.

Drexel's mission was to explore the potential for asynchronous learning in the domain of information and software systems design for part-time and full-time master's students on and off campus, as well as students participating in Drexel's cooperative education program (co-op).

TECHNOLOGY IN 1994

In 1994, collaboration software was all the rage, but collaboration primarily referred to e-mail. One of the earliest e-mail communications platforms was developed by the Lotus Development Corporation, a company founded by Mitch Kapor and Jonathan Sachs. The Lotus Development Corporation was perhaps best known for the development of the Lotus 1-2-3 spreadsheet.

Lotus developed amazing, ground-breaking collaboration software based on a new client-server architecture. IBM acquired Lotus in 1995. Drexel's ALN used Lotus Notes to support communications and problem solving. Students accessed the ALN via Microsoft Windows personal computers (PCs) and Apple Macintoshes. Each student had Lotus Notes and a suite of cross-platform compatible design tools pre-loaded onto their personal computers.

Lotus Notes was a "groupware" tool that permitted students to interact asynchronously—that is, anytime, anyplace via a technique known as replication—which permitted Lotus Notes users to get on to a network, send comments and messages, and simultaneously receive comments and messages that were sent since the last time they logged onto the network. They could then leave the network and work offline until they returned to the network to "replicate" what others had done.

Replication, or the process by which students accessed the network to send and receive comments, messages, assignments, and the like, was the functionality that enabled the learning process. When students accessed the ALN (via direct dialing into the network), the server immediately sent them all of the messages, comments, and assignments that had been posted since the last time they logged on. The server also received their input to the discussion or their assignments. As soon as this exchange was completed, Lotus Notes "hung up." The students then responded to the new information offline, accessing the network again when they finished their work. This meant that students did not need to spend much time at all actually connected to the ALN; instead, they were only actually on the network for short periods of time (usually five to ten minutes). Most of the work was done locally, on their own computers.

This was not a real-time, continuous learning process.

Five courses were initially offered with the Lotus Notes technology platform. We used Lotus Notes to orchestrate *all* course activity, including discussions, content, and assignments. Students and instructors accessed the Lotus Notes server to transmit and receive discussion points and assignments. Each student, however, had his or her own course materials, software applications, and other data necessary to take the course on their individual personal computers.

Figures 2 through 6 present some screen displays from Drexel's ALN just as they appeared in 1994. These displays present the basics of the ALN interaction process. Most importantly, they convey the structure of ALN course delivery that was—and remains—essential to success. Students and faculty must know an entire course's plan before the course begins. Students must be able to "see" the entire course on the first day of class. It is also imperative that the learning environment be user friendly. Students and faculty should find the system easy to use and intuitive. We established some crude rules of thumb for assessing the usability of the ALN: ideally, for example, students were able to learn how to use the network and its supporting applications programs in two hours or less. We also wanted to make sure that network access was reliable. We wanted to be confident about the tools we integrated into the learning process.

Note that these screenshots were taken from an Apple Macintosh.

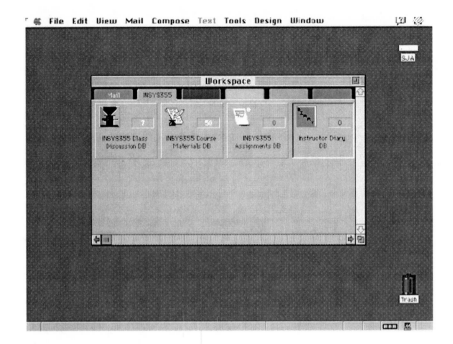

Figure 2: The Lotus Notes cockpit for class discussions, materials and assignments.

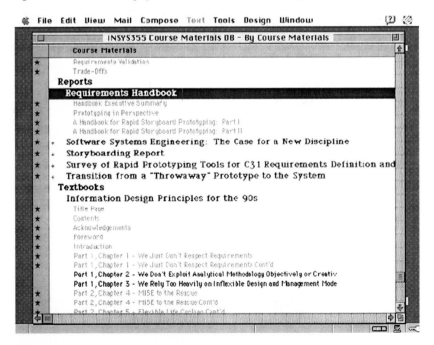

Figure 3: Course materials.

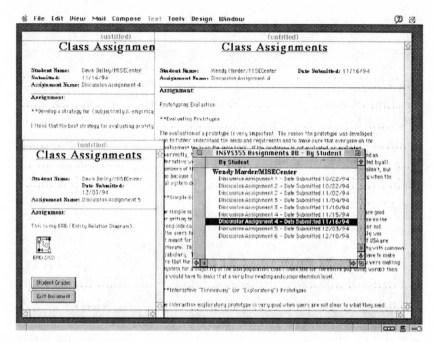

Figure 4: Course assignments.

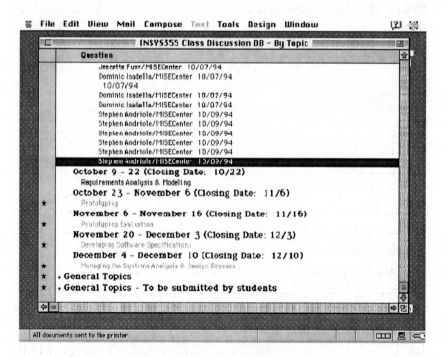

Figure 5: The course discussion data base (DB).

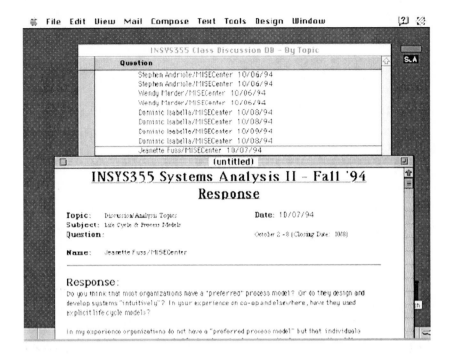

Figure 6: Sample response to discussion questions.

PEDAGOGY

The initial objectives of the 1994 Drexel ALN project included the following:

- Provide asynchronous learning opportunities for students on-campus, and students in and outside the region on co-op
- Demonstrate the integration and use of off-the-shelf computer-aided software engineering (CASE) tools into Lotus Notes to facilitate group learning and problem solving
- Simulate industrial information and software systems design on an ALN
- Measure the impact of asynchronous learning across a broad spectrum of indicators (student satisfaction, retention, degree completion time, cost-effectiveness, etc.)

- Implement self-pacing learning strategies and tactics

Information and software systems design and development was the targeted learning domain. We organized courses around the methods, tools, and techniques that support the conversion of user and software requirements into maintainable information systems. The domain focus was practice-oriented: the majority of students aspired to industrial careers. The student population included part- and full time students on campus, near campus, and on co-op. Many of the undergraduates in the network had part-time jobs; most of the graduate students were employed full time. The initial courses that were converted (from face-to-face courses) and delivered asynchronously included Systems Analysis & Design, Business Process Reengineering, and Information Systems Policy and Administration. Two additional courses, User Computer Interaction and Information Systems Implementation, were also offered.

The network was accessible to students and the Lotus Educational Consortium—of which Drexel University was a member—and the University of Illinois, another Sloan grantee, which hosted the Sloan ALN server that supported an ongoing discussion of ALN issues, problems, and challenges. Sloan wanted all of the participants in their program to share experiences, knowledge, and best practices. The Sloan server enabled this goal.

A special aspect of the project was *self-pacing*, which provided opportunities for students who fell behind or who wanted to proceed faster than average students. This aspect of the project was important since ALN-based education (and training) should offer the same quality as conventional educational processes, but also provide some additional benefits. In the fall of 1994 we made the course in *Systems* Analysis and Design continuous, that is, we offered the course term after term. This was significant because students who fell behind could stay in the course until they completed its requirements. Students took incomplete grades in one term and completed requirements for the same course in another.

WORKLOAD

The Drexel ALN project required much more work than anticipated. While we converted existing face-to-face courses to online equivalents, we nonetheless had to convert them with both technology and pedagogy in mind, anticipating how they would play online. This required us to extensively simulate course processes with special reference to how assignments could be assigned, performed, and assessed.

We also had to integrate and align course content and pedagogy to Lotus Notes and the network that connected the students, making sure that the technology worked as invisibly and unobtrusively as possible. We did not want the technology to overshadow the pedagogy, so we worked hard to keep the technology as invisible as possible. At least 250 hours was spent testing, retesting, and adapting the platform and network to make sure that everything worked as seamlessly as possible.

We also spent a great deal of time developing performance metrics. The Sloan Foundation wanted to know—empirically—exactly what was happening, and how ALN's enhanced or degraded the learning process. Frank Mayadas, the ALN Sloan program director, helped us enormously here: he and Ralph Gomory, president of the Sloan Foundation at the time, were appropriately and insightfully insistent on measurement. So we spent a lot of our—and their—time on identifying and defining performance and outcome metrics that could be empirically measured. Hundreds of hours were spent here as well.

Three professionals spent half of their time from January to August on the design, development, deployment, and testing of five courses prior to the launch of the MSIS program in the fall of 1994. This amounts to 4,080 hours of work, or roughly two person-years of effort, to develop five courses (approximately 800 hours per course). This work included the conversion of courses to Lotus Notes, the selection and integration of CASE tools into at least one course's processes, the extensive testing of the network and the learning tools that supported Lotus-Notes-based course delivery, and the simulation of alternative pedagogies.

Once the courses launched in the fall of 1994, approximately thirty hours per week was spent offline and online for each course by each professor. This time commitment greatly exceeded expectations. We hypothesized that each course would require approximately ten hours of work by each professor responsible for all aspects of each online course. The "design-once/deliver-often" concept was not supported by our experiences.

OUTCOMES

As suggested above, the project was committed to evaluation. We collected data about simple and complex outcome measures. Early results suggested that ALN-based education (and, by inference, training) was surprisingly cost-effective. We collected a great deal of online data and administered a questionnaire to determine the most effective ALN evaluation formulae.

The early results were encouraging and, in spots, even startling. Based on the data we collected in 1994 and 1995, there was every reason to believe that ALN-based education could be extended into additional domains and that whole (especially professional) degree programs could be delivered over ALNs. This was a real finding in the early-to mid-1990s. We wanted to know if the whole delivery concept would work technologically and pedagogically, while maintaining face-to-face-like quality. We discovered that it could.

As described above, the Sloan/Drexel ALN project began in January of 1994; by June of 1994 the ALN was up and running. The first courses were offered in the fall of 1994. Three courses were converted to ALN form; the conversion of several others quickly followed. The methodology for the project was anchored in systems engineering, which calls for requirements modeling prior to design and development. We thus began with a set of educational objectives and then developed a course conversion/design methodology that permitted us to satisfy those objectives.

The evaluation methodology required that a set of knowledge and ability capabilities be achieved via the learning process. Those capabilities were in turn converted into a set of topics, subtopics, and assignments. Readings were then matched to the topics, subtopics, and assignments. We developed a set of tools and processes for monitoring ALN activity, a back-up server, and an online grading system that permitted instructors to grade student assignments as they were submitted, and we integrated the cross-platform-compatible CASE tools into the network.

So what did we learn about ALN-based course design and delivery?

There were two kinds of observations. One set was based on a questionnaire administered after every course; the other was based on inferences made from questionnaire results, the experiences of the instructors, and empirical data about network behavior and patterns.

Summary interaction data for the courses given to date appears below:

- Number of interactions for approximately eight weeks:
    * 800 (for an average course of ten students)
- Preferred interaction times of day:
    * 8 PM - 12 Midnight (36% of total)
    * 4 PM - 8 PM (22% of total)
    * 12 Midnight - 4 AM (14% of total)

Questionnaire results included the following:

- 80% would take another ALN course
- 85% felt they had more access to the instructor than in "conventional" course delivery
- 80% felt that conventional courses were more boring than the ALN course
- 75% did not miss in-class lectures
- 75% felt they had more communication with fellow students than in conventional courses
- 70% felt they learned more on the ALN-based course than they would have expected to learn in a conventional course

- 95% felt that seeing the ideas and assignments of others was useful

After several courses, patterns emerged. Students found the ALN more convenient and—much more importantly—a superb learning environment. This was a gratifying—and somewhat surprising—finding.

The second set of results was inferential. It appeared—after several course deliveries and questionnaire data analyses—that the following was true: there was an enormous need for structure in an ALN environment, including:

- Opening and closing of discussion windows
- Clear discussion topics, readings, and assignment schedule
- Completely predictable course schedules
- All materials online and accessible
- Common course "look and feel," especially in a multiple course ALN
- Real-time monitoring of student performance

We also learned that online education *could* be made cost-effective:

- Hypothesized (maximum) quality ratios:
    * One instructor for every thirty students
    * One instructor plus one ALN assistant per fifty students
    * One instructor plus two ALN assistants per seventy-five students

- The methodology was repeatable:
    * The communications hardware and software is off-the-shelf and relatively inexpensive, and on the right price/performance trends
    * Industrial information and software systems design processes can be "simulated" via ALNs

* We can design a learning process and an interactive asynchronous learning environment that accommodates self-pacing CASE tools and can be integrated into a groupware environment

While we worked to identify the critical success factors for online education, there was a set of organizational conditions likely to predict ALN success. First—and perhaps foremost—we recognized that ALN-based course and curriculum design and delivery was an educational (and training) specialization that not all faculty or institutions can—or will want to—practice. It was also likely that faculty will—ideally—be motivated to participate in the ALN educational and training process as part of their normal duties and not as an overload. We determined in 1994, that if ALN-based course design and delivery was an overload for faculty, then it would become too expensive to deliver and eventually end up competing with normal workload responsibilities. This was an early yellow flag.

We also learned that institutions as a whole must be committed to ALN-based education and training. If organizations regard the technology as a fad or something in which they must become involved because of perceived competition, they will not sustain ALNs as part of their primary educational delivery process.

ONLINE LEARNING IN 2015

In the summer of 2015, I completed two sections of an online MBA course called Information Technology as a Strategic Lever for Villanova University's MBA program. I designed and developed this required course in winter/spring 2015 and delivered it in the summer of 2015. This was a 1.5 credit course that began on June 29, 2015 and ended on August 21, 2015. I delivered two sections of the course. I had twenty-five students in each section (for a total of fifty students).

What changed in twenty years?

Obviously the technology changed, but what about the pedagogy, workload, and outcomes?

As we investigate these changes, there's another change that deserves special mention: the *business* of online education and training enabled by technology and accreditation has exploded over the past twenty years. Twenty years ago, the business of online education and training was small. Very few companies sold online certificates for profit and very few universities offered online undergraduate or graduate programs. By 2015, the number of companies, colleges, and universities offering online certificates—and degrees—of one kind or another is easily well into the hundreds. What we referred to as "ALNs" in the 1990s is now a major revenue stream for countless companies, colleges, and universities.

TECHNOLOGY

The ability to connect, work, browse, and *live* online has obviously increased dramatically in the last twenty years. This is perhaps the understatement of the century. What we called "groupware" has yielded to social media and messaging platforms capable of performing all sorts of tasks. What we called "replication" in 1994, is what we now call real-time collaboration. Students today can mix and match their communications tools and techniques through access to a variety of professional and personal devices, networks and applications.

There are also now learning management systems (LMSs) created specifically to support online education and training. Note that in 1994 we customized Lotus Notes to support the learning process, an assignment it was never designed to complete. We used Blackboard as our LMS. In fact, today there are numerous open source and proprietary LMSs, including the following:

- Open Source Learning Management Systems
  * aTutor
  * Canvas
  * Chamilo

* Claroline
* eFront
* ILIAS
* LAMS
* Moodle
* OLAT
* OpenOLAT
* Sakai
* SWAD
* Totara LMS
* WeBWorK

- Proprietary Learning Management Systems
  * Blackboard Learning System (the LMS used in Villanova's MBA Program)
  * CERTPOINT Systems Inc.
  * Desire2Learn
  * Digication
  * eCollege
  * Edmodo
  * Engrade
  * WizIQ
  * GlobalScholar
  * Glow (Scottish Schools National Intranet)
  * HotChalk
  * Informetica
  * ITWorx CLG (Connected Learning Gateway)
  * JoomlaLMS
  * Latitude Learning LLC
  * Meridian Knowledge Solutions
  * Ning
  * QuestionMark
  * Uzity
  * SAP

* Sclipo
* Schoology
* SharePointLMS
* SSLearn
* Spongelab
* Skillsoft
* SuccessFactors
* SumTotal Systems
* Taleo
* TeamWox
* Vitalect

The sheer number of learning management systems suggests that the business of online education and training has been professionalized, a far cry from where we were twenty years ago when we customized LMS functions in a groupware application.

Note also the changes in bandwidth and network access. In 1994, access and bandwidth were relatively constrained. In fact, most of the work the students did was offline: they replicated when they logged on—but they seldom stayed online very long. In 2015, many of the students spent huge blocks of time online, often responding to discussion posts as soon as they appeared—and for hours on end. Our data suggests that students would often spend hours online participating in course discussions (in real-time), posting assignments and looking at course content continuously and from device to device.

Nor was there the ability to "Hollywood Square" up in synchronous video. In 2015, we used Adobe Connect to connect us all once a week. In 1994, this was impossible.

We also used simple content to support the 1994 courses, like books, papers, and journal articles. In 2015, we expanded the concept of content to include books, papers, journal articles, videos, interactive cases, spreadsheets, and audios. While we used computer-aided software engineering (CASE) tools back then, today these tools are a click away from a laptop, tablet, or smartphone.

In 2015, students accessed the course through (a cloud-hosted) Blackboard from any device they chose. This four-screen (desktop/laptop/tablet/smartphone) approach made it possible for students to discuss topics in their home offices and continue the discussion on their smartphones while jogging or traveling (which many of them actually did).

Finally, Blackboard (and other learning management systems) provided the capability to watch and learn in real-time through a set of embedded analytics. This capability proved very useful during grading (also an embedded capability) and for assessing participation rates, frequencies, and the depth of participation in discussions and regarding group and individual assignments.

PEDAGOGY

The course had seven modules, shown in Figure 7.

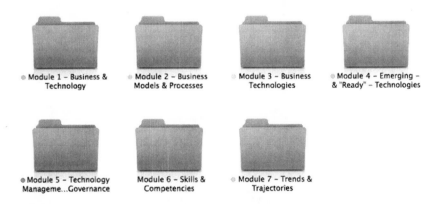

Figure 7: Course modules.

There were required and optional materials for each module that the students received. There were fifty-two required readings and eighty-three optional readings. There was one optional book. There were audio files for the required readings and one video for each of the seven modules, all shown in Figure 8.

Figure 8: Audio, video, and traditional content.

Figure 8 suggests that the course was organized around audio and video files attached to required readings, with optional materials that the students could use to widen and deepen their understanding of each module's subject matter. (While it was clear that the students read the required materials, most did not read the optional requirements—until they wrote their final essays.)

Figure 9 presents an example of one module's contents.

Figure 9: Typical module content.

The discussions were organized around discussion points, which were provided for all modules. Here is an example:

MBA 8710 Summer 2015

Information Technology as a Strategic Lever

*Module 2–**Business Models & Processes**–Discussion Points*

- What is a business model?
- How are business models differentiated?
- Do you understand your company's business model?
- What changes would you make to your company's business model?
- How is your company's business model updated and improved?
- How significant are business models organized around Gen X, Y, and, especially, Gen Z?
- How will mobility change business models?
- Do you understand the value of 'business process modeling' and 'business process management'?
- Have you ever used any BPM tools?
- Do you think that formal process modeling would be helpful at your company?

The importance of organization and structure and the communication of both to the students was extremely important. Students needed to know what was in the course, what they were expected to do (and when), and how they would be graded. No changes should occur during the course, because every in-course change ripples through process, structure, and expectations. For example, the identification of content with discussion points for each module was essential to anchor discussions and learning momentum: discussion points were published for each module on the first day of the course. The final essay exam was also published the first day of class so students could reverse engineer course content to their final essays.

WORKLOAD

The number of hours devoted to course development (by one professional) during the period from February to June 2015 was approximately 580. The number of hours devoted to the delivery of the two sections of one course was approximately 390 hours (approximately forty-nine hours per week, or twenty-five hours per section), for a total of 970 hours. (This was similar to our 1994 experience of approximately thirty hours per week/per course.) Delivery consumed Thursdays, Fridays, Saturdays, Sundays, and Mondays. Live sessions were given on Thursday evenings, back to back, starting at 9 PM.

As was the case in 1994, the number of hours spent designing, developing, and delivering the course was unexpectedly high, and greatly exceeded our estimates around the level of design/development/delivery effort required for a traditional face-to-face course. Note again: both in 1994 and 2015, the workload around the design, development, and delivery of online courses significantly exceeded the workload for a conventional face-to-face course.

Four months were spent developing one course and two months delivering two sections of that (1.5 credit) course. All told, this amounted to the identification of 135 required and optional materials, the recording of sixty audios, making seven videos, reading and responding to over 3,000 posts, reading, commenting on, and grading ten group projects, and reading and grading fifty final essays.

Assumptions that the same responses can be used in discussion boards within and across sections were proved false. The course's structure required students to respond to discussion points with reference to their former and current companies. So each response had to be customized to each post. This perhaps may not be the case for all courses, but if an instructor wants master's students to relate course content and discussions to their companies, then there's little or no chance of "canning" responses to oft-repeated questions.

Assumptions about "design once/deliver often" again proved false, at least for a technology course. Given the velocity of technology change, it's impossible to deliver the same course twice without significant updates. While this might be unique to technology education, it may also apply to other fields as well. It would be impossible to deliver a quality course in business technology without significantly updating the course each time it was taught.

OUTCOME

In terms of the metrics reported for our 1994 ALN courses, we can report on many of the same metrics in 2015.

For example, summary interaction data for the 2015 courses appears below:

- Number of posts (for two sections of the same course) for approximately eight weeks:
- 3,227 posts (for average course of twenty-five students)
- Preferred interaction times of day:
- Continuous—no preferred times/almost equal distribution of access times

Our 2015 data consisted of CATS (Course and Teacher Surveys) scores (see Figures 10 and 11) and informal, unsolicited student comments. Both sets of data indicated the following:

- 100% would take another ALN course
- 90% felt they had more access to the instructor than in conventional course delivery
- 80% felt that conventional courses were more boring than the ALN course
- 85% did not miss in-class lectures
- 85% felt they had more communication with fellow students than in conventional courses
- 80% felt they learned more on the ALN-based course than they would have expected to learn in a conventional course
- 95% felt that seeing the discussions and projects of other students was useful

- 90% felt that connecting course material to real companies improved the learning process

As in 1994, students in 2015 found online learning more convenient and equally effective as face-to-face courses. Similar to our 1994 experience, there was an enormous need for structure in the 2015 online learning environment, including the following:

- Opening and closing of discussion windows
- Clear discussion topics, readings, and assignment schedule
- All materials online and accessible

We learned in 2015 that there are strong relationships among levels of necessary-and-sufficient effort versus what may be overkill. Very conscientious teachers may find the online experience to be gratifying in terms of student satisfaction, but overwhelming in terms of workload.

We also learned that it's important to measure quality against workload. My students enjoyed the interaction they had with me within Blackboard and outside of Blackboard (through conventional e-mail and phone calls, and face-to-face meetings with students, at their request). I made it a point to be always and nearly immediately accessible, which may not be necessary.

As the course progressed, the students started to post earlier than required, reflecting rising enthusiasm for the course. The two sections generated thousands of posts (I had 375 total posts in the first week/module for one section of twenty-five students alone). Many of these posts were part of a thread that represents community, threads in which I participated directly, frequently, and quickly.

Fortunately, by 2015, most colleges and universities have adopted a course evaluation methodology embodied in Course and Teacher Surveys, or CATS, scores. The CATS scores for the two sections of the course appear in Figures 10 and 11.

The CATS scores suggest that the course was well received. In fact, the CATS scores are higher on some dimensions than the (same) face-to-face course. The scores for the "Overall Quality of

Instruction" metric were 4.6 and 4.8 (out of 5). Other important metrics include the perception of organization, responsiveness, and the likelihood and quality of faculty responses to student queries.

These metrics are the ones that explain the success or failure of conventional face-to-face courses. The online courses performed extremely well objectively *and* relatively.

BEST PRACTICES, THEN & NOW

The comparisons across the decades are very instructive. In fact, the overall experiences in 1994 and 2015 were amazingly similar. The major differences were technological. The pedagogical, workload, and outcomes data was similar, if not almost repetitive.

So what did we learn?

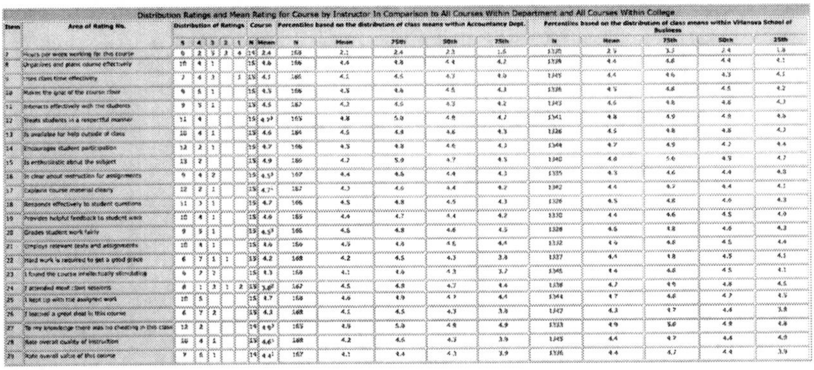

Figure 10: CATS Scores for Section 1 of Information Technology as a Strategic Lever.

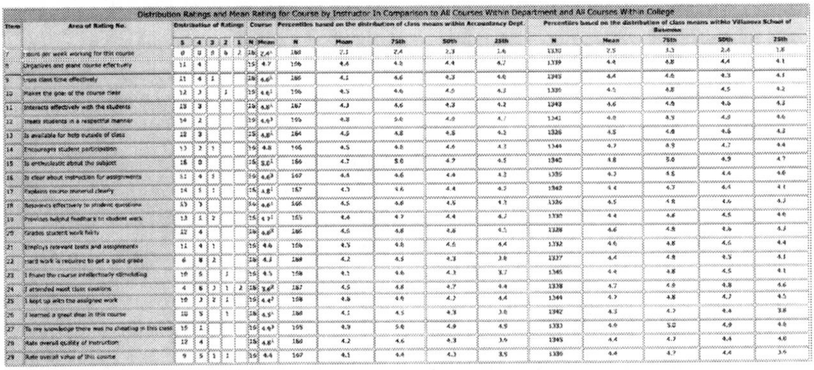

Figure 11: CATS Scores for Section 2 of Information Technology as a Strategic Lever

What are the design, development, delivery, and measurement best practices? Here's a short list of observations and emerging best practices:

- Online course objectives, content, assignments, and delivery processes must be incredibly well defined and organized well in advance of course delivery–and left unchanged throughout the course.
- Faculty must own the content, structure, and pedagogy–not third-party consultants or "design engineers."
- Course learning objectives and student participation/assignment expectations must be crystal clear and frequently repeated to students.
- Faculty must be fully trained on the delivery platform and tools (ALNs, Blackboard, Adobe Connect, Blackboard Analytics, grading, etc.) well before the course begins.
- Development time is much greater than expected. It takes a great deal of time to develop quality video and audio content; it also takes an enormous amount of time to deliver and measure online courses. Appropriate resources should be devoted to the design, development, delivery and evaluation process.
- There should be "course cohorts" comprised of one or two full-time faculty members and one or two adjuncts, which enable staffing, back-ups, rotation, and scalability.
- Students need to be led through the learning process through a combination of techniques, but mostly through discussion points published when the course launches and republished throughout the course.
- Faculty engagement stimulates student engagement, though it requires a great deal of faculty time.
- Learning outcomes are better achieved in a "high-engagement" class, defined around levels of student *and* faculty participation.

- Online education is not a direct transfer of a classroom experience to a virtual one: the delivery platform and process is different from the classroom experience and these differences should be optimized through the skilled exploitation of the capabilities of the learning platform, and by developing an "online personality" to which students can relate. Online pedagogy is a science and an art that should be learned and practiced prior to offering an online course.
- Alternative faculty compensation models should be explored.

GOING FORWARD

Faculty members manage their online workload through a variety of techniques. For example, some online professors do not comment on many student posts. Nor do they respond in timely ways. Some restrict the number of student projects. The trade-offs among quality/workload/compensation may justify (and even require)—even when weighting quality high—lighter versions of online courses. This is a core issue. Some colleges and universities tout their commitment to the quality of their online instruction, but fail to acknowledge that quality is driven by preparation and engagement. But engagement requires lots of work (and resources), so commitments to quality may suffer because of other commitments, like profitability.

Compensation and incentives remain an issue. Some faculty, especially the overly-conscientious ones, may not feel that the compensation model is adequate. Adjuncts may feel especially challenged by workload and compensation. Full-time faculty should be permitted to count online courses as part of their teaching loads. If online teaching is not part of faculty teaching loads, then only some faculty will participate. Over time we will learn if the participating faculty are the best faculty for online education. Relatedly, if full time faculty do not participate extensively in online college and university educational programs, instruction will default to adjunct faculty, who are seldom motivated by the same incentives as full-time faculty. The increased use of adjunct faculty to design/develop/deliver online courses and whole academic programs requires additional coordination and management and may, over time, threaten the quality of online education. This is an issue that must be addressed by colleges and universities engaged in the business of online education.

What about technology, pedagogy, and outcomes?

Technology will obviously continue to evolve. Learning management systems will become more functional, more intelligent, and much easier to use. Access to learning networks will be ubiquitous, on-demand, and therefore continuous. Linkages to academic programs and for-profit courses will be seamless. Accreditation will continue to admit new players to the market. Pedagogy will exploit new technologies like virtual reality, automated reasoning, location-based services, and wearables. We'll measure the effectiveness of online education not through quizzes, tests, and projects, but through students' ability to simulate, create challenging problems, and develop creative solution spaces. The structures of the nineteenth and twentieth centuries will continue to disappear as we march into the twenty-first century. The whole concept of course/program-based "start-and-stop" education will be replaced by continuous learning models where students immerse themselves in self-paced learning defined and constrained only by lingering accreditation requirements: the whole concept of "courses" and "programs" will be replaced by evidence of evolving skills and competencies. Self-pacing will become a best practice.

Learning will adapt to domains, individuals, teams, and ultimately, the business of education and training. This will require the educational establishment to change, so all this may take a while. Nevertheless, we can be certain that online education and training is here to stay, will dramatically increase, and will permanently alter the way learning occurs within and beyond the ivory tower.

This is just the beginning of major educational disruption.

In 1994, we successfully experimented with Asynchronous Learning Networks (ALNs) with the generous support of the Alfred P. Sloan Foundation. In 2015, online education and training is a major business. By 2025, education and training will seamlessly integrate with traditional education and training as it exploits technology and pedagogy in disruptive ways that are hard to precisely define today.

But make no mistake, disruptive change is already well underway, and the business of education and training will never be the same.

THE ANNUAL REPORT ON ONLINE LEARNING

An Interview with Jeff Seaman

Director
Babson Survey Research Group

WILLIAM PATRICK: How did you get started with the Annual Report on Online Learning?

JEFF SEAMAN: It was Frank Mayadas, who administered grants at the Alfred P. Sloan Foundation, who got the ball rolling. He approached Elaine Allen and myself and said, "I have one simple question for you. How many students are learning online?"

WP: Yeah, that's not so simple a question.

JS: In response, Elaine and I put together a proposal to the Sloan Foundation to address Frank's question, which they approved. We had no idea this would turn into an annual report; we assumed we were planning a one-off. These early years were very interesting ones for online learning, with many people in higher education asking, "Well, what is this online learning?" There had been ten years of Sloan Foundation investment in online education at that point, but no one knew the big picture impact because there were no tracking mechanisms in place.

WP: How did you decide on what to include in the report?

JS: As is typical with the Sloan Foundation, there was a lot of back and forth about exactly what we'd be most interested in learning. One of the first questions we had to address was what is our universe of interest—all of higher education or just particular types of institutions? The decision was clear; we were interested in all degree-granting organizations.

The next question was, "What is it we're measuring?" At that point, there was no universally accepted definition of what constituted an online course. We conducted a number of pretests, using multiple definitions to settle on a definition that was both meaningful and one we could measure. Our first definition was very strict: that all content had to be online for a course to be classified as an online course. After extensive testing, we revised the definition to require at least 80 percent of the content to be delivered online. It wasn't an ideal definition, but it was the closest to an ideal definition that was actually answerable.

The definition had to allow for some non-online content in order for people to be able to respond. From the Sloan Foundation's point of view, if institutions were delivering 80 percent of the content online, the foundation would consider that an online course. However, if, for example, only 50 percent was being delivered online, then they would conclude that the institution wasn't fully invested in online as a delivery method. Testing in succeeding years found that virtually all of the courses that were listed as being at least 80 percent online were, in fact, 100 percent online, so we were happy to continue with the metric. Functionally, if we had picked 95 percent, or 90 percent, or 85 percent, the results would have been virtually identical.

WP: With all the unknowns at this point, how did you decide who on campus to survey?

JS: We were not after the opinions of those running online programs (such as the online program director), as they have a vested interest and would give us a biased view. We needed respondents at the highest decision-making level to be able tell us if online learning was critical for the institution's long-term strategies. That led us to focus on the chief academic officer, defined as the highest-ranking individual at the institution with direct responsibility for the academic programs. They typically have a title of provost or academic vice president.

WP: And what were those early numbers revealed by the survey?

JS: The first report in 2003 found that 1.6 million out of 16.6 million total students in higher education were taking at least one online course; or in other words, 9.6 percent of all students had experienced online education during the previous academic year. The number came as a shock, and many did not believe it.

WP: Since the Sloan Foundation had been giving out grants since 1993, I'm surprised there was no means of measuring the effects during those years. But I'm more interested in your ideas about why there wasn't an agreed-upon definition for online learning then.

JS: Well, nobody knew the numbers because there was no mechanism in place to collect them. Part of the reason was that the definitional issues were complicated. The Sloan Foundation had their own definition; their journal was called the *Journal of Asynchronous Learning Networks* because of their focus was asynchronous learning. But there was no coalescing around any particular definition across all of higher education. People were building online courses and programs, inventing their own approaches as they went. Some were saying, "If I have at least one online session it is an online course," and others were saying, "Everything needs to be conducted online to be an online course," and others would ask, "What if it's done over the phone—online versus distance?" The net result was a lot of confusion.

WP: So how did you and Elaine finally decide on the definition that you wanted to use?

JS: Our approach was to conduct a number of pretests, using small samples to test various alternatives. We quickly discovered that we needed a definition that was short, clear, and somewhat flexible. The need to be flexible wasn't that we were trying to be imprecise, but because respondents didn't have data to answer a very specific question. If we used a very specific definition, for instance, "100 percent of everything delivered online," respondents would tell us, "Most of the course is online, but we send some materials out through the mail. Does that mean it's not an online course?" Or some said, "What if we have an organizational meeting on campus before we launch into fully online—is that an online course?" The result of all this feedback was basically, "I can't answer this."

WP: What did you learn when you first began conducting the survey?

JS: Two things were immediately clear; there were a large number of people in higher education who thought that the advent of online was going to cause massive changes, and there was little agreement on what those changes would be. Some thought that online education would usher in a new golden era; others saw it as the death of higher education as they knew it. Of course neither of these came to pass, although there was enough truth in each of the views to provide some interesting topics to investigate for the next thirteen years.

Of particular interest was examining the role of online education as a catalyst for radical change in higher education. The argument was that technology had made massive changes in other industries, and now it was higher education's turn. The view was that an online, highly-enabled education was going to completely change the way that students viewed their college educations. There wasn't a lot of agreement on what that change would be, but there was considerable speculation: one view was that geography was no longer going to be a factor; people would enroll wherever they wanted to go. This would lead to a huge consolidation with name recognition and brand awareness being the driving forces—not proximity—and small, local, and regional institutions would be pushed to the wayside, with the big names capturing all of the students.

WP: I can see that as a reasonable fear back then.

JS: Our results showed that local never stopped being important, and the vast majority of online students came from within fifty miles of campus. Federal data now tracks how many distance students come from the same state as the institution and, once again, we see that local still rules. Most institutions do not see a substantial change in their geographic service area when they add online offerings. When we probed why this was the case, it turned out that while the range of college options may have expanded for the online student, the process by which they made their choice was still basically the same. They selected institutions that they were most familiar with because of a local sports team, local advertising, or where fellow workers attended. The same recognition and familiarity with the local institutions continues to trump most of the distance and independence issues.

WP: While we're on this, how did you end up selecting the topic questions for the early surveys?

JS: They came from a number of sources. We began with the core set of questions from the Sloan Foundation. They were very simple: "How many people are learning online? Is it growing? Where is it growing?" The foundation was also interested in the institutional perspective: "How do institutions view online learning? What are their strategies for using it?" They wanted to understand not just if institutions had online offerings, but if they were a sideline or part of their core mission.

Most of the other questions came out of our own personal curiosity. We've always had three types of questions. First, core questions, which we ask every year address enrollment, strategic decisions, faculty acceptance, and perceptions of quality. Then we have a set of questions which we include every second, third, or fourth year, typically because the rate of change does not require annual monitoring. Finally, we have topical questions, typically related to economy issues. When the economy was tanking, we wanted to ask about the impact on online programs and enrollments. And when the economy was recovering, we wanted to understand that impact.

WP: So you just tweaked it as you went along year to year?

JS: Yes. The core remains the same; 60 percent of the questions have not changed over the thirteen years. A few evolved over time. We had a few that did not work well and were dropped, but most questions asked in 2003 were still asked in the last survey.

WP: Now I know that your survey is directed at people who work in higher education, but do you have a sense of how the general public regards online learning?

JS: Getting greater awareness and understanding of online education among the general public was one of the original goals of the Sloan Foundation in supporting these reports. The strategy was to reach the public through the popular press, so we wanted to educate reporters about the nature of and growth on online learning. Questions from these reporters have changed dramatically over time. At first, there was a tone of mystery and misunderstanding about online learning, as the reporters had no frame of reference. Early reporters thought online was the same as correspondence courses that you signed up for on the back of a matchbook. Their questions were very basic: "Do I need a computer? Is this done on a telephone? Will I know any other people who are in my class? Will I have a book?"

Because a primary objective for the Sloan Foundation was to convince the public that online learning was viable, we released the first report at the National Press Club. The coverage in the popular press meant that the message, "There are millions of students who are learning online, and it's working for them," could begin to resonate in the populace. The plan from the beginning was for the reports to be as widely distributed as we could manage, so it has always been a free download, to get as many copies out there as we possibly could. We also did our own marketing, unusual for most academic reports, by buying mailing lists and sending announcements with download links to multiple groups in higher education.

WP: So the Sloan Foundation wanted that first survey to act as something that was informative and persuasive simultaneously, right?

JS: Correct. And that worked extremely well for us, because the foundation understood that we have two audiences. One was the popular press, to get the information in front of the general population; and the other was the academic community, because those groups needed to be convinced that online learning was real and that it had merit. The Sloan Foundation also understood that the report needed to be not just independent, but also *viewed* as independent. That meant we were free to ask and to publish questions that were negative for online as well as positive. We had complete autonomy to design the survey and include whatever we thought was most important—warts and all—which was critical for gaining credibility among the academic community.

WP: Apropos of that, what do you make of the ways that people in higher education have responded to your questions? From the beginning and all the way through, what trends did you see?

JS: When we began, the amount of information about online education was extremely limited, for both reporters and academics. It was pretty scary how poorly informed both academics and the journalists who wrote about academia were, given there were already over a million and a half students involved. For the first two or three years, all of our sessions with reporters started out with basic questions about what was an online course. They did not understand how they operated or that they could serve "regular" students. There was an assumption that these online students had to be somehow different from "real" students.

Similarly, only a small fraction of administrators and faculty had any hands-on or direct experience with online. If you wanted to characterize most academics, it would be "unaware." The lack of awareness changed very rapidly among academics, moving to where they were aware but unconvinced of its merits. It took only a few years to change from very low levels of awareness of online education to one where awareness became pervasive.

The acceptance of online as a viable delivery mechanism has also seen a big shift. In the beginning, there was an aura of experimentation about online. The early pioneers often tailored new offerings for a specialty population—people who can't make it to campus for some reason, not as a delivery mechanism for the mainstream, on-campus population. That's not the case today. Many schools now treat online as their primary, or at least their equal, delivery mechanism.

WP: Who downloads the Annual Report on Online Learning? Who is interested in this?

JS: There have been close to two million copies of our reports distributed over the first twelve years, not counting secondary distribution. The fact that more than a million people have decided to download these reports is indicative of the level of interest in the topic and the lack of alternative sources.

About 60 percent of the downloads come from US higher education. There's also a huge amount coming from businesses—and not just businesses that are linked to higher education, but businesses in general, who are interested in online education for their employees for enrichment programs, etc. There is a sizeable international distribution to over 100 countries every year. The reports have been translated into Spanish, into Thai, into Chinese, and the survey has been replicated in multiple other countries. It appears that many countries look to the United States as the world leader in online education and hope to learn from what is happening here.

There is a significant level of interest in the entire series, not just the latest report. The current report averages about ten thousand downloads per month, while the year-old report has three thousand, and the two-year old report about a thousand downloads a month. Even the very first report is still being downloaded hundreds of times per month.

WP: What general trends have you seen over the last twelve years of doing this?

JS: The overall opinion about online education has been continually improving. Every year, most of the how-good-is-online questions show continuous improvement. The number of people reporting that online education is "as good as or superior to face-to-face learning" continues to increase.

But then there's another set of indicators that just do not change. There is a group of institutions that continue to report that, "online does not fit our mission. We will not do it." These institutions have been steadfast in that belief. They tend to be small, teaching a traditional-aged student, and they place considerable value on the on-campus experience. They believe that the value of an education is not just what happens in the classroom; it's also what you experience through the entire time at Alma Mater U. Online is not for them, and they have not budged from that belief.

Institutions are in three groups: those that have a positive view of online and that are trying to build it into their system, those who are negative, and those that were in the middle or neutral. Early on, the biggest group was the neutral group. Over time, what we've seen is a continuing movement of institutions from the neutral group into those that are positive about online. But, there has been little movement among institutions that were negative; there are almost as many now as there were ten years ago.

WP: Yeah, because they believe their clientele doesn't include adult learners or people who need to access distance learning, right?

JS: Yes. What's driven the belief in online, even among those who don't like it, is the concept of access. When most people talk about online, they typically don't describe it as being a better way to teach and learn, rather, they say, "It allows people who would not have access to this program or course to participate." Even faculty members who don't like online are still positive about the access issue. The more an institution's mission is driven by access, such as community colleges with government mandates to improve literacy and provide education to members of the community, the more likely online education will be a core part of their strategy.

WP: Let's talk about some of the beliefs and attitudes that have surrounded this endeavor. I am, first of all, fascinated by the notion that online learning has been viewed as a possible financial savior for higher education.

JS: There is a fairly persistent belief that higher education has financial problems. We're all aware that the cost of education keeps growing; other than health care, it's the fastest-rising sector of the economy in terms of cost. The concern about cost is present in the public policy discussions today.

Then there was a belief—this is before there were millions of online students and before most schools had online offerings—that online had the potential to be far more efficient, to leverage a small amount of resources to teach a large number of students. The institutional thinking was, "This teacher now teaches twenty-two students. If we record all the lectures and post the material online, we can enroll hundreds of students in that same class." But it didn't work. The initial perception of, "Oh, we can just point a camera at faculty as they teach their current classes and then we have the online version," didn't work either.

The truth is that it typically takes more time and effort to develop an online course. It's a different way of teaching, and the biggest difference that we heard from faculty members was, "I can no longer wing it. I have to think out the entire course before I launch it online," whereas with a lecture course, you can be halfway through and still change the final lectures if something isn't working out very well. The production processes for an online course mean you don't have that same luxury.

WP: I am amazed that so many professors were and still are so adamantly opposed to it, citing poor quality, among other reasons.

JS: Talking about faculty resistance and course quality puts us on a slippery slope. There is no universally agreed-upon measure of quality—course quality, learning quality, institutional quality, etc. How do you compare the quality of a face-to-face course at one institution with that at another? There's no clear answer and, in fact, probably the reason that we have indirect reputation rankings like *US News* is because there is no good universal measure. The federal government college scorecard measures do not directly address quality either, but instead look at debt burden, or the proportion of the students who complete their degrees within a specific time period.

We realized that we could never measure quality per se, but we could measure the *perception* of quality—in particular, the perception of relative quality—among academic leaders. The approach was to ask the chief academic officer—responsible for both the face-to-face and the online courses at their campus—what they thought the relative quality of those two delivery mechanisms. Of course, this comes with multiple caveats: we know that quality varies from course to course, quality varies by which faculty member is teaching, and what may be perfect for one student might be terrible for another. Key decision makers were making long-term, strategic decisions and resource allegations based on their perceptions, so it was important to understand what was driving these decisions.

We asked the relative quality question of key decision makers and faculty members. There is a clear pattern that emerges: those people and institutions with the greatest exposure to online tend to see the two as equivalent. There's a small minority who see the online as superior, and often for very specific reasons. Then there's a bit larger group that report, "No, it's not quite as good, but access trumps the other quality issues."

The biggest predictor for having a positive view as to the quality of online learning is exposure to online. That's true for leaders and for faculty. If a faculty member has ever taken an online course, taught an online course, or been part of a group which has designed an online course, then they are much more positive than others who have not had any exposure. They understand what it takes to deliver an online course and the effort involved, and they are less skeptical because they have been through that process.

If you ask all faculty members, not just those teaching online, they are much more suspect about the quality of online than their academic leaders, and they tend to be very negative about online education in general. Faculty members will overwhelmingly tell you that online is inferior to face-to-face instruction. There is a large group that says it's the same; very, very few will tell you that online is superior.

However, if you ask that same group of faculty, "Have you ever recommended an online course to one of your students or advisees," they report, for the most part, "Yes, I have." Many who believe online quality is abysmal will have recommended online courses. When you probe about why, the answer is "access"—"This student couldn't fit it in her schedule any other way to graduate on time," or, "This course is not available this term any other way," or, "We didn't offer it at our institution and they had to get it somewhere else to fill out their major." Access trumps any of the other issues.

WP: So has the percentage of faculty resistance reported to you remained fairly steady for the last twelve years?

JS: Yes. It has barely budged, even among the largest institutions, those with more than 5000 online students. Clearly there are large numbers of faculty at these institutions who are designing, delivering, reviewing, and planning online courses. Yet, the leaders of those schools report that the percentage of their faculty members who accept and approve of online has barely budged. It says something about academic leaders that they are able to staff programs to enroll thousands of online students when they report that "my faculty doesn't accept it."

WP: Now I know in your report that you deal with MOOCs (Massive Open Online Courses), at least recently. What's your personal feeling about MOOCs? Do you think they're going to last?

JS: Well, I think they're going to morph. It's the same thing as online. When online first began, everybody had these grandiose ideas: "We're going to deliver education completely differently." However, you'll never lose money betting that higher education will take the conservative approach. I expect the same thing will happen with MOOCs. We've moved from the hype stage, "Everybody's talking about this so we better think about it," to the next level. In the beginning there was no compelling reason for most schools to offer a MOOC other than "because everybody is talking about it." Now the hype is down from what it was, however, there are still only a small number of schools involved. The number of schools with MOOCs went from two and a half to about five percent. That is a huge growth—doubling in such a short period—but you're still talking about only one in twenty.

So I don't see that MOOCs are going to radically change higher education. I'm somewhat disappointed that that's the case, but I don't see that as what's happening. I do see that people are beginning to understand that it's yet another tool. It's another way to build and learn.

WP: Do you think the general public understands any of what we're talking about here?

JS: Yes. I think the general public has accepted online far faster and more openly than higher education has, because it fills a need. People ask themselves, "How do I improve my education or my employment prospects while I continue to work?" Or, "I have a family. What can I do with my education and still take care of them?" Taking online courses has been the answer for millions of these individuals.

Among academics there are concerns about retention rates, the quality of learning outcomes, and the effort required to develop and deliver online courses. The evidence on retention rates is not definitive; the sixty-four-thousand-dollar question is, do retention rates reflect the nature of course or the nature of the student? Are retention rates lower for online courses because they attract those students with greater likelihood to have work, family, or other life issues intercede? Or is it that online doesn't have that kind of intimacy that classroom learning does, and therefore it's harder for students to continue? Or perhaps it's that online courses place a much greater requirement on students to manage their own schedule and control their own education? The answer is, "yes." It's all of those. But the differences in the students cannot be ignored.

WP: What impact has online education had for higher education students in general?

JS: While we can't know if an online student might have attended a face-to-face program if online were not an option, a back-of-the-envelope calculation, using fairly conservative assumptions, is that over the ten years we were measuring, about one half of the growth in higher education enrollments are due to the availability of online options. During that time, the number of higher education students increased from sixteen million to twenty-one million. Our belief is that about half of that increase would not have occurred if online offerings did not exist.

WP: So access has made a huge difference for those students.

JS: Access has been one of the drivers, with the ability to reach this new class of students, for more than a decade. A substantial portion of the overall growth in higher education enrollments over the last decade would not have happened without the advent of online learning.

WP: I understand the federal government will be taking over the survey this year. How is that shift going?

JS: There is now a much greater level of conversation about higher education with federal policy makers, now and in the past five or six years, than there was when we first started. At the beginning, probably the biggest issue was the absence of any attention. There was concern on the part of institutions that there were no mechanisms or controls in place to know how online would be judged. There were the issues about some old existing laws that were in place, related to how many students were not on campus and what that meant about your ability to get students loans in federal programs. There were questions about how the regional accrediting organizations would view online learning. Higher education is a reasonably regulated institution, with accrediting organizations and substantial funding from federal programs, so institutions have to tiptoe lightly to make sure they're doing it correctly. When there are a lot of unknowns, there is a lot of uncertainty.

It's typical with the federal government that they were not proactive but reactive. It wasn't until online was well established, with millions of students—and with some clearly not-ideal marketing and recruiting structures in place—that they took action.

WP: So is that how the switch happened, or did you approach the federal government and tell them, "You should be in charge of this"?

JS: For the tracking of distance enrollments, the Sloan Foundation approached the Department of Education when we released our first report in 2003. We met with people from several divisions in the

Department of Education and presented our results. Our message was, "There are already over a million online students—you should be tracking these numbers." We did not think it was a federal role to explore opinions and strategies, but measuring enrollments was central to their role. Now, twelve years later, they have taken up the effort.

WP: During those twelve years, did they give you any indication that they were making progress?

JS: Well, for the first nine years, we heard nothing. And then there was a proposal circulated on an approach to track distance education. We provided feedback once we heard about the proposal. Basically, we were supportive for the direction they had proposed. Their approach was not identical to what we had been doing, but it was clear why from the point of view of the federal government and their needs. We understood that there would be a transition, and our numbers, based on a sample and somewhat different definitions, would not translate to the new federal numbers, but the overall picture would be similar enough to allow for long-term trends to be apparent.

WP: What do you see for the future of online education?

JS: I expect the growth to slow. The numbers of people learning online will reach a natural equilibrium point. It's not there yet, but it is coming.

WP: What do you mean by natural equilibrium point?

JS: At any given time, people prefer different kinds of delivery mechanisms and different kinds of programs—for example, the number of people enrolling in humanities versus social sciences versus hard sciences, or the number taking particular degrees, will vary. That has not been the case for online education, where the numbers have gone up every year. That will not continue. Inevitably, every degree or program will stop growing and reach a point where we will see both increases and decreases over time. Online programs have not yet reached this point, but will soon. Supply and demand will become more in balance, after which steady growth will be replaced by the normal variability that we see for other types of programs.

WP: Are there things that people in higher education still don't understand about online learning?

JS: I think we're still dealing with some of the same expectations we saw at the beginning, that online education is going to change the world of higher education. It may yet change the world, but certainly hasn't done so yet. The typical online course has a structure very similar a face-to-face course: thirteen weeks, same number of credit hours, delivered on the same schedule, with the same requirements. At many institutions, there is no distinction between a course online and a classroom-based course—they are totally interchangeable. That is not the original view, which was that online courses were going to be new and different.

The natural question is therefore, "Why did online instruction evolve to be so similar to face-to-face instruction?" One part of the answer is that if online was similar to face-to-face it was easier for administrators running programs, for people doing registration, for those monitoring enrollment, and for teachers delivering information, advising students, and giving grades. If you made radical changes, then these changes that would ripple through the entire institution.

Given the substantial level of resistance from faculty members, the more different an online program is from the face-to-face courses they are teaching, the harder to convince them to teach online. Faculty are the most important political group on campus, so getting their buy-in is critical.

A far as I can tell, however, the real driving force for why we didn't have massive change was the students. Students have a mental picture of courses and education. They are interested in a degree, in getting an education, not in radical change. Their ideas are based on their friends or family members' educational experiences. The closer that online learning was to that ideal view, the more likely they were to understand it and to enroll.

The strategy of the Sloan Foundation was based on the realization that they had to win the battle from within: they couldn't propose a radical alternative and expect to win. The question has always been, has online course delivery changed higher education? The answer is, absolutely no, and absolutely yes. The "no" is that online courses are basically the same as face-to-face, as close as you can get to them, given the different delivery mechanism. But the "yes" is that close to three million students are currently taking all of their courses online. If the online delivery option did not exist, where would they be? There are probably ten million students over the past thirteen years who would not have an education without this alternative.

WP: Have you and Elaine now done your last survey?

JS: We have done our last survey of the original structure. We will no longer collect online enrollment data. However, we will do detailed analysis of the enrollment data collected by the federal IPEDS (Integrated Postsecondary Education Data System) program. We will also continue to collect what the federal data does not address, such as opinions, strategies, or barriers, so we will continue those, but in a different format, with additional partners.

We were lucky in finding a topic that was fun to do, interesting, and was valuable enough to the Sloan Foundation that they were willing to support it for eight years. An indication of the value of what the Foundation created in starting this project was that, when their program ended, other sponsors immediately approached us to continue the series.

THE ONLINE LEARNING CONSORTIUM
Charting a Course for the Future of Digital Learning

Meg Benke
Professor, SUNY Empire State College
Former President of the Board of Directors
Online Learning Consortium

Jill Buban
Senior Director, Research and Innovation
Online Learning Consortium

Kathleen Ives
CEO and Executive Director
Online Learning Consortium

OVERVIEW
Background
For more than twenty years, the Online Learning Consortium (OLC) has served as an institutional and professional leadership organization dedicated to integrating digital learning into the mainstream of

higher education. Recognizing the impact digital learning technologies promulgate for both learners and educators, the organization took the opportunity to redefine its strategic direction and brand upon moving away from the Alfred P. Sloan Foundation at the end of 2013. Not only did this effort represent how the organization had changed on the outside, but it also had a considerable effect on how OLC operated on the inside, laying the foundation for the future of the organization.

Achieving the Mission

As detailed in an earlier chapter written by John Bourne, OLC has extensive experience in research, pedagogy, and learning solutions, with a dedication to the continuous quality improvement approach. It is a respected and credible source of information as well as a trusted advisor for online and digital learning adoption and evaluation. The OLC Quality Scorecard is a one of the major tools used to evaluate and improve online learning classes and programs and has been adopted by hundreds of institutions. Building on the Five Pillars of Quality Online Education promulgated in 1997, the OLC Scorecard is one of the major tools to help colleges and universities conduct self-assessments and peer assessments of online administration, services, academic programs, and courses. This tool has been used by many institutions as part of their accreditation reviews. Not only does OLC assist member institutions in extending access to nontraditional learners, the organization has become known for stimulating on-campus pedagogical innovation through its programs and services. Thus, the organization's new vision setting the global standard in digital learning, coupled with its mission of creating community and connections around quality online learning while driving innovation, very ably encapsulated its illustrious past and sets its path for the organization's future.

Organizational Impact

In true reflection of the organization's mission, the OLC community consistently exhibits an innate ability to unite to achieve a common objective. This was clearly evidenced in 2005, when hurricanes

Katrina and Rita caused severe destruction along the Gulf Coast from central Florida to Texas. The Sloan Semester was an initiative supported by individuals and institutions and, combined with special funding from the Sloan Foundation, it provided the opportunity for thousands of displaced students to continue their education with minimal disruption. More than 3,000 students enrolled in the Sloan Semester, a one-semester virtual university. The students were able to choose from more than 1,500 courses from 150 institutions across the country. Participating institutions offered the courses online and free of charge. Coupled with the foundation's financial support, the rapidity with which this community coalesced to tackle this national tragedy served as a defining moment, demonstrating the passion and power of community. Today, OLC member institutions continue to make positive and meaningful contributions to the digital learning community. Most recently, OLC was awarded a grant by the Bill & Melinda Gates Foundation that has helped recognize both institutional and faculty-led teams' contributions toward advancing student success through the adoption of digital courseware.

Focus on Professional Development
OLC Institute for Professional Development
In today's current climate, colleges and universities are charged with addressing ever-increasing demands: reducing the achievement gap, adopting evidence-based practices, meeting adequate yearly progress goals, managing the requirements of first-generation and underserved students, and remaining current on the increasing amount of pedagogical and content area research as well as evolving digital technologies. Often, insufficient resources or lack of expertise within institutions hinder the implementation and adoption of professional development best practices. This is where the OLC Institute for Professional Development acts as a resource for many institutions. For over ten years, the institute has offered educational and professional development in online teaching and learning through online workshops, webinars, mastery series, and certificate programs facilitated by leading subject matter experts in the field.

OLC workshops enable colleagues worldwide to collaborate with peers and experts via synchronous and asynchronous methods. The webinar series includes interactive, sessions covering industry hot topics, best practices, and special interests. The mastery series programs emphasize theory and application of research on key topics culminating in a recognition of mastery. The Online Learning Consortium certificate programs are offered as a sequence of one foundation course and three electives leading from the conceptual to the implementation of online learning effectiveness best practices. All of the institute programs stem from OLC's Five Pillars of Online Quality Education: student satisfaction, access, learning effectiveness, faculty satisfaction, and scale. While many learn through professional development opportunities such as those offered through the Institute for Professional Development, we recognize that others learn from reading a variety of publications, as represented in our suite of research and publications.

Conferences

Conferences have played a very important role in digitally powered higher education. In planning OLC's national, international, and regional events, the organization recognizes that today's higher education institution very much values updated information on key issues that administration, faculty, and staff face daily. Participants can spend a reasonably short period of time and get substantial information on a variety of topics. The other aspect to OLC's conferences and events that makes them a unique learning opportunity lies in the creation of "learning communities," that bring together individuals from like-minded institutions. The learning environment encourages participants to exchange experiences, ideas, and practices from their own institutions. Participants can interact with colleagues from institutions who may be experiencing similar issues and problems. It allows them to tackle issues together and in turn it broadens their perspectives. This information exchange helps delegates benchmark their institutions.

OLC's international conference, OLC Accelerate, is offered in the fall and is devoted to driving quality online learning advancing best practice guidance and accelerating innovation in learning for academic leaders, educators, administrators, online learning professionals, and organizations around the world. OLC Innovate, hosted in the spring, focuses on how institutions thrive in a rapidly changing learning environment whether embracing emerging technology, incorporating intelligent learning management systems, or designing blended classrooms. OLC's regional events, OLC Collaborate, are modeled after the Chautauqua. Originating in the late 1800s, the Chautauqua was an adult educational gathering that moved from town to town. OLC partners with member institutions around the country for these one-day events which focuses on a deep dive into regionally specific issues.

Digital Learning Professional Development
Institute for Emerging Leadership in Online Learning
In 2007-08, OLC and Penn State formed a partnership recognizing that as the online learning landscape continued to evolve, the demand for skillful leaders was outpacing supply. The partnership between OLC and Penn State to create the Institute for Emerging Leadership in Online Learning (IELOL) was instituted at a pivotal time for online education. There was a recognized need to begin succession planning as many of the first generation of online leaders would be retiring or continuing their career trajectory into broader leadership roles. For many of these senior leaders, their passion still lay in the field of online learning so for them it was even more important to provide leadership development for those who would assume their roles. Additionally, the online learning, landscape was evolving at a rapid rate, and the IELOL would be poised to play a pivotal role in providing the leaders with the leadership skills necessary to navigate the ever-changing landscape.

IELOL consists of four components offered over a five-month time frame. The program begins with a three-week online primer, enabling participants to become familiar with program content and format. The online primer is followed by a four-day, face-to-face immersion experience to create community and expand the participants' network as well as approach an in depth study of the leadership issues around the OLC Five Pillars. Following the immersion experience, the third component, a three-week online experience, offered the opportunity for participants to define a project based on their institutional needs and use the IELOL faculty and other IELOL participants for input and guidance. The fourth and final component is a half-day workshop or conference session at OLC's Accelerate conference. This preconference session reunites the IELOL program participants, faculty, and alumni provides an opportunity to share insights and perspectives about issues impacting on the field.

An extensive network of over 300 administrators and faculty have become a self-directed leadership learning community that engages and collaborates as new challenges arise. These participants are now entering the highest-level positions in online learning and becoming our next leaders, policy advisors, and advocates for the field fulfilling the need identified by the founders of the program from Penn State University and the OLC leadership and board. After nearly 10 years at Penn State University, this program will reinvent itself in 2018 as it moves from campus to campus with new academic partners and an evolving experience.

The Leadership Network
The Online Learning Journal

In 2016, OLC launched the Leadership Network in order to best serve senior leaders in digital learning positions. The Leadership Network provides leaders in the field the opportunity to learn from each other, as well as network with peers. Resources are available for leaders through the Leadership Network web pages offered on OLC's website. It is expected that the network will continue to expand and become the leading resource for leaders as they continue refine their skills in this ever-changing field.

Online Learning (OLJ), now in its twentieth year of publication, continues to provide scholars, practitioners, administrators, students, and policy makers with rigorous, peer reviewed research in the field. Published quarterly, "the journal promotes the development and dissemination of new knowledge at the intersection of pedagogy, emerging technology, policy and practice in online environments." (Online

Learning Consortium, 2016). Oftentimes the publication schedule includes special issues that focus on pertinent topics in the field such as learning analytics, accessibility, K-12 online learning, and the annual conference edition, which features papers from selected presentations at OLC conferences over the course of the given year.

Formerly the *Journal of Asynchronous Learning Networks* (JALN), the journal's name was changed to *Online Learning* in 2013 to reflect the organization's name change. Since that time, the journal's editorial board has undertaken a sustained effort to transform OLJ into the premier scholarly journal dedicated to research in online education. Under the oversight of editor-in-chief Dr. Peter Shea who took the helm in 2013, OLJ merged with the *Journal for Online Learning and Teaching* (JOLT), the flagship publication of the Multimedia Educational Resource for Learning and Online Teaching's (MERLOT). The merger of the two journals greatly expanded the OLJ's author and reviewer communities. Utilizing double-blind peer-review process, OLJ accepts roughly 25 percent of submissions. The OLJ editorial board has been expanded to provide expertise in online and blended education, K-12, community colleges, and a variety of focus areas in the field of higher education. The editorial board's goal is to see the journal continue to rise in stature on the metrics that reflect the quality standards of a reputable scholarly journal.

OLC Publications

For over fifteen years, OLC has provided the online learning community with publications that provide theoretical and practical knowledge in the field. Many publications, such as the *Quality Scorecard for the Administration of Online Programs* (Shelton & Saltsman, 2014), and the *Criteria for Excellence in Blended Learning Programs* (Mathes & Pedersen, 2016), pertain to elements of OLC's 5 Pillars of Quality Online Education that include learning effectiveness, scale, access, faculty satisfaction and student satisfaction. Others, such as *Leading the e-Learning Transformation of Higher Education: Meeting the Challenges of Technology and Distance Education* (Miller et al., 2013) provide perspectives from thought leaders in the field.

Research

The organization was founded on research grants provided to a series of individuals beginning in 1992 and continues to expand its research focus not only through the *Online Learning* Journal, but also through a variety of research projects (Picciano, 2013). For the past thirteen years, the organization has supported an annual online learning survey, with research sanctioned by the Jeff Seaman and Elaine Allen of the Babson Survey Research Group. The survey serves as a state-of-the-state of online learning with a focus on quality of online programs, faculty perception of online learning, and enrollment trends among other topics. In response to the many changes in the field since the seminal study was completed in 2003, future iterations of the study will feature different topics that are relevant to the current climate of the field.

While the organization has featured other research studies, including a K-12 online survey, OLC is increasing its visibility in the field of digital research in 2016. To differentiate OLC from other organizations in the field, OLC is strategically moving into the research field for digital learning as it launches the OLC Research Center for Digital Learning and Leadership. In collaboration with the OLC professional and institutional community, the center will further knowledge of the field, create networked collaborations among like-minded professionals with similar knowledge bases, and provide original evidence-based and theory–based research. Offerings will include research publications, as well as podcasts, infographics, and blogs. Additionally, the center will become a resource for researchers and practitioners seeking just-in-time news and opinion on topics such as digital learning trends, innovations, and effective practices in the field.

Consulting Solutions

OLC formed its consulting arm, formerly called OLC Advisory Services, on to assist institutions in developing and managing their online programs smoothly and efficiently. Every institution has a unique set of circumstances, which means that what works for one college or university may not work for another. OLC's rich history and dynamic connection to researchers and practitioners enables customized and relevant solutions. Given the ever changing environment our institutions operate in, OLC supports continued research on current topics. It also identifies best practices in online and blended learning through *Online Learning Journal* partnerships with multiple institutions that serve as sources of research, Effective Practice award winners, and multiple conference opportunities.

Examples of services include:

- Comprehensive program reviews
- Custom training or professional development
- Instructional design support
- Organizational change and transformation
- Institutional effectiveness
- Accreditation and assessment analytics
- Infrastructure design and deployment
- Professional development
- Online learning, blended program design, and deployment
- Enrollment management
- Student experience

Strategic Collaborations

Focus on Policy: Advocating for the Nontraditional Learner

In 2015, OLC formed a partnership with the University Professional Continuing Education Association (UPCEA) to advance the interests of nontraditional (sometimes called "contemporary") learners and the programs that support them. This partnership comes at a time of great importance to the higher education federal policy landscape, as Congress reviews the reauthorization of the Higher Education Act. As Congress comes together to amend the most important legislation for our country's colleges and universities, UPCEA and OLC are working together to advocate for advancing access, innovation, and creative solutions to help realign federal policy with the current higher education landscape. This early work morphed into the formation of the National Adult Learner Coalition. This coalition includes additional organizations and other stakeholders interested in ensuring that nontraditional learners have access to high-quality courses and programs that allow them to meet the competing demands of work, family, and education.

Organizational Collaborations

The Online Learning Consortium leadership team feels the organization brings greater value and impact to the educational community by building and leveraging relationships among its members and peer organizations. Figure 1 includes key relationships established during the period of 2013-16:

Organizational Discovery and Partnerships	
American Association of Community Colleges (AACC)	Intentional Futures
	League for Innovation
American Association of State Colleges and Universities (AASCU)	National Institute for Staff and Organizational Development (NISOD)
American Council on Education (ACE)	
American Indian Higher Education Consortium	Network for Change and Continuous Innovation (NCCI)
Association of Public and Land Grant Universities (APLU)	American Education Research Association (AERA)
Association of Catholic Colleges and Universities (ACCU)	College Student Educators International (ACPA)
Association of Jesuit Colleges and Universities and JesuitNET	Higher Education Resource Services (HERSnet)
CAEL	NACADA
Council of Independent Colleges (CIC)	Presidents' Forum
	SRI International
EdSurge	Student Affairs Administrators in Higher Education (NASPA)
Hispanic Association of Colleges and Universities	Tyton Partners

Figure 1: OLC relationships, 2013-2016.

Institutional Membership Organizations	
American Association of Community Colleges (AACC)	Association of Jesuit Colleges and Universities and JesuitNET
American Association of State Colleges and Universities (AASCU)	Council of Independent Colleges (CIC)
American Council on Education (ACE)	Hispanic Association of Colleges and Universities
American Indian Higher Education	League for Innovation

Figure 2: OLC relationships, 2013-16.

Organizations That Have Programming Overlaps with OLC	
Center for Learning Innovations and Customized Knowledge Solutions (CLICKS)	National Center for Accessible Media (NCAM)
Competency Based Education Network (CBEN)	Open Education Consortium (OEC)
CREAD	Quality Matters
Creative Commons	The Campus Computing Project
Educause and ELI	The NUTN Network
IMS Global Learning Consortium	University Professional and Continuing Education Association (UPCEA)

Figure 3: OLC relationships, 2013-16.

Other Organizations	
American Society for Association Executives (ASAE)	Huron Consulting Group
Babson Survey Research Group	Inside Higher Ed
Chronicle of Higher Education	International Association for K-12 Online Learning (INACOL)
Clayton Christensen Institute	Kresge Foundation
Educational Advisory Board (EAB)	Lumina Foundation
Eduventures	MIT Online Education Policy Initiative

Figure 4: OLC relationships, 2013-16.

AWARDS

Recognizing Excellence in the Field

Digital Learning Innovation Award (DLIA)

Many collaborations in the digital courseware field have come as a result of the organization's Digital Learning Innovation Award (DLIA). The Bill & Melinda Gates Foundation granted the OLC funding to support the use of digital courseware to improve student success, especially among minority, first-generation and other disadvantaged student groups. With a focused lens on increasing the number of under-represented students who complete general education or gateway courses, the funding aims to build awareness, assess readiness, and provide guidance on the use of digital courseware. With online environments as the platform for digital courseware, the grant furthers the reach of the OLC mission through the continued expansion of online learning for students.

Research indicates that low-income, underrepresented, and first-generation students are most likely to struggle in any academic setting. While many technology innovations and learning management systems utilized in education have revolutionized mass delivery through efficiencies of scale, our targeted student population often requires personal interaction and mentoring to create a high-touch experience. OLC is interested in student-centered active learning solutions that advance the world of digital learning for all students.

Several funding initiatives have informed the emerging use of digital courseware in postsecondary education, but continued adoption is needed to better understand design features, implementation strategies, and student related outcomes. More institutions need to add their own experiences with digital courseware initiatives to what is currently known in the field.

To accelerate the adoption of digital courseware for general education or gateway courses, OLC is offering two award categories for funding for three years (2016-18):

• Institutional Award – $100,000 (up to three awarded)

- Faculty-led Team Award – $10,000 (up to ten awarded).

Honorable mentions may be recognized for both the institutional award and the faculty-led team award.

Recommendations and lessons learned related to the following dimensions will be included in the growing body of knowledge related to digital courseware: access, accountability, adoption/scale, affordability, interoperability/implementation, innovation, organizational learning, and quality. OLC is dedicated to sharing these recommendations in a series of public forums including webinars, white papers, and conference presentations. Communities of practice may evolve to further engagement and sharing. In addition to expanding the current digital courseware body of knowledge, an auxiliary OLC quality scorecard focused on the implementation/integration of digital courseware in colleges and universities will be created in a direct alignment with OLC's mission to support quality online education.

The Digital Learning Innovation Award (DLIAward) was granted through the Bill & Melinda Gates Foundation Postsecondary Success Program. The Postsecondary Success Program aims to help US higher education become more personalized, flexible, clear, and affordable. As the focus of the funding is US higher education, so is the focus of the OLC DLIA.

Annual Awards, Effective Practice Awards, and the OLC Fellows

The Online Learning Consortium annual awards recognize significant contributions to online education, announced at each year's annual conference (OLC Accelerate). Awards include: Gomory-Mayadas Leadership Award in Online Education, John R. Bourne Outstanding Online Program, Online Learning Journal Outstanding Research Achievement Award in Online Education, Excellence in Faculty Development for Online Teaching, and OLC Excellence and Innovation in Online Teaching. Nominations are reviewed by a subcommittee of the

OLC board of directors, as well as a group of experts in the field. In addition to annual conference awards, the OLC recognizes effective practices biannually at its fall Accelerate conference and spring Innovate conference. Those practices submitted for nomination are put through a rigorous evaluation process. In 2016, award winners were asked to present their practices at the conferences.

In 2009, the OLC board of directors established the OLC Fellows Awards. This award recognizes outstanding and extraordinary qualifications in the field of online learning, significant experience in online learning or an allied field, a record of distinguished service to OLC or the field, and extraordinary contributions to leadership the field of online learning.

Whether an effective practice award, conference award or Fellows award, the OLC suite of awards recognizes individuals at different stages in their careers and provide recipients with a distinguished honor.

QUALITY IN ONLINE EDUCATION

Quality is a cornerstone of the mission of the Online Learning Consortium. A quality online course provides the scheduling flexibility for learners, but does so with institutional support, technology support, course development and instructional design, course structure, teaching and learning, social and student engagement, faculty support, student support, and evaluation and assessment. These criteria serve as the foundation for OLC's suite of quality scorecards.

The OLC Suite of Quality Scorecards

The Quality Scorecard for the Administration of Online Programs provides a way for institutions to evaluate administrative practices (Shelton, 2010). Developed through a Delphi study that surveyed experienced online administrators and building on OLC's Five Pillars of Quality, the Quality Scorecard achieved consensus on the quality indicators that had been published a decade earlier by the Institute for Higher Education Policy (IHEP); (Merisotis & Phipps, 2000).

The OLC Quality Scorecard process helps institutions measure and quantify elements of quality within online education programs in higher education. It is an easy-to-use tool for online program evaluation and continuous improvement. By evaluating each of the respective quality indicators within the established categories, an online program administrator can determine strengths and weaknesses of their program, which may also be used to support program improvement and strategic planning initiatives. The scorecard could also be used to demonstrate to accrediting bodies elements of quality within the program as well as an overall level of quality. The scorecard contains seventy-five quality indicators. Each indicator is worth up to three points. The administrator will determine at what level their program meets the intent of the quality indicator after examining all procedures and processes.

The Quality Scorecard may be used to:

- Evaluate existing online education programs
- Improve online education programs
- Demonstrate to accrediting bodies the breadth of quality in program administration
- Plan and create new high-quality online education programs
- Develop strategic objectives for program improvement
- Benchmarking against other programs of like size and type

The OLC Quality Scorecard is now being utilized by institutions all over the United States and Latin America. Online education program administrators are finding that by using the scorecard for quality evaluation, they are able to develop strategic objectives for program improvement and demonstrate to accrediting bodies the breadth of quality in program administration. As more institutions have adopted the scorecard, there have been requests for "official reviews" of the Quality Scorecard by the Online Learning Consortium. Now, for a reasonable fee, OLC will provide an official scorecard review by three trained evaluators to assess your an institution's submission.

After self-scoring with the scorecard, the program administrator develops justifications and submits documenting artifacts that are placed inside the OLC online repository (available to OLC institutional members). Trained scorecard reviewers virtually examine each score, justification, and artifact and certify that each quality indicator was scored correctly. This process includes a report prepared for the institution with recommendations for possible improvements, if applicable. Programs that score 202 points or more after the official review, will be awarded an Online Learning Consortium Exemplary Program logo that may be displayed on their website and other materials.

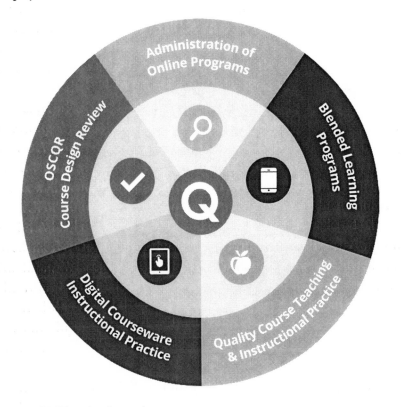

Figure 5: OLC Exemplary Program logo.

MEMBERSHIP AND COMMUNITY ENGAGEMENT

While many of our publications and resources are open resources, it is our members who benefit greatly when they access scorecard resources, receive conference and institute discounts, and join a community of networked professionals in the field. OLC offers different types of memberships including a free community membership, a professional membership for an individual, and institutional memberships, which allow entire institutions to take advantage of OLC offerings. OLC membership spans nearly 800 organizations including academic, association, consortium, and corporations, with academic institutions constituting the largest number of organizations. Among these organizations, OLC serves both private and public, profit and not-for-profit universities and colleges, community colleges, and vocational schools.

OLC LEADERSHIP
OLC Board of Directors
The OLC board composition is representative of the organization's membership. The board provides strategic oversight of all activities that enhance the strategic goals of OLC and the effectiveness and sustainability of the organization. It ensures that initiatives adhere to applicable laws and align with vision, mission, and purpose of OLC as well as make sensible and practical use of all OLC assets. The board also makes and shares connections. OLC membership spans nearly 800 organizations including academic, association, consortium, and corporations with academic institutions constituting the largest number of organizations. Among these organizations, OLC serves both private and public, profit and not-for profit universities and colleges, community colleges, and vocational schools.

Executive Leadership Team and Senior Leadership
The OLC staff members possess a unique combination of experience in higher education, corporate. and association management. This skillset proves imperative to the success of a self-sustaining nonprofit.

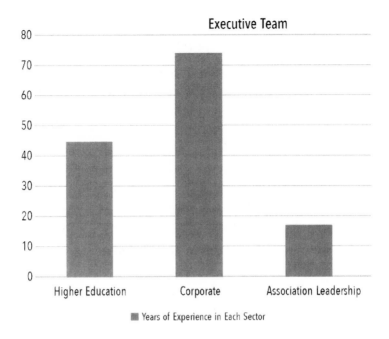

Figure 6: Leadership, years of experience.

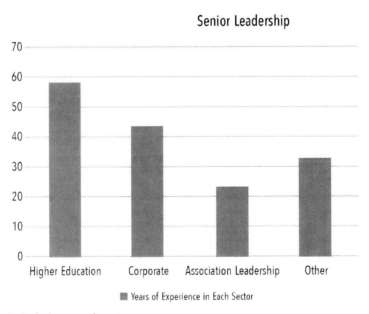

Figure 7: Senior leadership, years of experience.

LOOKING AHEAD
The Future of the Online Learning Consortium
Today's colleges and universities are not like yesterday's, as they straddle two worlds. One world consists of leather-bound books and voluminous lecture halls. The other is saturated in technology such as learning management platforms, open educational resources (online), mobile applications, MOOCs (Massive Open Online Courses), and new pedagogical best practices such as competency-based education, flipped classrooms, and learning analytics. The Online Learning Consortium has evolved as its membership evolved, from those first Sloan Foundation-funded initiatives to todays institution-wide and often global program offerings. In order to ensure OLC's long-term relevance and solvency, the organization continues to monitor the academic digital frontier so it can best serve the membership base and the community in an ever-changing academic landscape.

REFERENCES
Mathes, J., & Pedersen, K. (Eds.). (2016). *Quality Scorecard Handbook: Criteria for Excellence in Blended Learning Programs.* Newburyport, MA: The Online Learning Consortium.

Miller, G., Benke, M., Chaloux, B., Ragan, L., Schroeder, R., Smutz, W., & Swan, K. (2013). *Leading the e-learning transformation of higher education: Meeting the challenges of technology and distance education.* Sterling, VA: Stylus.

Online Learning Consortium (2016). About the *Online Learning* Journal. Retrieved from: http://onlinelearningconsortium.org/read/journals/.

Picciano, A. (2013). Twenty years timeline of the Anytime, Anyplace Learning Program. Retrieved from: http://aalp-sloan-report.gc.cuny.edu/timeline/.

Shea, P. (2016). Introduction. *Online Learning Journal,* 20(1), 7-9.

Shelton, K. & Staltsman, G. (Eds.). (2014). Quality scorecard 2014: Criteria for excellence in the administration of online programs. Newburyport, MA: Online Learning Consortium.

SHEPHERDING CHANGE
Creating the State Authorization Reciprocity Agreement (SARA)

Paul H. Shiffman
CEO, Presidents' Forum

James W. Hall
Founding President, Empire State College

INTRODUCTION

In 2013, a broad spectrum of our nation's higher education institutional and policy leadership agreed to advance a newly crafted State Authorization Reciprocity Agreement (SARA). SARA is an agreement that will permit each of the states and territories to accept programs and courses offered by higher educational institutions from other participating states without requiring an additional authorization in each SARA establishes comparable national academic standards for approved participating institutions for all members of the agreement. The agreement is intended to rationalize and make more efficient individual state processes for authorizing colleges and universities, improve the capacity of each state's regulators to manage a demanding workload, save the institutions significant costs, and encourage expanded opportunities for students in all participating states to take online courses offered by postsecondary institutions based in another state. Implementation of SARA is managed by the four regional higher education compacts [Western Interstate Compact for Higher Education (WICHE), New England Board of Higher Education (NEBHE), Midwestern Higher Education Compact (MHEC) and Southern Regional Education Board (SREB)] under the aegis of the National Council for State Authorization Reciprocity Agreements (NC-SARA). By Spring 2017, forty-eight states and over 1,000 postsecondary institutions had opted to participate in SARA. In an environment where any form of change, especially one that fosters the relinquishing of control, is too often met with avoidance, apathy or open hostility, this is a remarkable accomplishment. How did this happen?

BACKGROUND

Unfortunately, the existing structure for the approval of institutions to operate in each of the fifty States, the District of Columbia, five major territories, and the nation's various possessions, often hinders the full realization of the benefits offered by online and distance learning. Institutions that seek to offer instruction to students in multiple state jurisdictions are typically required by law to secure independent authorization in each state. Federal law also requires an institution to hold authorization from each state in which it chooses to operate. But every state maintains its own unique definition of when an institution has established a "physical presence," as well as widely diverse associated standards and regulations for authorization to operate. Moreover, some states totally ignore online institutions or exercise minimum oversight and qualitative control, reducing their ability to accept and evaluate approvals on an interstate basis. Others have rigorous requirements with high educational standards. These factors present serious complex issues for postsecondary institutions and significant barriers to students, often resulting in reduced educational access and increased costs to both.

The Presidents' Forum at Excelsior College believed that it was in the best interest of the nation's goals, and its students' need for choice in learning, to explore and advance means for states to reform and streamline these processes. SARA emerged as a product of these policy considerations. Excelsior College, originally founded in 1971 as the Regents College of the University of the State of New York, is an independent not-for-profit institution located in Albany, New York. In extending its mission to serve adult learners at a distance, the college created the Presidents' Forum in 2002 as a collaborative convening body of accredited, national, adult serving institutions and programs that have embraced the power and potential of online distance learning. The Presidents' Forum serves to advance innovative practice and excellence by convening institutional leaders and stakeholders to share their knowledge, learn from others' best practices, and frame recommendations for national policy.

At the time of the Forum's creation, postsecondary education confronted the rapidly growing impact of the telecommunications revolution. No longer was the residential campus the sole place for learning. Dramatic new and transformative technologies offered students, wherever they lived or worked, significantly enhanced opportunities to access and attain a college degree and the skills needed to participate in an increasingly competitive workforce. Initially, the nation's online postsecondary sector was dominated by well financed for-profit institutions. Only a limited number of public and independent not-for-profit colleges and universities had invested resources in online learning and the instructional technology necessary to mediate delivery to external students. The Presidents' Forum, seeking to share the knowledge of those most innovative and experienced programs, invited participation from both for-profit and not-for-profit online purveyors of postsecondary learning. The initial Advisory Council to the Presidents' Forum, representing this cross-sector approach, included leadership from Excelsior College,

Charter Oak State College, SUNY Empire State College, Western Governors University, Capella University, American Public University, Franklin University, Walden University, Dow Lohnes LLP, and the American Council on Education. The one unifying factor that all had in common was a desire to serve students, absent the boundaries of fixed time and geographic location, that produced student outcomes equivalent to or exceeding the high standards set for campus-based programs.

At the first meeting of the Presidents' Forum (April 16, 2004, Albany, NY), and throughout the years that followed, the most pervasive concern for institutions serving students nationally was the patchwork of state authorization rules and regulations that served as costly barriers to serving students across state borders. Though many states had taken steps to introduce and encourage technology mediated teaching and learning at all levels, in most cases state regulation had not kept pace with the emerging reality of technology-driven innovative educational delivery systems that facilitated learning across state and national boundaries.

THE EMERGENCE OF SARA

Presidents' Forum participants and professional colleagues held many discussions about the barriers to the acceptance and accessibility of online distance learning. An obvious impediment was resistance by states, established campuses, and their residents to "outside intruders" who might compete for students. Whenever the Forum advanced the topic of establishing some form of agreement for inter-state reciprocity with the leadership of such national organizations as the State Higher Education Executive Officers (SHEEO), Western Interstate Commission for Higher Education (WICHE), American Council on Education (ACE), or others, we were instructed that this was a low priority issue, a topic best left to fester, and that our vision was naive, if not foolish, if we thought that any level of consensus or agreement for reciprocity between the states could be achieved.

Given the individual state histories, significantly different approaches to regulation and support, and the plethora of competing interests, it was not surprising that this initial outreach for reform by the Presidents' Forum was met with skepticism. Some of those responding had championed prior attempts to resolve state regulatory diversity, as well as to provide uniform and transparent measures upon which to base judgments for program integrity and consumer protection - none of which had met with lasting success.

Notable among these was the *Project ALLTEL Report*, issued by the Council on Postsecondary Education and the State Higher Education Executive Officers Association (SHEEO) in the 1970s. That report identified disparate and onerous state licensure requirements as posing a significant threat to the ability of institutions to effectively and efficiently offer telecommunications supported learning. The impact of this earlier attempt at regulatory reform may be assessed through the realization that "the barriers erected a quarter century ago against the most modest incursions wrought by telecourses have become more common and increasingly robust in the face of the growth of online learning." (Michael Goldstein–July 13, 2009 - Letter of support to Lumina for Grant #6325)

Another failed attempt at regulatory reform occurred in the 1990's through federal actions to advance the State Postsecondary Review Entity (SPRE) program. The SPREs, created through the 1992 amendments to the Higher Education Act, were conceived as a federal–state partnership to strengthen regulation and monitoring of postsecondary education and the administration of student financial aid with specific attention to preventing abuses by for-profit institutions. However, when the envisioned regulatory reach of these bodies and the Department of Education's (USED) proposed implementation measures were perceived as more intrusive than helpful to states and institutions, this initiative was terminated in 1995.

It is not the intent to provide here an in-depth analysis of the lessons learned from these prior efforts at postsecondary regulatory reform. Suffice to say, in each case the demands for accountability and the reporting requirements were advanced as mandates that did not reflect the needs of nor garner the support from the communities they were meant to serve. The continuing downside of these involuntary reforms has been a reflexive avoidance of such collaborative measures by those on the front line of postsecondary institutional authorization: the states and their designated agencies.

Change is too often a product of a chance opportunity rather than genius. In 2008, Paul Shiffman asked Charles S. Lenth, then Vice President for Policy Analysis and Academic Affairs at SHEEO, to provide program time at the SHEEO Annual Meeting for a panel discussion of the costs and issues associated with cross-state offering of online distance postsecondary learning. The intent was to determine if there was interest in elevating this concern to a national policy agenda. The panel presentation did occur and was well received by panel attendees, even as the topic of access to online learning through reciprocity remained below the radar of the gathered postsecondary leaders.

This occasion provided the first big step on the long path that led to SARA. On departing from the SHEEO presentation, Shiffman happened to enter an elevator with Dr. James Applegate, then vice president of the Lumina Foundation. Still "fired up," in full presentation mode, and quite effusive about questioning the wisdom of those who did not yet recognize the rationality of reciprocity for state authorization, Shiffman subjected Applegate to a full presentation of concerns during the short transit between floors. As a creative listener, Applegate invited further discussion of the issues with his office. From this chance exchange in the elevator, subsequent introductions were made by Applegate to Kevin Corcoran, strategy director and Suzanne E. Walsh, senior program director at the Lumina Foundation. The Lumina Foundation recognized that these inquiries held the potential to advance the foundation's goal to boost degree completion by the nation's citizenry to 60 percent by 2025, and invited the Presidents' Forum to apply for a grant.

THE TASK FORCE AND ITS REPORT

The resulting report of this inquiry, entitled *Aligning State Approval and Regional Accreditation for Online Postsecondary Institutions: A National Strategy* (a report of the *Presidents' Forum Task Force*, Excelsior College, Albany, NY, 2008.) focused on the need to update regulatory systems. Such reform would recognize current changes in the modes of learning, embrace the opportunities offered by innovative technology mediated learning systems, and facilitate the successful outreach of interstate higher education institutions. At a time when both young and adult degree completion continued to decline in the United States, the foundation's goals could be advanced by addressing these issues.

This report was endorsed by a task force (those who accepted the invitation to participate and supported the report, including several regulators, are noted in Appendix A) organized under the convening authority of the Presidents' Forum, Those who comprised the membership of the Presidents' Forum Task Force represented a broad collection of experience across all levels of postsecondary regulation, accreditation, distance learning, institutional leadership, policy development, and legal affairs.

The task force considered and recommended new models for cooperation and reciprocity among the states, thereby reforming outdated systems for state authorization. In order to accomplish this task, the Forum needed to identify a number of individuals who might be invited to address the question linking many of these issues: *What do states need to know to assure institutional credibility and consumer protection?*

This initial engagement with leaders and practitioners in the field, supported by the Lumina Foundation, reinforced several issues of concern. Although the meeting ranged over a wide and detailed number of related issues, there was remarkable unanimity about the reality of the problems, the need for reform, and the attractiveness of certain pathways to action.

Perhaps the most important, and obvious, was that reform is needed in the policies and processes of state regulatory review and approval for postsecondary educational institutions, and especially for those colleges and universities with a national footprint that offer degrees across multiple political boundaries. Current state practices were found to be redundant, inefficient, and costly for both the states and the institutions seeking approval to operate. None denied the importance of and necessity for state regulation. But it was apparent that significant benefits could accrue to students, institutions, and states if the patchwork of state regulation could be reformed through shared policy and processes. The task force concluded that states could share in a common, high quality, and consistently applied system of processes and standards. Mutual confidence in such a process would be increased with enhanced state participation, and institutions seeking approval to operate in multiple state jurisdictions would participate in a significantly more efficient and consistently demanding process of review for authorization throughout the nation.

The task force advanced four recommendations for actions to bring about policy and operational enhancements in the state regulatory environments, encourage acceptance by the states of reciprocal agreements to streamline regulatory processes, while encouraging expanded access to learning for students: (1) *define a common sharable template of requirements and processes*; (2) *establish collaboratively a model for reciprocal institutional evaluation and approval between states*; (3) *develop new statutory model laws that provide state authority to participate in reciprocal compacts*; (4) *create new financial and consumer protection models*.

As in other areas of public regulation reserved to the individual states, some states are highly effective and efficient in exercising authority over delivery of postsecondary learning. Many others have instituted procedures and rules more recently, often reinventing the wheel. And, a number of states continue to exercise very little oversight of higher education, thereby providing a fertile environment for dishonest actors. Ironically, this pattern has had the effect of encouraging even more protective and restrictive barriers to operation in other states. The challenge before the Forum, and those institutions desiring to serve students across the nation, was not simply one of rationalizing the maze of regulation; it was also one of proposing an appropriate system of regulation acceptable to all states. The Presidents' Forum advanced the belief that movement toward a high degree of inter-state reciprocity would help states to offer effective oversight and consumer protection to their citizens, to build confidence across the nation in the quality of approved educational offerings, and to reduce the substantial costs for administering and staffing regulatory compliance for both states and institutions—costs that were too often passed on to students through increases in tuition and fees.

VALIDATING THE NEED WITH JOURNEYMAN STATE REGULATORS AND STAKEHOLDERS:
The Pathway to the Dallas Convening

As early as April 16, 2004, at the first Presidents' Forum annual meeting, the gulf between state authorization rules and innovative online access for students was cited as one area among those that inhibited student access. Some intervention was suggested. The Forum continued to voice this topic of concern to the higher education community at large by convening seminars and webinars involving a broad spectrum of recognized stakeholders from the regulatory, policy, and institutional sectors. These activities culminated in the aforementioned *Report of the Presidents' Forum Task Force: Aligning State Approval and Regional Accreditation for Online Postsecondary Institutions: A National Strategy.*

In consideration of this report, the Lumina Foundation expressed continued interest in exploring the relationship between state authorization, student access to academic credentialing and reciprocity. As a result, on September 1, 2009, the Lumina Foundation awarded a grant "to convene The Presidents' Forum to develop recommendations for demonstration projects in order to improve efficiency and encourage better alignment of individual state regulatory requirements, as well as support increased reciprocal agreements among states in order to offer instruction across multi-state boundaries." (Grant No. 6325, September 1, 2009.) We now needed to find an appropriate audience to further validate the findings of the task force and to delineate strategies to realize its recommendations. Moreover, it was now incumbent upon us to demonstrate in greater detail that our plan for action would advance the stated goals of the Lumina Foundation.

As a practical matter, we made a clear choice to consult with those individuals whose daily work at the state level would provide the hands on information and detailed experience essential to undertaking a successful effort. During our initial inquiries, members of the Forum Task Force attended meetings of the National Association of State Administrators and Supervisors of Private Schools (NASASPS), the professional association serving the majority of state regulators, and found that this organization provided a vehicle for ongoing consultation and dialogue with a broad representation of the state officials currently charged to oversee institutional authorization processes. Based upon the discussions and assessments provided by these individuals, we decided that the Presidents' Forum convening should center upon eliciting more detailed information regarding institutional authorization practices and processes at the state level, and that state regulators should constitute the core of attendees. The convening was held on September 21-22, 2010 in Dallas, Texas. (Attendees and regulators are listed by title in Appendix A.)

The Dallas convening was a critical step in understanding more fully the barriers posed by state authorization for students, states, and educational institutions. In preparation for this gathering, Kevin Corcoran, strategy director at Lumina, suggested that, in addition to state regulatory personnel, we invite participants with specific expertise in law and policy related to interstate agreements. He recommended outreach to John Mountjoy, Director of Policy, Research & Special Projects, from the Council of State Governments (CSG). The constituencies of CSG span all the major areas of state government policy, he noted. Moreover, the mission of CSG is to help state officials shape public policy through interstate collaboration and problem-solving partnerships. Much of this expertise is exercised through CSG's National Center for Interstate Compacts, which has overseen or assisted in the development of numerous interstate agreements. That office was headed by Crady deGolian, who later became the moderator for drafting panel meetings. The decision to partner with CSG was pivotal in broadening the appeal of the Forum's inquiries to the national postsecondary education and state regulatory communities, and in exploring the specialized issues associated with the development of an interstate reciprocity compact, eventually leading to SARA.

The importance of the Dallas meeting cannot be overstated. It has often been cited by SARA project participants as the turning point where policy makers, regulators, and institutional representatives, often averse to collaboration, agreed to work together to explore SARA. This convening essentially allowed the Forum to establish a network with representative stakeholders in state authorization, to engage in a continuing partnership with CSG in the proposed project, and to strengthen our commitment to engage state regulators in subsequent policy development.

The following narrative summarizes the issues, findings, and information gained from the participants in Dallas, as well as the prior seven years of discussions, outreach, and development led by the Presidents' Forum, all of which established the foundation upon which the current SARA initiative rests:

State employees who hold positions that are tasked to monitor and enforce rules created by legislatures and governors have a rough road to travel. As regulators and invigilators, they must establish working rules that support existing legislation. They must establish procedures that allow the applicable individuals and organizations to understand requirements, to apply and maintain compliance with these requirements, and to enforce due process in identifying and disciplining those who fall short. In many cases, perhaps most, they are expected to find individuals or organizations that are operating in their state but which have avoided compliance, through ignorance of the law or purposeful obfuscation. Such are the tasks assigned by the state regulators of whom we speak and who played a central role in the development of SARA.

Needless to say, regulators tend not to be the most popular of public employees. Especially in higher education, where traditions of institutional self-governance in matters of academic purport are long-standing, the whole concept of external regulation is generally unwelcome. Colleges and Universities have long-standing private arrangements with regional accreditation associations, themselves organizations of, by and for the institutions. They expect approval of new programs of study leading to degrees, and periodic review of the qualitative characteristics of existing programs, to be a collegial process, conducted by teams of peers with a common purpose of continuous improvement. Actions that inhibit a member organization or second guess its own professional judgments are not common, and, at least in the past, issued only in fairly extreme cases of institutional malperformance. Given this predilection, the addition of an additional layer of regulation from the resident campus's state is especially onerous.

There is an important exception to this state of mind. When a new institution suddenly intends to offer its services, or when an existing institution opts to offer a new program that is highly competitive with existing similar programs of study, then external regulation takes on a more benign attractiveness. When state regulators seek to regulate such intruders, they are perceived as protectors of turf, an important member of the team.

Perversely, this factor does not endear state regulators with leaders of new postsecondary educational programs. Such intruder organizations often bring special attributes that could, in certain cases, serve the citizens of a state. They may be highly innovative, offering new and needed services. They may be well funded through private equity, able to move quickly in offering services. They may be extended branches of very strong out-of-state universities with powerful attractive reputations. Conversely, they may be entrepreneurial operators who seek out needy but poorly qualified potential student who are nonetheless able to access federal financial aid. They may be the product of a single person's creativity, with little sustainable capability. They may, in too many cases, be completely fraudulent, profiting from unsuspecting students and student aid systems. In such cases, we were told, regulators do not *become aware of these organizations until some student complaint is referred to the office of the regulator. Such intruders, in surprisingly large numbers, operate beneath the regulatory screen. Ultimately, regulators spend an inordinate amount of their time on this aspect of their daily work.*

The matter is perhaps even more difficult in some states. Many states compartmentalize postsecondary regulation, assigning regulatory authority to different offices or divisions. Thus public institutions may fall under one authority; two-year community colleges under another; independent non profit or for-profit institutions under yet another; and typically religious or Native American institutions operate under yet another authority. Professional licensure, whose applicants may prepare for licensure through specific programs of study in every kind and level of institution, may appear in yet more diffuse offices or related organizations. State postsecondary regulatory officials thus face difficult but essential assignments.

Given this voluminous, detailed insight gained from the Dallas meeting, the Forum, the Council of State Governments, and the Lumina Foundation were persuaded that these issues were important to states, institutions, and students, both immediately and into the future. When Lumina provided a second substantial grant (ID#7100, Making Opportunity Affordable - $300,000 - November 5, 2010) "to explore the potential for a voluntary, interstate agreement to broaden the availability of accredited online degree programs by reducing state regulatory barriers while ensuring strong consumer safeguards", the Forum, in partnership with CSG, moved forward to implement the proposal.

THE FEDERAL MANDATE FOR STATE AUTHORIZATION

Even as the Dallas meeting was examining state authorization practices, the USED clarified its existing rules about state authorization, creating for the Forum project an immediacy that stimulated a broad concern across all of the higher education establishment. As noted earlier, from the 1980's through the present, the federal interest in curbing perceived abuse of student financial aid programs has emerged frequently. In the view of policy makers and consumer rights advocates, some postsecondary institutions abuse student aid programs by collecting and retaining the student's financial aid award whether or not the student drops out or proves incapable of college-level study. Students too often become "victims" of loan programs that leave them saddled with debt and no credential of value. These federal interests were reflected in the 1992 reauthorization of the Higher Education Act (HEA) that called for reforms to address student loan default rates, abuses of student loan programs, unscrupulous conduct by proprietary institutions, and enhanced accountability for postsecondary education by the triad of the federal US Department of Education, states, and recognized accrediting bodies.

Following the 1992 HEA reauthorization, a perception developed that *for-profit* postsecondary providers are a primary source of abuse of federal student financial aid programs and a threat to public support for their continuance. These concerns continue through highly publicized congressional/state legislative hearings and exposés in the media. Much of this heightened scrutiny has occurred in parallel with the rapid expansion of the availability of online postsecondary courses of study. As technology-mediated learning systems have matured, entrepreneurs and innovators have invested resources in creating access to online distance learning for students who have been underserved by traditional campus-based institutions. But this has amplified the challenges to consumer protection and maintenance of institutional and program integrity.

The federal constitution leaves regulation to the individual states. The federal Department of Education requires state authorization of any organization that seeks to qualify for federal financial aid. The result, historically and practically, is a patchwork of state regulation. Every state has established its own particular version of requirement and processes for state authorization. Every state determines how and in which offices regulation occurs.

Some states choose to not regulate at all. Some have modest regulation, or may simply require that institutions hold regional voluntary accreditation. Many states have substantial, often complex, requirements that must be reviewed at periodic intervals. And some states have very demanding and qualitatively challenging requirements. The result is fifty-four different state and territorial demands.

All of this worked reasonably well in years past, when with a few unique exceptions, all post secondary offerings within a state were also offered by in-state residential or campus-based instruction. Regulators knew their institutions and where the trouble spots were likely to occur. Over time, experienced regulators also came to know other regulators in a loose national network. They could deal, often informally, with student complaints when the student happened to live in another state, such as students in the military services and corporations, who moved frequently.

In the past few years, there have been many developments in the area of state authorization. On October 29, 2010, the USED published fourteen new regulations intended to prevent abuses of federal financial aid programs by establishing new consumer protections, ensuring that only eligible students have access to federal student financial aid programs, and by defining courses and programs of study approved for student use of federal financial aid. These "Program Integrity Rules" focusing on the integrity of federal student financial aid programs under Title IV of the Higher Education Act of 1965, as amended, addressed five areas of concern: institutional eligibility to participate in Title IV student financial aid programs, recruiting and admissions, eligibility of specific programs of learning for Title IV assistance, student eligibility to receive Title IV assistance, and Title IV aid disbursements and refund policies. Although largely directed towards curbing perceived abuses of federal student financial aid programs by for-profit postsecondary institutions, and especially those extending their footprint and student demand for federal financial aid through online offerings, it quickly became apparent that there were also significant implications for non profit, independent, and public postsecondary institutions.

In order to be eligible to receive federal student financial aid for students, an institution must be legally authorized to provide an educational program beyond secondary education in the state in which the institution is physically located. In an attempt to define what constitutes sufficient state authorization for purposes of compliance with this requirement, a new *State Authorization Rule* was advanced. The rule required that an institution must be authorized to provide both educational programs beyond secondary education in the state in which it is physically located and in the state in which a student resides. In its proposed application, institutions administering Title IV student financial aid for their students would now be required to show evidence of compliance with state rules and regulations to serve students wherever they resided. The possible institutional penalties for noncompliance with this rule were draconian and could possibly result in the loss of eligibility for administration of all Title IV funds.

The evolution of the state authorization requirements caused significant consternation and confusion. At the onset of this rule, institutions were faced with the massive challenge to acquire knowledge of the physical location of all of their students, as well as an in depth understanding of each state's rules, regulations, and administration of institutional authorization. For states, there was a corresponding need to address increasing numbers of non resident institutions serving students within their geographic boundaries, as well as to respond to requests for authorization approvals from these institutions now required by federal mandate.

In 2012, the US Court of Appeals for the District of Columbia affirmed a district court decision vacating the portion of the program integrity regulations related to the state authorization requirements for distance education. However, the "wake-up call" to states and institutions served to clarify that institutions have been, and will remain, subject to state laws that may require authorization for distance education programs independent of any ancillary federal requirements. As a result, state authorization agencies have become more aggressive and active in requiring comprehensive compliance by non resident institutions serving their citizenry at a distance. In addition, there is nothing to prevent the US Department of Education from seeking to reinstate and enforce its state authorization rule at any time. All of these considerations served to support the Presidents' Forum's contention that a state authorization reciprocity agreement was now possible and essential to the future success of institutions and their students.

DELIBERATION AND DESIGN: THE DRAFTING PANEL

During the several stages of inquiry described earlier, we had met and engaged in conversation with a number of individuals who appeared to have the requisite knowledge and experience and a demonstrated ability to work together with others. We had established no rigid expectations for either the number of panelists nor the several characteristics that would enrich the panel's deliberations. Clearly, however, from the outset we had placed considerable value on engagement with those most immersed in the daily authorization for and regulation of higher education institutions at the state level. Moreover, the ongoing Forum discussions had emphasized that the most successful approach would be to work from the grass roots, avoid the usual Washington professional association tendency to politicize the process, and, above all, avoid a federally dictated process. Alan Contreras underlined that decision, saying "Well-meaning education organizations with little knowledge of the practicalities of how state approvals actually work will decide that they should simply invent such a system without bothering to involve actual regulators. To preclude this kind of bumblehandedness, we need the states to simply get to work ..." (*Inside Higher Education*, March 1, 2009.) The later USED interventions into *state authorization* were not as yet on the screen. Shiffman personally discussed the project with individuals, many of whom had attended the earlier Dallas convening, issuing invitations to participate as mutually agreed. The final Drafting Panel included twelve members and remained unchanged, remarkably, throughout the several years of SARA development that followed. (For the list of drafting panel members, see Appendix B.)

In summer 2011, the drafting team completed a draft *white paper* that presented much of the panel's current thinking, including some important new approaches to reciprocity. Key new policies were proposed, importantly including a clear definition of "home state," fixing responsibility for the recommendation of eligible institutions for participation in SARA with the state of origin or charter. The purpose of this provision was to overcome the confusion among students, state regulators, and attorney generals as to who would be responsible for dealing with student complaints, legal issues, and oversight. Another key decision defined a governance model for SARA, initially calling for an interstate compact as the basis for authority. The white paper went on to propose a listing of the kinds of qualitative factors that states would agree to consider in recommending an institution for participation. Among these were expectations for faculty, curricula, credit, admissions, and finances. Finally, a financial model was proposed that would provide adequate support to the governance mechanisms, while assuring a very modest institutional fee, clearly a significant savings from the enormous costs in travel, personnel, and authorization fees under the prevailing practices. The white paper was clearly a first draft, to submit a number of panel decisions for critical review.

UNDER THE GUN: THE UMUC CONVERSATIONS

Common to collaborative efforts in the philanthropic community, the representatives of the Lumina Foundation apprised Thomas C. Dawson, senior policy officer for the Bill & Melinda Gates Foundation, of possible joint interest in the Forum's activities. As a result, the Gates Foundation had been following with interest the work of the drafting panel. In March, 2010, we joined a one-day seminar in Washington DC, hosted by the Gates Foundation, to share information regarding the reciprocity project with Gates staff and representatives of Washington-based postsecondary associations. Although no special outcome emerged from the meeting, it indicated the Gates interest, no doubt stimulated by approaches from at least three other national educational organizations (SHEEO, APLU, AASCU).

In July 2011, Gates sponsored an assembly of interested parties held at the University of Maryland University College, sponsored by Chancellor William C. Kirwan. While the aim of the meeting was unclear, it appeared to be an opportunity to allow the various perceived stakeholder parties from the public institutional sector, who expressed grave misgivings about the Forum/CSG project, to vent their concerns. The majority of comments centered on the assumption that non profit public institutions would be immunized from state authorization requirements imposed by the federal government or other states. Though the pending USED rules on state authorization had also increased the concerns of the Washington-based associations in the topic, the "hell no, we won't go" message was clearly advanced. Many had perhaps hoped that their attendance at the meeting might portend a larger interest from Gates in funding one of their organizations with a "more national" approach.

The meeting elicited a number of concerns about the white paper, which was an early model for discussion purposes only. Among these concerns was that an interstate compact might foster a new level of standards of performance for institutions that might supplant or result in an additional level of institutional accreditation. Also, institutions currently were constituents of a number of representative associations competing for dues-based revenue, and the outlined compact model might add to institutional costs and disrupt existent revenue streams. The unspoken concern, however, was how our panel of regulators, lacking direct institutional representation, could possibly be qualified to produce such a far reaching project plan at all. We took the concerns and criticisms to heart, promising that a revised draft would take their concerns into consideration.

As an additional recollection, the UMUC meeting ended abruptly as cell phones erupted throughout the audience with the announcement that Thomas Dawson (Gates sponsor of the meeting) had accepted a senior administrative position with Laureate Education, a for-profit provider of postsecondary education. In the midst of surfacing the concerns of the public sector with restrictive regulation that this audience believed was best applied only to for-profit institutions, the telecommunicated announcement served as the segue to adjournment.

THE EMERGENCE OF OTHER POSSIBLE APPROACHES

W-SARA: The Regional Higher Education Compacts. Although David Longanecker, president of WICHE, participated in the earliest task force discussions and report, he announced that he was preparing WICHE's own reciprocity plan entitled W-SARA. In testimony offered at a special open hearing for comments from the public at large, Longanecker appeared again and spoke in the most definitive terms about his plan to prepare a proposal for the Regional Higher Education Compacts to consider. In doing so, he accepted many of the key innovations and language of the model Forum/CSG model. He assumed leadership of this reciprocity effort on behalf of the other three regional higher education compacts (SREB, MHEC, NEBHE). Both groups, Presidents' Forum/CSG and WICHE, eventually agreed that the introduction of multiple models to policy makers and stake holders would result in a fragmented community unable to achieve the necessary changes sought in the state institutional authorization process. Kevin Corcoran had counseled, "Don't let the perfect be the enemy of the good." We resolved to seek unity.

As a result of these parallel initiatives and the desire to put forward a singular model, the groups had a series of meetings, made compromises, and agreed to implement a limited time—(three-year)—transitional approach (referred to by both groups as the SARA Implementation Plan) that resulted in a unified and single SARA model with oversight of implementation vested in the regional compacts.

One step toward achieving this goal was an "in the passageway" meeting between Hall and Longanecker, who was moving between our meeting and another in the same location (Lumina headquarters in Indianapolis, IN). After the discussion, a compromise plan was offered to the drafting panel. Basically, the panel gave up the central governance concept of an interstate compact, and agreed to support a unified plan that included governance by the regional compacts, organizations that would later seek implementation funding from Lumina. The Forum's panel, with much reluctance, recognized that its early hopes that between five and ten states might participate after a year or two could be significantly enhanced if the regional compacts, whose members included all but three of the states, took the lead in implementation. Longanecker had indeed edited the core of the Presidents' Forum/CSG proposal into a more acceptable format, and all concurred that the resultant unified approach to SARA would enhance education and outreach to the growing number of affected constituencies.

COMBINING ALL PRIOR EFFORTS
The Commission on the Regulation of Postsecondary Distance Education

On May 2, 2012, Paul Lingenfelter, president of the State Higher Education Executive Officers Association (SHEEO) and M. Peter McPherson, President of the Association of Public and Land-Grant Universities (APLU), convened The Commission on the Regulation of Postsecondary Distance Education, with former Secretary of Education Richard W. Riley as Chair. The twenty-one commissioners, the majority from institutions, represented leadership from a broad spectrum of stakeholders in postsecondary distance education policy. Paul Shiffman and Marshall A. Hill, Executive Director, Nebraska Coordinating Commission for Postsecondary Education and a member of the Presidents' Forum/CSG SARA Drafting Team, were invited to serve as commissioners.

At its inaugural meeting, the direction for the commission was proposed by its two primary proponents. Lingenfelter expressed strong interest in strengthening the traditional higher education triad of state, accreditation, and federal roles to address the changing environment of postsecondary education wrought by online distance learning. McPherson, concerned about the effect of expanding regulatory demands on institutions, expressed a need for a greater institutional voice in any proposal that would diminish institutional flexibility. Shiffman and Hill presented and summarized the unified SARA model to the commission and invited this body to adopt and validate this work as a guide to their exploration of the regulatory environment for postsecondary distance learning. Both promoted their belief that the prior work of the Forum/CSG and WICHE teams had already revealed that the primary immediate concern was the regulation of institutional authorization by the states, and that the commission was the appropriate body to further validate this finding, as well as to provide input from and unify the postsecondary community to advance implementation of SARA.

Ultimately, the commission shaped its mission "to develop and provide recommendations that will address the costs and inefficiencies faced by postsecondary institutions that must comply with multiple (often inconsistent) state laws and regulations as they endeavor to provide educational opportunities to students in multiple state jurisdictions." On April 15, 2013, the commission released its final report, *Advancing Access through Regulatory Reform: Findings, Principles, and Recommendations for the State Authorization Reciprocity Agreement (SARA)*. The report built upon and enhanced the earlier proposed SARA models. It explored key issues, not yet fully addressed in the prior versions of SARA, associated with appropriate government regulation and oversight, consumer protection, quality assurance of distance education offered by institutions across the nation, and a methodology for funding and administering implementation of SARA.

On April 16-17, 2013, immediately following the release of the commission report, the Presidents' Forum and the Council of State Governments convened a reciprocity symposium, in collaboration with the Commission and the four regional higher education compacts, to invite state teams to review the proposed SARA and to explore the implementation processes recommended for states and their designated authorization agencies, institutions, and accreditors to advance and implement SARA. Representatives from forty-seven states came to Indianapolis, Indiana, to review SARA and to meet in region-specific groups to explore implementation issues and establish collaborative approaches. The collaboration and harmony of approach evident in this meeting had rarely, if ever, been achieved across all sectors of the higher education community.

The Indianapolis reciprocity symposium marked the movement of the all of the parties involved in the creation of SARA from development to implementation. The initial state engagements with the partnering organizations suggested that there was strong interest in SARA, but also a good deal of confusion and misinformation about necessary steps and their impact. Because the issues raised relating to SARA were complex and revealed that state participation would often require legislative action to permit participation, the need for clear, consistent, and accurate information emerged as a critical concern. The Presidents' Forum/CSG team engaged in ongoing conversation with Travis Reindl, program officer with the Bill & Melinda Gates Foundation, seeking support to develop informational and messaging materials that could increase the understanding of and participation in SARA, thereby allowing states, institutions and students to realize the benefits of SARA. On April 1, 2014, the Presidents' Forum/CSG partnership received a $200,000 award from the Bill & Melinda Gates Foundation to direct their efforts to address this need through 2016.

SUMMARY

Following the completion and publication of the generic model by the Forum/CSG Drafting Panel in January, 2014 (The final report of the SARA Drafting Panel is called: *Model for State Authorization Reciprocity Agreement*, the Presidents' Forum, January, 2014), and a regionally tailored implementation proposal by NC-SARA, a substantial proposal for initial funding was submitted to the Lumina Foundation by the four participating regional higher education compacts. Lumina, building upon the report of the commission on the Regulation of Postsecondary Distance Education focused its continuing support upon the establishment of a National Council for

State Authorization Reciprocity Agreements (NC-SARA) incorporating many of the participants from the PF/CSG SARA project, the W-SARA initiative, as well as the Commission. The national council is a policy body assisting the regional compacts in developing and implementing consistent SARA policy and procedures and formulating legislation and procedures to permit states' participation in SARA in their regions.

That proposal provided for support of a small staff at each of the regional compacts, and, with the Forum's insistence, a national council that would develop shared policy, procedural, and qualitative consistency across the nation. In 2014, Lumina provided a substantial award for an initial two-year development cycle, assuming that SARA would become self-supporting after that period. The NC-SARA Board appointed Marshall Hill, earlier a member of the drafting panel, as SARA's first Executive Director. Paul Shiffman serves as a Commissioner and member of the executive committee.

Although some time must pass before the full understanding of what SARA means for students, educational institutions, and states, the initial successes suggest some early observations. First, a very high level of interest has been expressed by the states. By Fall 2017, forty-eight individual states had applied for, been recommended by their home states and regional SARA, and been accepted for membership. Many have gained legislative law changes in order to join SARA. Additional states are in communication with SARA and should join in the coming years. Second, the initial financial plan proposed in the Forum/CSG model has proven to be viable. By setting the annual fees for the institutions at a three-tiered modest level based upon total enrollment, over 1000 member colleges and universities now provide sufficient support for the regional and national organization to operate successfully. It appears that the institutions are saving very large sums of money compared to the former level of expense for state authorization. The individual home states for these institutions are able to charge reasonable fees in state to support the costs of periodic evaluation and review. And state regulatory staff may be experiencing a more rational flow of work, given that it is no longer necessary for each state to authorize every out-of-state institution that wishes to offer courses of study.

What cannot be known at this point in time is how effective the network of NC-SARA is in maintaining strong and comparable performance standards. Most recently, several challenges have been raised from external groups concerned with performance quality, in particular of for-profit corporate institutions. Consumer groups have questioned whether SARA merely opens the door to some low performing institutions, thereby disadvantaging enrolled students who may lose substantial financial aid funds they have borrowed, or gain worthless degrees. In our view, these concerns are valid questions that have been addressed and carefully vetted by NC-SARA and its staff.

Only institutions carefully certified as meeting required high performance standards are accepted into SARA membership, and provision is made for addressing directly any student issues that may appear. Moreover, every member institution must hold full regional accreditation as a prerequisite to membership. In addition, the home states also require institutions to meet their own stated standards prior to recommendation to SARA.

In conclusion, the grand experiment called NC-SARA seems likely to achieve all of the hopes and expectations described in the model defined by the Forum/CSG drafting panel. Truly, the design constitutes one of the most significant changes in higher education in the US in some years. It provides the companion structures to address the radically changed and challenging issues of the technology revolution—a revolution that makes it possible for students to learn wherever and whenever they are able and ready. For many years, institutions have lagged behind in meeting these challenges. SARA has opened that door with a design, structure, and safeguards that can ensure its success to an extent once only imagined.

APPENDIX A

Members of the first Presidents' Forum Task Force

Bruce Chaloux, Executive Director, Sloan Consortium, and Director, SREB Electronic University

Steven Crow, Past President, The Higher Learning Commission

John F. Ebersole, Past President, Excelsior College

Richard Garrett, Program Director and Senior Research Analyst, Eduventures, LLC

Michael B. Goldstein, Co-chair of the Higher Education industry practice at Dow Lohnes, PLLC

James W. Hall, Chancellor Emeritus Antioch University/ President Emeritus, SUNY Empire State College

Darcy Hardy, Assistant Vice Chancellor and Executive Director, University of Texas TeleCampus

Edward Klonoski, President, Charter Oak State College

Alan Davis, President, SUNY Empire State College

Charles Lenth, Vice President, State Higher Education Executive Officers

Paul Lingenfelter, President, State Higher Education Executive Officers

Bernard Luskin, CEO, Touro University Worldwide

David Longanecker, Executive Director, Western Interstate Commission for Higher Education

Gary W. Matkin, Dean, UCI Extension, University of California, Irvine

Linda Thor, President, Rio Salado College

Michael Offermen, President, Capella University

Julie Porosky Hamlin, Executive Director, Maryland Online

Joseph Porter, Past Vice President and General Counsel, Excelsior College

Terry Rawls, Vice Chancellor, Jones International University

John Sabatini, Vice President, Walden University

Paul Shiffman, CEO, The Presidents' Forum

Roger Sublett, President, Union Institute and University

Terrance Thompson, Director of Congressional and Public Affairs, US Chamber of Commerce

APPENDIX B

The Drafting Panel

Bruce Chaloux, Executive Director of the Sloan Consortium, and former Director of the SREB Electronic University, and had extensive experience in regional accreditation, working with the Virginia Board. A champion of reciprocity, he did not live to see SARA succeed.

Alan Contreras, Director, Oregon Office of Degree Authorization, and Member, NASASPS

Shane DeGarmo, Associate Vice-Commissioner, Ohio Board of Regents

Crady deGolian, Director, National Center for Interstate Compacts, Council of State Governments

James W. Hall, Chancellor Emeritus Antioch University/ President Emeritus, SUNY Empire State College

Marshall Hill, Executive Director, Nebraska Coordinating Commission of Higher Education

Russell Poulin, Director of Policy and Analysis, WCET

George Roedler, Manager Institutional Registration and Licensing, Minnesota Office of Higher Education.

Paul Shiffman, CEO, The Presidents' Forum, (Lumina Grant Project Director)

Sharyl Thompson, State Authorization Compliance Officer, Capella University

LeRoy Wade, Deputy Commissioner, Missouri Department of Higher Education, and past President, NASASPS

ABOUT THE CONTRIBUTORS

STEPHEN ANDRIOLE, PhD, is the Thomas G. Labrecque Professor of Business Technology at the Villanova School of Business at Villanova University, where he teaches courses and conducts research on digital technology.

Dr. Andriole was the director of the Cybernetics Technology Office of the Defense Advanced Research Projects Agency (DARPA), where he supported the development of spatial data management and multimedia systems, decision support systems, computer-aided simulation and training systems, and intelligent technology-based command and control systems.

He was the chief technology officer and senior vice president of Safeguard Scientifics, Inc., where he was responsible for identifying technology trends, translating that insight into the Safeguard investment strategy, and leveraging trends analyses with the Safeguard partner companies to help them develop business and marketing strategies.

Dr. Andriole was the chief technology officer and senior vice president for technology strategy at Cigna Corporation, where he was responsible for the enterprise information architecture, computing standards, the technology research and development program, data security, as well as the overall alignment of enterprise information technology investments with Cigna's multiple lines of business.

Dr. Andriole was professor of information systems and electrical and computer engineering at Drexel University in Philadelphia, Pennsylvania, and was professor and chairman of information systems and systems engineering at George Mason University.

Dr. Andriole is the author of over thirty books, including the *Sourcebook of Applied Artificial Intelligence* (McGraw-Hill, 1992), *Cognitive Systems Engineering* (1995), a book on user interface technology for Lawrence Erlbaum Associates, and co-authored with Len Adelman, Managing Systems Requirements: *Methods, Tools & Cases* (McGraw Hill; 1996), *Technology Due Diligence* (IGI, 2007), and *Ready Technology* (CRC Press, 2014). He has published articles in the *Communications of the AIS, Communications of the ACM, Journal of Cases in Information Technology, Journal of Information Technology Education* and *IEEE IT Professional*. He is also a regular contributor to *Forbes*. Dr. Andriole received his BA from LaSalle University and his master's and doctoral degrees from the University of Maryland.

MEG BENKE, PhD, is a professor at Empire State College's School of Graduate Studies and coordinates the programs in adult learning and emerging technologies. Dr. Benke has had an extensive administrative career at Empire State College, serving as dean of the Center for Distance Learning, vice provost, provost, and acting president.

In 2015, Dr. Benke served as a Fulbright Research Scholar at the Waterford Institute of Technology, in Ireland. Dr. Benke was inducted into the International Adult and Continuing Education Hall of Fame for her contributions to adult and online learning. Dr. Benke was recognized for the "Most Outstanding Achievement in Online Learning by an Individual," by Sloan-C (now Online Learning Consortium), a national consortium for distance learning providers, in 2007. Benke was honored by the board of directors of the Sloan Consortium, by being named to its inaugural class of Sloan-C fellows for her extraordinary qualifications, significant experience, distinguished service, and leadership in the field of online learning. She was president of the board of directors of the Online Learning Consortium from 2011 to 2014.

Dr. Benke also serves as a commissioner for the Middle States Association for Higher Education, and was a commissioner for the National Commission on Interstate Regulation of Distance Education, the nationally appointed group that reviewed State Regulation of Distance Education. She also serves as a member of New York State's Regents Advisory Council.

RICHARD F. BONNABEAU, PhD, joined the faculty of SUNY Empire State College in 1974 as an Eli Lilly postdoctoral mentor intern. He received his PhD in 1974 from Indiana University, where he specialized in history and cultural anthropology. Bonnabeau was the recipient of a Fulbright scholarship for graduate studies at the University of San Marcos and the Catholic University, both in Lima, Peru. At Empire State College, Bonnabeau has served as a member of the faculty, as an administrator, and as faculty chair of the Empire State College senate. He was a founding member of the Center for Distance Learning and co-authored and co-taught one of the first online learning courses in the US. He joined International Programs in 1993. His work focused on academic quality initiatives, including the use of courses developed by the Center for Distance Learning. Bonnabeau is the founding coordinator of the Empire State College Dual Degree Program with Anadolu University, Turkey, which is part of a SUNY system-wide initiative. He is the author of a number of distance learning course guides and a co-author, with founding Empire State College President James W. Hall, of a chapter on nontraditional education focused on SUNYESC and published by Jossey-Bass. Most recently, he authored a chapter with Turkish scholars on ethno-political conflict in Turkey, sponsored by the International Academy for Intercultural Research and published by Springer. This was followed by another coauthored chapter on Turkey for a global study on gender and culture. Dr. Bonnabeau is the college historian and archivist, and has a special interest in oral history as a research tool. He is the author of *The Promise Continues*, the history of Empire State College.

JOHN R. BOURNE, PhD, received his doctorate in electrical engineering from the University of Florida. He was professor of electrical and computer engineering and professor of biomedical engineering at Vanderbilt University from 1969 until 2000. In 1982, he served as a visiting professor at Chalmers University in Goteborg, Sweden, and in 1990, he was a visiting researcher at Northern Telecom. He was professor of electrical engineering at Olin College of Engineering and professor of technology entrepreneurship at Babson College from 2000 until 2010. He was executive director of the Sloan Consortium until 2010. He was provost, chief academic officer, and chief innovation officer at American Sentinel University from 2010 to 2014. Since 2015, he has been editor-in-chief of the *International Journal on Innovation in Online Education.*

Dr. Bourne has had varied research interests over the last four decades that include: quantitative electroencephalography, visual evoked response studies, syntactic pattern recognition, and paradigms for online learning. Dr. Bourne was the editor-in-chief of the *Begell House Critical Reviews in Biomedical Engineering* from 1979 until 2003. He founded the *Journal of Asynchronous Learning Networks.* He established the Sloan Foundation supported Asynchronous Learning Network (ALN) Web in 1996. Dr. Bourne is a fellow of the Institute of Electrical and Electronic Engineers (IEEE) and a fellow of the American Institute of Medical and Biological Engineers (AIMBE).

JILL BUBAN, PhD, has worked in online learning for the past ten years and is currently the Online Learning Consortium's senior director of research and innovation where she oversees the organization's research and publications strategy. Prior to joining the Online Learning Consortium, Dr. Buban was the assistant provost for research and innovation at Post University. In this role, Dr. Buban instituted university-wide initiatives with a forward-thinking, student-centered focus. These initiatives included, but were not limited to, the university's transition to digital course materials, the creation of an online academy for high school students, competency-based learning initiatives, professional developing credentialing, articulation agreements, enrollment management, and oversight of all academic publications, as well as a variety of teaching and learning initiatives.

Prior to joining Post University, Dr. Buban worked in academic affairs at SUNY Empire State College. She collaborated on a variety of online learning initiatives including the implementation of ePortfolios, open learning access and opportunities, and prior learning assessment.

Dr. Buban continues to study and present on topics surrounding effective technology use for adult learners in online environments. She is a member of the SSEA Communications Committee, an organization for which she was named an Emerging Scholar in 2012. Buban continues to teach in the areas of adult and online learning.

CHRIS DEDE, EdD, is the Timothy E. Wirth Professor in Learning Technologies at Harvard's Graduate School of Education (HGSE). His fields of scholarship include emerging technologies, policy, and leadership. His funded research includes grants from the National Science Foundation (NSF), the US Department of Education's Institute of Education Sciences, and the Gates Foundation. From 2001 to 2004, he was Chair of the HGSE department of teaching and learning. In 2007, he was honored by Harvard University as an outstanding teacher, and in 2011 he was named a fellow of the American Educational Research Association. From 2014 to 2015, he was a visiting expert at NSF, Directorate of Education and Human Resources.

Chris has served as a member of the National Academy of Sciences Committee on Foundations of Educational and Psychological Assessment, a member of the US Department of Education's expert panel on technology, a steering committee member for the Second International Technology in Education Study, and a member of the 2010 National Educational Technology Plan technical working group. In 2013, he co-convened a NSF workshop on new technology-based models of postsecondary learning; and in 2015 he led two

NSF workshops on data-intensive research in the sciences, engineering, and education. He has co-edited four books in the last decade: *Scaling Up Success: Lessons Learned from Technology-based Educational Improvement*; *Online Professional Development for Teachers: Emerging Models and Methods*; *Digital Teaching Platforms: Customizing Classroom Learning for Each Student*; and *Teacher Learning in the Digital Age: Online Professional Development in STEM Education*.

Chris has several fields of research in which he is considered an expert. These include online and blended learning, mobile learning, immersive learning (virtual reality, multi-user virtual environments, mixed and augmented realities), personalized learning, and scaling up educational improvements.

JOHN EBERSOLE, LpD, was the second president of Excelsior College, a post he held from January 2006 until his death in November 2016. Under his leadership, the College transformed itself from an institution primarily focused on assessment and credit aggregation to one of online instruction. The institution currently serves 42,000 students worldwide, with more than 600 online courses, including an award-winning curriculum for associate-degree-seeking nursing students.

In positions prior to Excelsior, at Boston University, Colorado State, UC Berkeley, and JFK, he was involved in moving these institutions online and, in the case of BU, building an online capability from scratch (with help from Susan Kryczka). As a trustee of the New England College of Finance (now "Business"), while at Boston University, he helped secure a Sloan grant to support the College's move online. Together, he, Gary Matkin, and Charles "Chuck" Hill worked to put the UC system's Center for Media and Independent Learning online, with Sloan Foundation support.

To build support for both online learning and the posttraditional student, he has produced two videos, the WOW Award Winning, *Access to Learning* (DVD) and the documentary film *Courageous Learning*, available online and on DVD. The latter was preceded by the book which he and Bill Patrick wrote in 2011.

Dr. Ebersole was inducted into the US Distance Learning Association's Hall of Fame in 2014 and into the International Adult Continuing Education Hall of Fame in 2015. He was a former chair of the American Council on Education's Commission on Lifelong Learning, a two-term director of New York's Commission on Independent Colleges and Universities, and a past chair of the American Association of Community College's Corporate Council.

ERIC E. FREDERICKSEN, PhD, is the associate vice president for online learning and provides leadership for the exploration of online learning initiatives across the University of Rochester. He is also associate professor in educational leadership in the Warner School, where he teaches in the classroom and online.

Eric has extensive experience in online education and instructional technologies. He was associate vice provost for academic and research IT at the University of Rochester from 2005 to 2012. Prior to the University of Rochester, Eric served as the director of academic technology and media services at Cornell University. Before Cornell, Eric was the assistant provost for advanced learning technology in the State University of New York, where he provided leadership for all system-wide programs focused on the innovative use of technology to support teaching and learning. This included the nationally recognized SUNY Learning Network, winner of the EDUCAUSE Award for Systemic Progress in Teaching and Learning and Sloan-C Awards for Excellence in Faculty Development and Excellence in Institution-Wide Online programming. Eric was the co-PI and administrative officer for three multi-year, multi-million dollar grants on online learning from the Sloan Foundation. He also received three grants for national research workshops on online learning from the Sloan Foundation. For the past fifteen years, he has been designing and teaching graduate online courses in education. He was also chair of the Sloan-C International Conference on Online Learning and served as chair of the Sloan-C Awards Program for Excellence in Online Teaching and Learning. In 2012, Eric was elected to the board of directors for the Sloan Consortium and was honored as a Sloan-C Fellow in 2013. In 2015, he was elected as the vice president of the Online Learning Consortium (formerly the Sloan Consortium).

JAMES W. HALL, PhD, served for twenty-seven years as founding president of the innovative Empire State College of the State University of New York, anticipating in 1971 the emergence of new approaches to distance and online teaching and learning. ESC offered open access, individualized mentored contract learning, evaluation of prior college-level learning gained through experience and work for credit, narrative evaluations, open academic calendar with year-round study, interdisciplinary curricula, and employment of distance technologies. It became the first regionally accredited such institution. Subsequently he served as chancellor of the six campus Antioch University and holds emeritus title from both institutions.

Hall earned the MA and PhD (1967) in American civilization from the University of Pennsylvania as a Danforth Graduate Fellow. Earlier he earned the bachelor of music from Bucknell University, and the master of sacred music from Union Seminary, NYC. A member of the Cedar Crest College music faculty as organist, conductor, and historian, in 1966, Hall joined the history faculty at SUNY Albany. He served the SUNY system chancellor's office in several capacities, including associate university dean for arts and cultural affairs, and vice chancellor for educational technology. He initiated a system-wide focus on using the technologies for instruction: State University of New York and Educational Technology for the Year 2000 (1990). Other publications include *Forging the American Character* (1971), *Access Through Innovation: New Colleges for New Students* (1991), *In Opposition to Core Curriculum: Alternative Models for Undergraduate Education* (1982), and numerous articles, such as *Planning and Management in Distance Education* (2003). In addition to lectures and consultancies, he has served as chair of more than a dozen teams for regional accreditors, helping to establish high academic standards and improved understanding and acceptance of new approaches to collegiate learning. He served as interim president of SUNY/Old

Westbury (1981-82). Hall has held board leadership posts at ACE, AASCU, AACU, CAEL, ICDE, Boyer Center, Rockefeller Institute, Monmouth University, Fielding Institute, and US Open University. He holds honorary Doctor of Humane Letters degrees from Thomas Edison State University, DePaul University, University System of New Hampshire, and the State University of New York. Currently he serves as consultant to The Presidents' Forum at Excelsior College, helping to create the model for a recent major innovation in postsecondary education, SARA.

JULIE POROSKY HAMLIN, PhD, has, since 2001, served as executive director of MarylandOnline, a consortium of twenty public and independent colleges and universities in Maryland that collaborate in online learning. Previously, Hamlin was senior vice president of University of Maryland University College (UMUC), having begun her career as a faculty member in UMUC's European Division. At UMUC, Hamlin oversaw a number of operational units, including undergraduate programs, military programs, international programs, contract programs, student affairs, marketing, a research institute, and a leadership institute. She also organized the annual UMUC-sponsored Conference on Improving University Teaching.

Hamlin's career in higher education includes appointment to several boards and commissions; publications and presentations related to quality assurance in online education; service as an accreditation team member and chair for the Middle States Commission on Higher Education; and service as an evaluator for the American Council on Education's Military Institution Voluntary Education Review (MIVER) program. She was the recipient of the 2012 Nofflet Williams Service Award from the National University Telecommunications Network. As time permits, Hamlin teaches online classes in the University of Phoenix's PhD in Higher Education program. Her professional interests and achievements are in the fields of online education, non-traditional students, and quality assurance. Hamlin holds a PhD in higher education policy from

University of Maryland College Park and a BA and MA in English from The University of Arizona.

DARCY W. HARDY, PhD, has over twenty-five years of experience in higher education, distance, and online learning. Darcy has served as assistant vice provost for technology education initiatives at the University of Texas at San Antonio, assistant vice chancellor for academic affairs at The University of Texas System, and executive director of the UT TeleCampus at the UT System. She has also served as an Intergovernmental Personnel Act (IPA) appointment for the Obama Administration at the US Department of Labor and the US Department of Education in Washington, DC. She currently serves as chair emerita with the United States Distance Learning Association (USDLA), and is the founder of the popular USDLA-sponsored International Forum for Women in E-Learning (IFWE), an event that focuses on issues faced by women in the industry as well as on the importance of networking and mentoring in the growth of women leaders for tomorrow. Darcy was inducted into the USDLA Hall of Fame in 2009 and received the Mildred and Charles Wedemeyer Outstanding Distance Learning Practitioner Award in Madison, Wisconsin in 2006. In addition, she was inducted into the Texas Distance Learning Association Hall of Fame in 2006, and received the WCET Richard Jonsen award in 2005. Darcy received her PhD in instructional technology from The University of Texas at Austin in 1992.

GERALD A. HEEGER, PhD, manages an active practice in higher education consulting, assisting universities and private equity groups in their efforts to develop transformational learning initiatives. Currently, he serves as senior advisor to MediSend International, a 501(c)3 focused on training US Armed Forces veterans and international health workers as biomedical technology technicians and on the distribution of medical instrumentation and supplies to emerging countries in Africa, the Middle East, and Latin America.

For more than forty-five years, Heeger has been passionately committed to the need to expand access for nontraditional students to affordable higher education opportunities, nationally and internationally. From 2005 to 2009, Heeger served as founding president of Whitney International University System (WIUS), a system of Latin American institutions, now enrolling more than 200,000 students throughout Latin America, and as president of the American College of Education (Indianapolis), an innovative initiative in graduate education for teachers.

Previously, Heeger was president of University of Maryland University College. Under his leadership, UMUC became one of the largest universities in the United States. During his tenure, UMUC received national and international recognition for its innovative leadership in online learning and in providing educational access solutions.

Prior to joining UMUC, Heeger served as dean of New York University's School of Continuing Studies, as dean of the New School, and as dean, provost, and executive vice-president of Adelphi University (New York) as well as a faculty member at the Woodrow Wilson Department of Government and Foreign Affairs at the University of Virginia. From 2000 to 2005, Heeger was a commissioner with the Commission on Higher Education of the Middle States Association of Schools and Colleges.

In 2005, Dr. Heeger was named to the International Adult and Continuing Education Hall of Fame, located at the University of Oklahoma. Dr. Heeger holds degrees from the University of California, Berkeley (BA) and the University of Chicago (MA, PhD).

CHARLES "CHUCK" HILL is the retired director, international alliances and business development for the Distance Learning Center at the University of California, Irvine. Prior to moving to southern California, he held the same position with the University of California, Berkeley Extension. A native of St. Paul, Minnesota, Chuck was involved in distance education beginning as an instructor in 1986 teaching business ethics for John F. Kennedy University in Orinda, California, via a 2400 baud modem through the Electronic University Network (EUN).

As one of the founding members of UC Berkeley Extension's Technology Initiatives Group, Chuck was a key member of extension's original distance education development team. He had hands-on experience in planning, course development, editing, budgeting, marketing, and creating hybrid delivery models to enhance student learning. Chuck designed and developed academic programs in collaboration with a number of universities worldwide. Those included videoconference programs via satellite to Finland and Spain; educational cable television in Argentina; and hybrid courses blending instruction via the Internet with traditional face-to-face classroom instruction in Hong Kong and Shanghai.

He has consulted on distance education with the National Research Council, Prentice Hall, the Pan-American Distance Learning Exchange, the Bavarian Virtual University, the Universidad Politecnica de Valencia, and Wolters Kluwer publishing, among others. Chuck is a graduate of Dillard University, earned a master's in industrial relations from the University of Minnesota and has completed post graduate work at Harvard University. He is a charter member of the International Project Management Education Union based in Beijing, China. Chuck is currently a Tennessee Supreme Court Rule 31 listed mediator and vice chair of the board of directors of the Nashville Conflict Resolution Center. He volunteers with the district attorney's office through their Victim Offender program and with the civil court. His private mediation practice focusses on family, civil, and intellectual property disputes. Chuck also holds an appointment with the US Department of Defense as an ombudsman/mediator for employers and service members disputing employment status following military deployment with the National Guard or Reserve.

KATHLEEN S. IVES, DM, has worked in online technology for over twenty years and is currently the Online Learning Consortium's chief executive officer and executive director where she oversees the organization's strategic direction. Dr. Ives assumes this leadership role after serving as interim CEO and executive director since October 2013. Additionally, she serves on the faculty of the Institute for Emerging

Leadership in Online Learning (sponsored by Penn State and OLC) and on the Leadership Advisory Board for the Center for Learning Innovations & Customized Knowledge Solutions (CLICKS). Formerly, Dr. Ives oversaw all forms of alternative instruction at Quinsigamond Community College in Worcester, MA (distance learning, accelerated programming). She serves as adjunct faculty for University of Phoenix, Denver-based American Sentinel University, and Wentworth Institute of technology in Boston. Dr. Ives began her career at CBS and helped to develop the service that evolved into Prodigy. She then spent fourteen years designing and implementing consumer online information services, first at AT&T and then at Verizon, where she spearheaded the development of the nation's first online Yellow Pages product, now called superpages.com. Dr. Ives has degrees in communication, communication management, and organizational leadership from the University of California at Davis, the University of Southern California, Annenberg School of Communication, and the University of Phoenix-Online, respectively.

SUSAN KRYCZKA, EdD, has over thirty-five years of distance education experience in higher education and served as assistant vice-president and chief academic strategist of the Extended Education unit at Excelsior College. Previously, she was executive director of the Center for Professional Development at Excelsior College and prior to that directed the distance education initiatives at Boston University, Northeastern University, Illinois Institute of Technology, and the City Colleges of Chicago. Susan holds a BA from Roosevelt University, and MA degrees from Loyola University Chicago and Northeastern University, and an EdD from Northeastern University.

GARY W. MATKIN, PhD, has been dean of continuing education, distance learning, and summer session at University of California, Irvine (UCI) since March 1, 2000, and oversees the Division of Continuing Education (DCE) and summer session, in addition to UCI's Open Learning Initiative. With a combined budget of $80 million for the two units, DCE offers 2,400 courses a year to approximately 50,000 students, and includes several community programs, such as the Osher Lifelong Learning Institute. Summer session serves 12,000 students with 800 course offerings. The UCI Open Initiative reaches millions of learners each year through open education channels and MOOCs.

Prior to becoming dean at UCI, Dr. Matkin was associate dean of university extension at UC Berkeley, where he was responsible for instructional technology initiatives, including online courses and various technology-assisted distance education programs. Dr. Matkin holds a bachelor of science degree from the University of San Francisco, an MBA and PhD in Education from UC Berkeley, and is a certified public accountant. An author of three books, *Effective Budgeting in Continuing Education* (1985), *Technology Transfer and the University* (1990), and *Using Financial Information in Continuing Education* (1997), Dr. Matkin has also written numerous articles and papers on the subjects of continuing education, distance learning, open educational resources, technology transfer, and university-based economic development.

Dr. Matkin also has served as principal investigator of several foundation grants, including grants from the William and Flora Hewlett Foundation to advise and support the foundation's Open Educational Resources initiative. He also regularly consults with US universities and international organizations such as the OECD (Paris) on subjects of continuing education administration and distance and online education.

GARY E. MILLER, EdD, is executive director emeritus of the Penn State World Campus. Until his retirement in June 2007, he served as associate vice president for outreach and executive director of continuing and distance education at The Pennsylvania State University. He was the founding executive director of Penn State World Campus, the university's online distance education program. He earlier served as executive director of the International University Consortium and associate vice president at the University of Maryland University College (UMUC). He is the author of numerous journal articles and book chapters on distance education and the undergraduate curriculum; most recently he served as lead author *Leading the E-Learning Transformation of Higher Education: Meeting the Challenges of Technology and Distance Education* (Stylus Press, 2013) co-authored with Meg Benke, Bruce Chaloux, Lawrence Ragan, Raymond Schroeder, Wayne Smutz, and Karen Swan.

He received the 2004 Weidemeyer Award from the University of Wisconsin and *The American Journal of Distance Education* for his contributions to distance education. In March 2004, he was inducted into the International Adult and Continuing Education Hall of Fame. He received the 2007 Irving Award from the American Distance Education Consortium, the 2008 Distinguished Service Award from the National University Telecommunications Network, and the 2009 Prize of Excellence from the International Council for Open and Distance Education for his contributions to the field. In 2010, he was named a fellow of the Sloan Consortium.

JEFF SEAMAN, PhD, serves as the co-director of the Babson Survey Research Group (BSRG) and as an independent technology consultant.

Dr. Seaman has worked in education information technology for his entire career, and holds degrees in demography/statistics, sociology, electrical engineering, and housing, all from Cornell University. He has taught social science, information technology and statistics at several colleges and universities, including Cornell University, the University of Wisconsin, the University of Pennsylvania's Wharton School, and Babson College.

Dr. Seaman created and ran the Computing Resource Center and served as associate vice provost for computing for the University of Pennsylvania and served as chief information officer for Lesley University. His industry experience includes serving as chief technology officer at HighWired.com where he led the development of an online learning system for US high schools and as the vice president of engineering for Vista Associates. Dr. Seaman has served on academic technology advisory boards for a number of information technology companies including Apple Computer, IBM, and Microsoft.

Dr. Seaman has been conducting research in the impact of technology on higher education and K-12 for over a decade. Recent BSRG work includes: *Online Report Card: Tracking Online Education in the United States*; *Grade Level: Tracking Online Education in the United States*; and *Opening the Textbook: Open Education Resources in US Higher Education*. In addition, he has partnered with Tyton Partners on a number of Gate Foundation-supported efforts, including *Time for Class: Lessons for the Future of Digital Courseware in Higher Education* and *Driving Toward a Degree: The Evolution of Planning and Advising in Higher Education*. His reports can be found at: http://www.onlinelearningsurvey.com.

PAUL H. SHIFFMAN, EdD, joined Excelsior College in 2002, and currently serves as the CEO of The Presidents' Forum, a policy institute comprised of a national membership of higher education leadership, focusing on policy, regulatory, and fiscal issues associated with adult serving and distance learning institutions. He has also served as the college's assistant vice president for strategic and governmental relations. Prior to joining Excelsior College, Dr. Shiffman served in a variety of administrative roles in academe and public service including vice president for institutional planning and advancement at State University of New York Rockland Community College, executive associate to the president and assistant vice president for government relations at State University of New York Empire State College, executive associate to the vice chancellor for Educational Technology of the SUNY System, coordinator of legislative and educational policy for the National Education Association of New York, executive director of the standing committee on education of the New York State Assembly, and educational planner for early childhood through secondary education in the Office of Planning and Budget for the Governor of the State of Georgia, to name a few. He has held faculty teaching appointments at Hahnemann Medical College and Hospital in Philadelphia, Temple University, North Georgia College, Georgia State University, The College of Saint Rose, and SUNY Empire State College. Dr. Shiffman earned a BA (Psychology) from Fairleigh Dickinson University, a MEd (Educational Administration) from Georgia State University, and an EdD (Educational Psychology - Classroom Behavior) from Temple University.

CAROL VALLONE is the CEO of Meteor Learning, a company focused on enabling top-ranked higher education institutions to close workforce skill gaps by delivering high-quality, workforce-aligned competency-based education (CBE) degrees for working professionals. Prior to Meteor Learning, Vallone served as board chair, president, and CEO of Wimba Corporation, the global leader in virtual collaboration software for higher education. Vallone also launched WebCT Inc. in 1999. As board chair, president and CEO, Vallone built a global higher education customer base in seventy countries until she sold the company in 2006.

Prior to her pioneering efforts in education, Vallone held several executive-level positions with companies breaking ground in the corporate technology sector, including UCCEL, Software Arts and Honeywell Information Systems.

Vallone currently serves on the board of trustees and chairs the Ventures Committee at McLean Hospital, a major teaching facility of Harvard Medical School that is world renowned for its research in neuroscience and psychiatric clinical services. For over ten years she served on the board of trustees of the Massachusetts Technology Leadership Council. And as Education Foundation Chair, Vallone spearheaded an effort to rewrite the Massachusetts Department of Education's instructional technology standards with a focus on integrating technology into the curriculum.

Vallone also served as a member of the National School-to-Work Advisory Council during the Clinton Administration where she worked with the US secretaries of Labor and Education to integrate school and career activities.

PATRICIA WALLACE, PhD, has held varied positions in higher education throughout her career, including tenured professor, head of information technology, academic administrator, and also executive director of a research center. She was the chief information officer and associate vice president at University of Maryland University College for almost ten years during the 1990s, when the virtual university was first launched. Before that, she lived in Japan from 1981 to 1990, teaching courses in the UMUC Asian Division and serving as director of information services. More recently, she was head of online programs and IT at the Johns Hopkins University Center for Talented Youth.

Wallace's research and writing focus on the relationships among technology, learning, and human behavior. She is the author of thirteen books, including *The Psychology of the Internet* (2016), and *The Internet in the Workplace* (2004), both published by Cambridge University Press, as well as many scholarly articles, book chapters, and several educational software programs. She holds an MS in computer systems management from UMUC, and a PhD in psychology from the University of Texas at Austin. Currently, Dr. Wallace teaches in UMUC's graduate school, and she is also working on the third edition of her book *Information Systems in Organizations*, to be published by Pearson.

INDEX

ABOUT HUDSON WHITMAN

Hudson Whitman is a small press affiliated with Excelsior College, which has administrative offices in Albany, New York.

Our tagline is "Books That Make a Difference," and we aim to publish high-quality nonfiction books in areas that complement Excelsior's academic strengths: education, nursing, health care, military, business and technology, with one "open" category, American culture and society.

If you would like to submit a manuscript or proposal, please review the guidelines on our website, hudsonwhitman.com. Feel free to send a note with any questions. We endeavor to respond as soon as possible.

OTHER TITLES BY HUDSON WHITMAN

See Me for Who I Am: Student Veterans' Stories of War and Coming Home
Edited by David Chrisinger

Retire the Colors: Veterans & Civilians on Iraq & Afghanistan
Edited by Dario DiBattista

Courageous Learning: Finding a New Path through Higher Education
John Ebersole and William Patrick

Competency-based Education & Assessment: The Excelsior Experience
Edited by Tina Goodyear

The Call of Nursing: Stories from the Front Lines of Health Care
William B. Patrick

Shot: Staying Alive with Diabetes
Amy F. Ryan

The Sanctuary of Illness: A Memoir of Heart Disease
Thomas Larson

CPSIA information can be obtained
at www.ICGtesting.com
Printed in the USA
FSOW02n0322091117
40944FS